International Shrine Clown Association

50th Anniversary

Acclaim Press
MORLEY, MISSOURI

Acclaim Press
— Your Next Great Book —

P.O. Box 238
Morley, MO 63767
(573) 472-9800
www.acclaimpress.com

Book Design by Steward & Wise

Steward & Wise
GRAPHIC DESIGN

Cover Design: M. Frene Melton
Editor: Randy Baumgardner

ISBN-10: 1-938905-26-1
ISBN-13: 978-1-938905-26-1
Library of Congress Control Number: 2013935239

First Printing: 2013
Printed in the United States of America
10 9 8 7 6 5 4 3 2 1

Photo: A.A.O.N.M.S. for North America 90th Annual Sesson, 1964 Imperial Council Session, New York City, NY, July 1964. Courtesy of Glen Wheeler and Richard Cain.

SPHINX
SPHINX
SPHINX
ISMAILIA
CLOWNS
EL RIAD
CLOWNS
A.A.O.N.M.S.
CA
SESSION
TY N.Y.

Contents

The Great Falls Shrine Club's "Jolly Rogues" in their stand-up car. Pictured l-r: Bill Briggs, Jim Alquist, Kerry Fagenstrom, Bob Bennetts, and John Ross III.

Acknowledgments

Mark G. Burgad
President, 2012-2013

Most people know Shrine Clowns by their goofy makeup, bright, colorful costumes and by their funny antics. ISCA and Shrine Clowns go hand-in-hand creating the history of the Nobles who spend their time for the kids.

ISCA has reached the fifty-year mark and again is recording some of its history with this 50th Anniversary book.

Contained within are only a few of the stories of Shrine Clowns who dedicate their time, monies and talent to simply make people smile. All of these Clowns work for the same reason, the kids. As long as there are Shrine Clowns, there are stories to be told and history to be recorded.

There currently are 2,800 Shrine Clown members of ISCA. Although they are not all included in this volume, they will be well remembered by those who they have made laugh or just smile. Through the years, our goals have not changed. We are dedicated to helping the children in our hospitals. The Sneaker Fund was established to do just that. The Sneaker Fund contributes thousands of dollars each year to our Shrine Hospitals.

During this year, 2013, it is appropriate to record the history of the International Shrine Clown Association with this 50th Anniversary book. Although time erodes memories and accomplishments of those who gave their time, monies and talent, this book endeavors to record some of the events during its time period.

Mark G. Burgad
President, 2012-13

Dedication

George "Patches" Pipes
President, 2013-14

Normally, a book of this type would be dedicated to one, perhaps two individuals who have made a lasting impression on the organization; however, over the last fifty years the many and varied contributions of our membership makes this an impossible selection.

With that in mind we dedicate this book to:

All the Joey's within the International Shrine clown organization that have made a difference, regardless of how large or small, in the life of a child;

To those who have worked tirelessly for the betterment of our hospital system;

To those whose efforts have focused on the Red Sneaker Philanthropy;

To our Ladies, whose support and assistance we so deeply appreciate and gratefully acknowledge;

To all the children who have been patients of our Hospitals and enjoyed our antics;

To the Administration, Doctors, Nurses, Volunteers, Road Runners, and other care givers within our Hospital system who supply the much needed care and love for our children;

To the Officers who, throughout the fifty years of our existence, have given generously of their time to build and maintain the International Shrine Clown Association;

And lastly, to Shriners International and all the Nobles who make up that organization for their commitment and support throughout our history.

In short, this book is dedicated to you—

Thanks so much for the work you do for the Shrine, your dedication to the craft, and your contributions to our future.

George "Patches" Pipes
President, 2013-14

SHRINERS INTERNATIONAL

OFFICE OF
ALAN W. MADSEN
IMPERIAL POTENTATE

MEMBER
OASIS SHRINERS
CHARLOTTE, NORTH CAROLINA

Shrine Clowns – The Laughter Behind the Healing

February 2013

On behalf of Shriners International, we are pleased to congratulate the International Shrine Clown Association (ISCA) on 50 years of providing smiles, laughter and hope to countless people of all ages. Because of your continued support of Shriners Hospitals for Children®, many children with burn injuries have recovered and gone on to live happy fulfilled lives. Since 1973-74, the Shrine Clown Sneaker Fund has raised awareness and support for our philanthropy and contributed toward our efforts to provide excellent pediatric care to children in need – especially those with burn injuries – and to conduct innovative research to improve treatment methods.

Lady Jan and I have been proud supporters of the ISCA for many years and are always very pleased to see the many ways the Shrine Clowns bring joy to our young patients. The Shrine Clowns have truly become the laughter behind the healing at Shriners Hospitals for Children.

At the upcoming 2013 Imperial Session in Indianapolis, our amazing Shrine clowns will lead the parade July 1, and we are hoping to set a world record for the most clowns in a parade. To accomplish such a feat, we need to break the current record of 850 clowns!

We're encouraging all clown units to participate in the Imperial Session Parade. Along with your units, Shrine Lady Clowns are also welcome. Come out, join the fun and help us set a brand new world record!

Let us show the world the family fun, fellowship and brotherly love of all our clowns!

Best wishes for continued years of improving the lives of children, one laugh at a time!

Yours in the Faith,

Alan W. Madsen

Alan W. "Al" Madsen, Imperial Potentate
Shriners International

International Shrine Clown Association

2013-14 Officers

ISCA 2013-14 Officers, back row left-right: Rupert Solis, Secretary; Imperial Sir Jim Cain, Imperial First Ceremonial Master; Ernest Pearlstein, Imperial Liaison and Past President 1995; Imperial Sir Wayne Lachut, Imperial Marshal; Mark Burgad, Junior Past President 2012; Randy Weldon, Treasurer and Past President 2011. Front row: Lon Burke, Second Vice President; George Pipes, ISCA President 2013; Imperial Potentate, Alan Madsen; Bob Bassett, First Vice President; and Cliff Hartmier, Third Vice President.

George "Patches" Pipes – President 2013

First Vice President:	Bob "Peaches" Bassett
Second Vice President:	Lon "Cactus" Burke
Third Vice President:	Cliff "Mr. Stripes" Hartmier
Secretary:	Rupert "Cy-Lo" Solis
Treasurer:	Randy "Wuzzles" Weldon PP
Sneaker Fund Chairman, U.S.:	Richard "RC" Cain PP
Assistant Sneaker Fund Chairman, U.S.:	Steve "Swampy" Marsh
Sneaker Fund Chairman, Canada:	Don "Milty" Hamilton
Assistant Sneaker Fund Chairman, Canada:	Robert "Buzz B" Gordon
Sneaker Fund Chairman, Mexico:	Leon "Joy" Portman
Assistant Sneaker Fund Chairman, Mexico:	Agustin "Windies" Martinez Sibaja
Clown Alley Editor:	Mark "Buzzy" Burgad PP
Education Director:	Kenneth "Diamonds" Whigham
Master of Ceremonies and Imperial Ambassador:	Earnest "Rollo" Pearlstein PP
Sneaker Fund Ambassadors:	Steven "Bubbles" Ackerman
	Mike "Splatter" Ford
Chaplain:	Don "Milty" Hamilton
Historian:	Richard "RC" Cain PP
Webmaster:	Clayton "PABO" Robertson
Parliamentarian:	Joe "Ol Coach" Cole PP
Sergeant at Arms:	Mike "Crackers" O'Neil
Junior Past President:	Mark "Buzzy" Burgad PP

CLOWNS

By Megan "Lollypop the Clown" Johnson

I wish every person had a clown in their life to help brighten up their day,
To make them smile, laugh, and have a good time the ole fashion clown way.
I wish every person knew what I knew about clowns and what makes them tick,
How their hearts are huge and they cry inside every time they see a child that's sick.
I wish everyone could see the person behind that red nose and made up face,
And see the love that radiates from within a clown for every child of every race.
I wish I could stand tall and yell to the world that clowns mean the world to me,
Cause behind those big feet and crazy hair is a person that is a hero indeed.
Yes, a clown is a hero in every sense of the word because they make kids forget they're sad,
As they make dogs out of balloons, chickens out of napkins and help sad turn into glad.
I thank God every night for the clowns in my life that have helped me through my pain,
Giving me the strength and courage to face life head on knowing I have everything to gain.
I wish everyone in this whole wide world had just one clown as special as the ones I know,
Because my Shriner clowns are the Best in the World and I love them from head to toe!!!

CAVALLO

AMARA
Clowns

ISCA HISTORY

Amara Clowns on parade.

The Barnum & Bailey Greatest Show on Earth circus poster showing clowns with performing animals including geese, roosters and a donkey, Stobridge Litho. Co., ca. 1900. Library of Congress photo, reproduction number LC-USZC4-9670.

History of Clowning

What is a clown?

"A divine spirit—to rejoice and delight the heart," according to a nine-year-old Egyptian Pharaoh who heralded the first recorded appearance of a clown around the year 2270 B.C. The comic spirit of clowning exists in just about every known culture. It is as old as civilization. This ancient craft speaks to that which is human in all of us.

The western tradition of clowning can be traced to ancient Greece, where strolling clowns were seen in Sparta as early as the seventh century B.C., called "deikeliktas" or "those who put on plays." These clowns portrayed everyone from soldiers, fools and witches to slaves and Greek gods.

Throughout the Middle Ages and early Renaissance, jesters or fools perpetuated the art of clowning in the palaces of kings and great nobles. Jesters played an important role in the social culture of Medieval Europe by serving as "safety valves" or the "social conscience." They could answer back to kings, bishops and all in authority. By making fun of anyone and satirizing social customs and more, jesters were often catalysts for social change.

It was also during this period that the colorful costumes associated with today's clowns had their beginnings. During this period, Jesters adopted a standard uniform of bright green and saffron colored coats, hose and a hooded cap that was topped by tiny bells designed to tinkle whenever the wearer moved.

Harlequin, painted between 1888-1890 by Paul Cezanne. Image courtesy of Wikimedia Commons.

Will Sommers, court jester to Henry VIII. This image was scanned from Robert Chamber's Book of Days (published 1864). Image courtesy of Wikimedia Commons.

Although many clowns entertained at court, the vast majority continued to be street performers. They were adept at a variety of skills, such as magic, contortion, juggling, acrobatics, story telling, puppetry, tightrope walking, exhibiting trained animals, ballad singing, and clever dialogue.

"Zany," "jester, "fool," "minstrel," and "mime" are but a few of the historical synonyms for "clown." The English equivalent used today did not appear until the sixteenth century. "Clown" originally meant "clod" and was often used to denote a clumsy country bumpkin. These rustics were considered very funny, and comedic actors soon imitated their ways. These actors were called clowns.

Whatever term is applied, the medieval clown's ability to perform unusual acts of skill in a daring, yet comic, manner became and important part of modern circus clowning.

But then came a somber period in the history of clowning. The Puritans closed the English theatres in 1642. When theatres reopened in 1660, clowns were not welcome in the sedate drama of the Restoration. Undaunted, English clowns continued to perform on improvised stages, at fairground booths and short farces known as "drolls."

During this same period, the spirit of improvisation reached new heights in Italy in the form of street theatre called "com-

Pierrot (Gilles), painted between 1717-19 by Antoine Watteau. Image courtesy of Wikimedia Commons.

media del'arte", or the comedy of professional actors. From the 1500's to the 1700's this form of Italian theatre thrived and gave birth to a roster of comedic characters that may still be seen today. These include Harlequin, with his popular patchwork costume, and Pierrot, one of the first clowns known to use whiteface makeup.

The "commedia" influence was noted in France, where clowns incorporated juggling, tightrope walking, and tumbling in front of fairground theatres. These performances were used to entice fairgoers to pay to see the main show inside the fairgrounds.

During the eighteenth century, this form of improvisational theatre came under attack by authorities who claimed that "more established" theatre had a monopoly on drama. Hence, the fairground zanies resorted to the use of pantomime, since English and French restrictions did not include silent acting.

Philip Astley's Ampitheatre in London, England, as drawn by Thomas Rowlandson and Augustus Pugin for Ackermann's Microcosm of London (1808-11). Courtesy of Wikimedia Commons.

As pantomime gained in popularity, Harlequin and Pierrot were transformed into romanticized heroes. This transformation, along with the emergence of a new entertainment form, allowed the reappearance of the lively, more versatile clown.

Joseph Grimaldi as Clown Joey, painted ca. 1820 by George Cruikshank. Image courtesy of Wikimedia Commons.

In 1768, on the outskirts of London, a former sergeant major in the British Cavalry, Philip Astley, presented a show that combined the comedic and acrobatic skills of the clown with the precision of military horsemanship. Immediately popular, what we now call the "circus" was born.

Dan Rice, ca. 1901. This image originally appeared in The Life of Dan Rice by Marla Ward Brown. Courtesy of Wikimedia Commons.

However, Astley never called his establishment a "circus," which refers to the circular riding ring. The modern circus received its name a few years later when in 1782 one of Astley's former horsemen, Charles Hughes, founded the Royal Circus.

The comic character that is usually associated with the word "clown"—often interchangeable with the nickname "Joey"—was originated by Joseph Grimaldi in the early 1800's.

Joey's comic gift was the flexibility and expressiveness of his face and body. His winces, glances, grins and scowls projected his emotions to the farthest reaches of the theatre. Grimaldi used makeup to exaggerate his rubbery features. His makeup designs, applied over a base of pure white, supplied the basic funny face on which clowns still compose their greasepaint variations today.

Dan Rice, whom some have called "the original American white-face clown," made his first circus appearance in 1840. With his distinguished goatee, top hat, blue leotard, and red and white tights, "Yankee Dan" is considered to have been the model for "Uncle Sam."

The importance of Dan Rice and the one-ring circus to nineteenth century America is best demonstrated by the influence they had on the people they touched. When Dan Rice's show played McGregor, Iowa in 1870, five brothers were fascinated by the performance and decided to start their own circus. The amateur presentations of the Ringling brothers would eventually evolve into the famous Ringling Bros. Circus.

Meanwhile, a new type of clown, created by Tom Belling in 1869, was emerging on the other side of the ocean in Berlin, Ger-

Five circus clowns, a color lithograph by Calver Litho. Co., 1890. Library of Congress photo, reproduction number LC-USZC4-727.

Ringling Bros., Crandall and his comic burlesque equestrain act on his riding mule Thunderbolt, by Courier Litho. Co., ca. 1899. Library of Congress photo, reproduction number LC-USZC4-10498.

many. Garbed in an eccentric outfit and performing a series of actions that seemed at once stupid and spontaneous, Belling was greeted by delighted German audiences with cries of "Auguste!", which was slang for "silly" or "stupid."

By the end of the nineteenth century, the smaller tents of the one-ring show had given way to the "big-top" and the circus enjoyed a golden age. As the large, new, three-ring format evolved, clowns were presented with their greatest challenge yet. Spectacular movement, bright costumes, oversized props, loud explosives, and flamboyant makeup became essential ingredients in the clown's new formula for laughs. By 1907 when the Ringling brothers purchased another popular circus, Barnum & Bailey, the profession of clowning had reached one of its highest peaks.

But only a few decades later, it seemed the ancient art of clowning was dying. By the late 1960s, there were estimated to be fewer than 200 professional circus clowns in the entire United States. When Ringling Bros. and Barnum & Bailey Circus was purchased by the late Irvin Feld in 1967, there were only 14 members remaining on the Circus' Clown Alley.*

To preserve the rapidly dwindling profession, Irvin Feld founded Ringling Bros. and Barnum & Bailey Clown College in 1968, providing the first formal training ground for clowns. Since then, the College has had more than 1,000 aspiring mirth makers pass through its doors, rejuvenating the Circus' Clown Alley.

Today, Clown College offers a varied and imaginative curriculum that reflects the skills and traditions of this ancient and international art. Boasting an impressive faculty roster and star-studded list of alumni, there is little doubt that the vision and dedication of Irvin Feld has been richly appreciated. Clown College graduates offer amusement—a legacy of gladness and goodwill to be shared with audiences for years to come. *This article originally appeared in the Dec 1990/Jan 1991 edition of "Clown Alley."*

**Clown Alley is a term that refers to the private section of the arena where clowns put on their makeup and store their props.*

Poster depicting the Barnum & Bailey Greatest Show on Earth (with portraits of P.T. Barnum and J.A. Bailey), Stobridge Litho. Co., 1897. Library of Congress photo, reproduction number LC-USZC4-921.

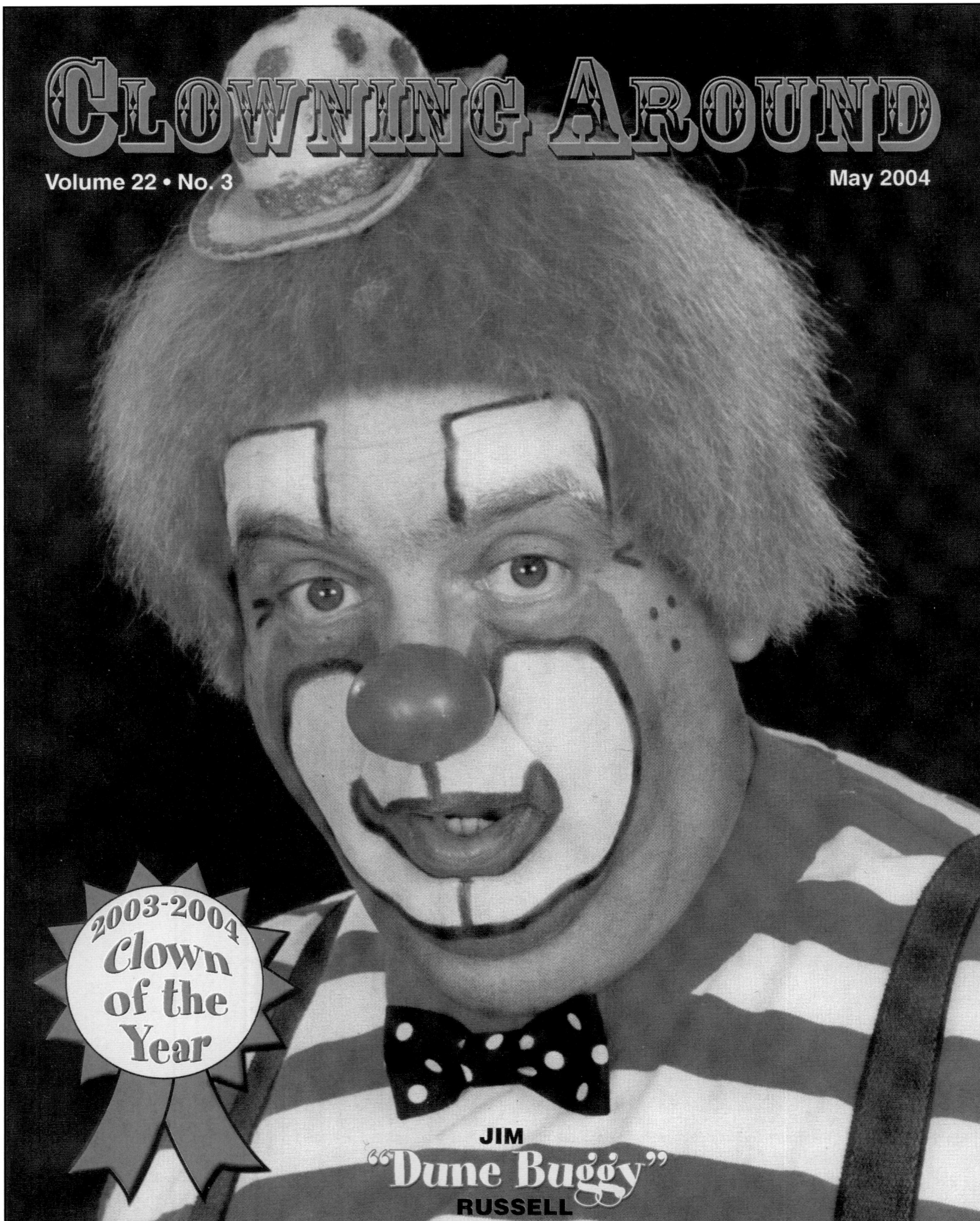
CLOWNING AROUND
Volume 22 • No. 3
May 2004
2003-2004
Clown of the Year
JIM
"Dune Buggy"
RUSSELL

The First 25 Years of the NSCA and the ISCA

By Glen W. Wheeler, Past Historian, 1987

The National Shrine Clown Association was started by Noble Joseph Silva, of Almas Temple, Washington, D.C., who contacted a group of Shrine Clowns and made arrangements for the first meeting to be held at the Imperial Session in July of 1963 at the Bismark Hotel in Chicago.

Of the 16 charter units, seven were present and established a set of common goals, as follows:

1. To promote acquaintance, friendship and fellowship among Shrine Clowns.
2. To exchange ideas, practices and methods of operations for the betterment of all Shrine Clowns.
3. To promote favorable publicity for all Shrinedom.
4. To promote fun and entertainment for any occasion on behalf of the N.S.C.A., since all members benefit from the exchange of ideas, stunts, etc.

A special measure of credit is due two individuals who acted as counsel from the Imperial, Past Potentate Rudy G. Larsen of Almas Temple and Past Imperial Recorder and Recorder Emeritus of Almas Temple, Frederick Wilken, who helped, encouraged and assisted in setting up the by-laws and constitution, which have subsequently stood the test of time.

A special measure of credit is also in order for Joseph F. Sliva, who had the dream of what could be done and took the responsibility that enabled NSCA to become a reality. He was secretary-treasurer for the first ten years.

In July of 1963, there were a total of 212 Shrine Clown members from 16 units. Five years later at the 1968 Imperial

Five of the first six Srekoj Clowns. Front, l-r: Joe Pearce (Wuz), Donald Kraft (Bumkin), and Max O. Slade (Cuzz). Back: Eddie Jones (Cuz the Cop) and Barney Koepp (Fuz).

The Sphinx Funsters at the Imperial Session in Miami, 1961. Pictured l-r: Ray Miller, Robbie Robbins, Fred Kenyon, Ray Provencal (in car), Chief of Police Fox, Art Jepsen, and Bill Scott.

The Syria Temple Harige Unit, 1965.

We clown for the kids!

Jim Russell speaks at the installation dinner for NSCA officers, 1973.

Session in Chicago, there were 61 units with 1,254 members in the NSCA. By 1973, the NSCA had grown to 180 units with over 4,000 members, due to a major emphasis in increasing individual, as well as unit, membership.

From 1963-71, clown competition was limited to parade and display boards. Awards were given for the best three displays of unit activities for the past year and the best three parade units.

In 1971-72 at the Dallas Imperial Session, competition in make-up and costume was initiated. James (Dune-Buggy) Russell was in charge of this original competition, which still follows the same format. Also during 1971-72, the project to sell giant checks in the amount of one dollar for $1.25 resulted in the first donations to the Imperial from the NSCA for the Shrine Hospitals of nearly $3,600.

During 1972-73, Abe Flaks brought the Sneaker Fund idea before the Executive Board to be discussed as a project for the NSCA. The concept was approved and adopted by the NSCA to be submitted to the Imperial for approval, which was granted.

NSCA Officers, 1973, back row (l-r): Leroy Canada "The Jolly Green Giant", First Vice President; Floyd Rinker "Uncle Mike", Third Vice President; David Beatty "Balloon Man", Secretary-Treasurer. Front row: Jim Russell "Dune Buggy", President; Bob Johnson "Freddie the Clown", Second Vice President.

Good times at the Mid-Winter session, Columbus, Georgia, ca. mid-1970s.

"Robo" cheering up a youngster in the hospital.

NSCA Officers, 1974. Courtesy of Jim Russell.

NSCA Officers, 1974. Courtesy of Jim Russell.

Shrine clowns checking in at the Mid-Winter session, 1975. Courtesy of Jim Russell.

Randy "Tinker" Holt

This was a project that no other association in the Shrine can come close to meeting. The first check for $700 was given to Imperial in 1974 by President James Russell.

The first mid-winter session was held from February 20-22, 1975 in Cedar Rapids, Iowa with El Kahir Shrine Temple as hosts. This was the start of general business meetings and elections held during the mid-winter sessions.

After proposing that the name be changed to International Shrine Clown Association in 1976 at the Imperial Session in Toronto, Quebec, Canada, the name change was approved at the Pensicola Mid-Winter Session. Final approval at the Pensicola Mid-Winter Session. Final approval was given by Imperial Potentate Val Preda in October of 1976 for the name and by-laws to be changed to International Shrine Clown Association and the organization to include all Shrine Clown member units from the United States, Canada, Panama, Puerto Rico, the Pacific and Europe.

The first annual meeting of the renamed International Shrine Clown Association was in Winnipeg, Canada on Feb. 24-26, 1977, with the Khartum Komedians as hosts.

A highlight of the ISCA Mid-Winter of 1979 in Jackson, Mississippi was another first: the Grand Wedding of Floyd and Sylvia Rinker and their entrance down the aisle under the arch of the Shrine Clowns all in costume. This session was attended by Imperial Potentate Warren Weck of Zuhrah Temple.

The Imperial Session at Minneapolis in 1979 provided another "first": the clowns were assigned a place in the parade and any Shrine Clowns in attendance could parade with the ISCA. This was a credit to Wayne McDowell and the other officers since it enabled clown members present without their unit to be in the parade.

The 1980 Mid-Winter at St. Paul, Minnesota hosted another "first": the ISCA clowns were asked to lead the nationally known St. Paul Winter Carnival Grand Parade.

The Mid-Winter session in February 1981 at the Hilton Inn Gateway in Orlando, Florida had 61 units represented from all over the U.S. plus Canada and the Canal Zone. There were 27 hours of lectures and seminars featuring Ron Severeni of Ringling's Circus World.

Ansar's Busiest Clown, "Pinwheel" Stelzer, autographs a child's circus coloring book.

At the 1982 Mid-Winter, hosted by Tebala Temple in Rockford, Illinois at the Clock Tower Inn, the Sneaker Check to Imperial had grown to $15,600.

At the June 1982 Imperial session in Orlando, Florida, all clown competition was at Ringling Circus World, with the judging by the Ringling clowns, who presented three large trophies to the three best all-around Clowns.

At the Mid-Winter in San Antonio in 1983 the Sneaker Fund check was $21,834.91.

The Sneaker check was $31,000 in 1984 at the Mid-Winter in Las Vegas.

"Jingles" at nursery school Christmas party.

The Allepo Temple Clown Unit hosted the 1984 Imperial hosted the 1984 Imperial Session at the Allepo Shrine Temple. It was reported that over one million people observed the 4th of July Parade, of which the ISCA was gladly a part.

At the Mid-Winter session in Tampa, the Sneaker check was $60,000 for Burns Research.

The ISCA Mid-Winter in 1986 was in Winnipeg, Canada and saw 60 unit delegates voting at the General Session. The Sneaker Fund rose to $85,000.

The Hadi Shrine Clown Unit hosted the Mid-winter in Evansville, Indiana in 1987—a record turnout of clowns as well a record Sneaker check of $139,535.45.

Some of the many who deserve a lot of credit for what the NSCA, now the ISCA, is today include: Joe Sliva, Doc. Rutkowski, Jack Cobleigh, Otto Miller, Lloyd Brace, David Beatty, Lloyd Webb, James Russell, Abe Flaks, Leroy Canada, Loren Buetler, W.C. Watts, E.C. Mitzel, Chris Johnson, and many, man of the other officers. The list goes on when you realize what Teeney Long, Doug Argent, Doodles, Rags Thomas, Mickey Rouse, Bob Hamilton, Al Ross, Jerry Steiger, Jack Anderson, Norm Skodje, and John Whipple have meant to clown competition as it is today (1987).

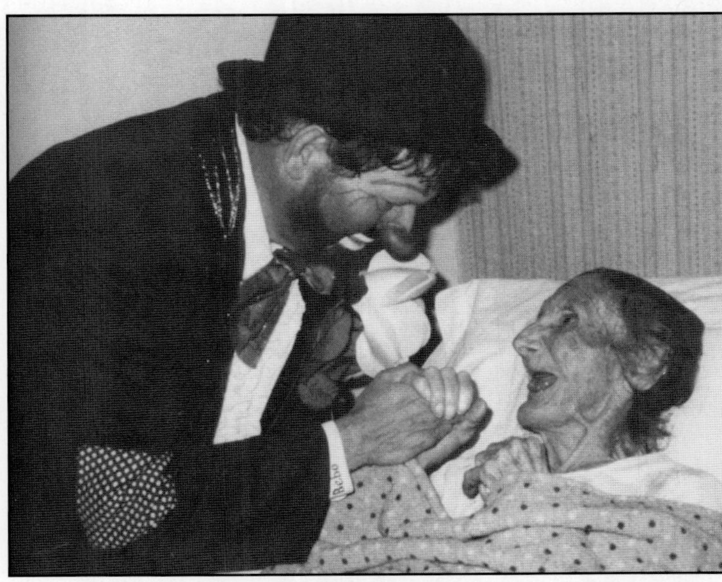

"Bebo" at Four Seasons Nursing Home, 1985.

We are also thankful for the great help given the Association by Imperial Recorder George Saunders, Imperial Sir Bob Turley, Bob Sconce and the help and guidance of the Imperial over the years. There are certainly many others who played an important part, but have been unintentionally omitted.

"Sir Ziggy" performs at an orphanage in Kerela, India. People all over the world love clowns! Courtesy of Lauren Zagoren.

See the smiles on their faces!

Newell Barker

Rich Sherriff, "MaGee"

Rich Sherriff, "MaGee"

The History of ISCA 1988-2013

By Richard "RC" Cain, Historian

As ISCA historian for many years, I was asked to assist in the preparation for the 50th ISCA Anniversary Book. I pondered several ways to present the facts and figures for the last 25 years, and so they say, here goes.

The year 1988 began the golden years of the ISCA. Membership was increasing, conventions were better than ever, and education was expanding, with more clowns and options for competition at both the regional and ISCA/ Imperial Conventions. Officer's positions began to expand to accommodate the ever-growing projects that required specific responsibilities. The Imperial really began to take notice of our accomplishments and our dedication to Burns Research. The *Clown Alley* magazine became of age when color was utilized and many new vendors were supporting the magazine and sharing their wares with the membership.

In the last 25 years, the Sneaker Fund has also evolved into a more complex undertaking with six figure numbers, sneaker ambassadors, an increase in the Red and Gold Nose Awards, and new incentive programs by ISCA presidents and sneaker fund chairmen to support our hospitals.

Officers

The elected officers remained the same from 1988 through 1995 with the president, 1st, 2nd, 3rd, and 4th vice presidents, secretary, treasurer and appointed officers. The 4th vice president office was eliminated in 1996, leaving only three vice presidents elected by the membership. Until then, the 4th VP had been responsible for the pins and patches.

The appointed officers made by the president changed as the years progressed. Until 1995, the appointed officers consisted of sneaker chairs of the U.S. and Canada, education director, historian, sergeant-at-arms, parliamentarian, editor, emeritus editor and chaplain. In 1994, the pins & patches chairman was added. In 1995, the Imperial liaison, goodwill ambassadors chairman, sneaker ambassador chairman, regional membership chairmen, and by-laws committee chairman (PP) were added.

Gaylord "Zeeby" Thomas served as the membership chairman as well as webmaster (one year) from 1996 until 2003 when the 3rd VP became responsible for membership. The webmaster changed in 2002 when Gaylord "Zeeby" Thomas was appointed. Randy "Wuzzles" Weldon became the webmaster in 2006, and then Clayton "Pabo" Robertson assumed the position and serves in that capacity today. By having only four webmasters, we have kept continuity within the program.

The public relations chairman was introduced in 2001 to share ongoing ISCA activities with the membership. In 2002, the quartermaster was made an appointed officer responsible for the flags and other equipment needed at meetings and conventions. An advisory board made up of all past presidents provides advice and assistance to the executive board as needed. Through the years, some appointments that have been introduced by the president have worked and some have not, so what you see is hit and miss—some good and some that didn't work and were eliminated as a position. Like all organizations, the ISCA has grown through change.

Richard "RC" Cain, Historian

The Lifetime Achievement Award has been awarded to past presidents and honorees for their exemplary and dedicated service to ISCA after serving in office as president or an appointed officer, and then seven consecutive years of additional service to International Shrine Clown Association. Those receiving this prestigious award include Chris "Sparkles" Johnson, John "Applejack" Whipple, Dale "Bago" Bieber, Walter "Troubles" Kendall, Ernest "Rollo" Pearlstein, Joe "Ol Coach" Cole, Gene "Geno" Harris, Richard "RC" Cain, Bill "10 Can" London, and Ed "Stripes" Whitenett. Their service to ISCA has perpetuated the craft of clowning for the last decade.

Membership

The ISCA Membership in 1988 was 5,461 as compared to current rolls of 2,856, with a steady decline due a great deal to age and not replenishing our own. Membership thrives when other clowns speak of their activities, joy and achievement of being a shrine clown. The economy has also dictated a decline in membership over the years. The membership dues have not changed that much during the 25 yr span.

In 1988 the dues were $10, with a $2.50 initiation fee (U.S.) for new members. The by-laws voted on by the membership increased the dues in 1990 to $13.00 plus an initiation fee of $5.00. The year 1992 brought the appointment of a membership deputy for each region to promote membership in his section of North America.

In July of 1994, there was an increase in dues to $16.00 with no change in the initiation fee. There was not another increase until 2007, when the by-laws voted on by the membership changed the dues from $16.00 with an initiation fee of $5, to $20.00 with the same initiation fee of $5 where it has remains until today. To increase membership, in July 2010 a new membership program, M+1 Program, was introduced to the membership. Each sponsor or a member without a sponsor would receive an incentive pin award for each new member they brought to ISCA. The program is still going strong.

Sneaker Fund

The Sneaker Fund for Burns Research at the Shrine Hospitals had funds totaling $173,795.00 in 1988 and this was presented at the Imperial Convention in February 22, 1989. Sixty (60) clowns earned the Red Nose Award that year as well.

The sneaker chairman is an appointed officer appointed by the ISCA president during his term of office. There have been only a few in number that have held this position between 1988 and 2013. William "Strawberry" Watts (PP) held the position for many years until 1994, when Charles "Pee Wee" Beumler (PP) was appointed.

In 1996, Chris "Sparkles" Johnson (PP) assumed the position

El Zaribah (Doug Fry)

Uthoff

Alfred E. Peveto. El Mina Shrine Clown.

Alfred E. Peveto, Fire Truck driver and "Tiny" Fowler.

Heroman

and was joined by the newly appointed Canadian Sneaker Fund Chairman Herb "Herbie" Grills. In 1999, Dale "Bago" Beiber (PP) was appointed with Herb "Herbie" Grills and newly appointed Mexico's Sneaker Fund Chairman Enrique "Cisco" Finkler, who remained in their positions until 2000 when Ed "Stripes" Whitenett (PP) assumed the position for Canada.

In 2002, Alan "Ding Dong" Bell was appointed the Canadian sneaker fund chairman and remained in that position until 2007. In 2005, Joe "Ol Coach" Cole (PP) was appointed to be the U.S. sneaker fund chairman along with Bell and Finkler. In 2006, Victor Montalvo served, followed by Leon "Joy" Portman, who became the Mexico sneaker fund chairman in 2007 along with Donald "Milty" Hamilton, who became the Canadian sneaker fund chairman. In 2010, Bill "10 Can" London (PP) was appointed and remained in that position through 2012 when Richard "RC" Cain (PP) was appointed in 2013 along with Hamilton and Portman.

There have been assistant sneaker fund chairmen for North America since 2004. Those gentlemen include, Mel "Happy" Cooper, Bobby "BooBoo" Byers, and Nick "Pooky" Clausen, and for Canada, Neil "HoHo" McNeilage, who served from 2004-2011, and Bob "BuzzB" Gordon.

The sneaker fund chairman appointed sneaker ambassadors in 1988 to promote the sneaker and its purpose to the membership throughout North America. In 2002, emeritus sneaker ambassador plaques were presented to members who had nine years of service as a sneaker ambassador.

The Sneaker Fund for Burns Research at the Shrine Hospitals for Children has continued to grow over the years, with many incentive programs in place by the ISCA president and executive board. President Randy "Tinker" Holt was the first to reach and surpass the $200,000 mark during his year of 1989, and President Richard "RC" Cain was the first to reach and surpass the $300,000 plus mark in 2002 with an ISCA presentation at the Imperial convention of $311,374.33.

In 1993-1994, sneaker pins were offered for a $100 donation to the Sneaker Fund. Some of the other incentive programs were the introduction of a sneaker pin in 1993, a sneaker patch in 1998, and in 2002, a man's sport's sneaker watch with the red nose logo for people who made a $1,000 donation. In 2006, a new sneaker fund pamphlet (in caricature) was presented, as well as a print of the officers, "Clowns of the ISCA" by Don Howard—a Disney Artist—who donated 15% of the proceeds to the Sneaker Fund. Little red sneakers were also sold for $10 a pair that year.

Many shrine clowns are receiving their red and gold nose awards for their many hours of clowning around and dedication to the sneaker. Public relations have fostered the record number of monies given to our hospitals and our philanthropy has been on an upward spiral over the years. It is our sincere desire to go even further in the next twenty-five years.

The ISCA *Clown Alley* Magazine

There have not been many executive editors for the ISCA *Clown Alley* magazine in the last 25-year period. A new home was established in Rockford, IL for the 1988 April/May Edition of *Clown Alley,* when Loren Beutler (PP) of Psilanti, Michigan handed the reigns over to new editor Chris "Sparkles" Johnson (PP) and Loren was named the emeritus editor. Chris remained as editor until 1993, when Richard "Salty" Burgess was appointed by President William "Patches" Knowles and served through 1994. Chris "Sparkles" Johnson (PP) was made the emeritus editor.

In 1990, a new by-law was passed that required the incoming president to have the executive board approve the appointments of the executive editor and sneaker fund chairmen. William "Patches" Knowles (PP) was appointed and approved as editor by President Lyle "Oppo" Boyd for the years 1996-97. In 1998, Gene "Geno" Harris of Rockford, IL was appointed and approved by President Dale "Bago" Bieber as the editor of *Clown Alley,* and remained as the editor until 2011 when due to a financial crunch, Mark "Buzzy" Burgad became the editor and found Simpson's Printing in Rapid City, South Dakota, who began publishing the magazine and continues to do so to this day.

In 1989, more regional news and other regular columns were introduced such as The Prop Shop ('89) and Uncle Jake's Sahib Tips ('89). As the years passed, Ask Betty ('90), News 'N Notes ('93), From Inside the Bago ('94), Card Swappers ('95), Bowzo's Corner ('98), RC's Convention News ('04), Ask Wuzzles ('04), the Public Relations Report ('05), and The ISCA Clowns Last Walk Around ('12) were also added as regulars to the magazine. In 1996, *Clown Alley* began using color throughout the magazine.

A magazine must have the support of advertisers. During the last 25 years there have been many advertisers from all over the United States who have purchased ads in the magazine. They include Costumes by Betty, St. Paul, MN; Mitzie's, Hopkins, MN; Mehron Inc., Valley, NY; Stein Make-Up Center, Boston, MA; T. Myers Magic, Austin, TX; Balloon Box; La Rock's Fun and Magic Outlet, Charlotte, NC; Fun House Magic, Baltimore, MD; Lynch's Dearborn, MI; The Circus Clowns, Minneapolis, MN; Creative Costumes by Judimac, Nashville, TN; Suits That Suit, Coeur d'Alene, ID; Artistic Clowns, Mt Clemens, MI; The Clown Factory, San Antonio, TX; Pricilla Mooseburger Originals; Clowns by the Bunch, Beallsville, PA; Apples and Co., Union, NJ; The Clowning Touch, Oklahoma; The Clown-So-Port Collection, Oconomowoc, WI; Spears Specialty Shoe Co., Springfield, MA; The Gag Bag, Kansas City, MO; Bubba's Clown Supplies, Orange Park, FL; Classics by Barbi, Houston, TX; Gilligan's Wheels, Springfield, MA; and American Balloons, Arlington, TX—just to recognize a few who have continued their support throughout the years.

Charter Members
National Shrine Clown Association

Al Koran Temple Clowns, *Cleveland, Ohio*
Almas Temple Clowns, *Washington, District of Columbia*
Kazim Temple Clowns, *Roanoke, Virginia*
Kena Temple Clowns, *Alexandria, Virginia*
Khedive Temple Clowns, *Norfolk, Virginia*
Kismet Temple Clowns, *Brooklyn, New York*
Medinah Temple Clowns, *Chicago, Illinois*
Moolah Temple Clowns, *St. Louis, Missouri*
Nur Temple Clowns, *Wilmington, Delaware*
Osiris Temple Clowns, *Wheeling, West Virginia*
Sharon Temple Clowns, *Tyler, Texas*
Sphinx Temple Funsters, *Hartford, Connecticut*
Tangier Temple Clowns, *Omaha, Nebraska*
Tigris Temple Clowns, *Syracuse, New York*
Zamora Temple Clowns, *Birmingham, Alabama*
Zem Zem Temple Clowns, *Erie, Pennsylvania*

James L. "DB" Russell

Although there had been an Editor's Award in the early years, it was reintroduced in 2012 by Editor Mark Burgad as an Editor's Award Patch. A person must submit and have published an article in at least four different issues during the year to receive the award.

Conventions

All clowns enjoy the camaraderie, excitement, education, and competition that are provided at a Shrine Clown Regional, Mid-Winter, and Imperial Conventions. There are also educational seminars and shrine leadership conferences provided by the ISCA, regional education chairmen and committees or other sponsors through the years. These events have been a lifeline of self-improvement for the individual clown. Many have traveled many miles to attend these conventions and seminars throughout North America in all types of weather.

From 1988 until the present, the ISCA Mid-Winters and Imperial Sessions respectively were conducted in the following host cities:

Toronto, Ontario, Canada,
Galveston, TX • Jackson, MS
Salt Lake City, UT • San Francisco, CA
St. Louis, MO • Orlando, FL
Sarasota, FL • San Antonio, TX
Columbus, OH • Denver, CO
Tacoma, WA • Indianapolis, IN
S. Portland, ME • New Orleans, LA
Las Vegas, NV • St Louis, MO
Gatlinburg, TN • Orlando, FL
Tampa, FL • Dallas, TX
Toronto, Ontario, Canada • Boston, MA
Indianapolis, IN • Las Vegas, NV
Atlanta, GA • Vancouver, BC, Canada
Victoria, BC, Canada • Minneapolis, MN
St. Louis, MO • Denver, CO
Louisville, KY • Baltimore, MD
Calgary, AB, Canada • Tampa, FL
Branson, MO • Anaheim, CA
Irving, TX • San Antonio, TX
Atlanta, GA • Indianapolis, IN
Des Moines, IA • Denver, CO
Billings, MT • Charlotte, NC
and in 2013 **Huntsville, AL** • Indianapolis, IN.
The International Clowns do get around!!

Competition

ISCA clowns look forward to the competition aspect at the Mid-Winter, Imperial, and Regional conventions. In addition, there are educational seminars presented on the local, regional, and international levels throughout the year.

As clowns participate in competition, they learn from other clowns and judges so that they can become better clowns as they perform for children of all ages throughout the world. The second 25 years of ISCA History has produced a much keener sense of competition. Competition makes the clowns improve to a point so that when they go to hospitals, birthday parties, nursing homes, schools, etc., they have a sense of pride in their make-up.

Of course, there will always be the one clown that just likes to dress up and have fun to support the sneaker fund and shrine hospitals, and isn't really interested in the competitive aspects of clowning. He is more interested in being a smile maker, and there is absolutely nothing wrong with this. He is to be respected and admired by his peers.

In the beginning, the main categories for the competition were make-up (white face, auguste, character, and tramp, with

Robert G. Bassett, "Peaches."

"Happy the Clown," Douglas Kroeger.

hobo added in later years), one-man skits, unit skits, and balloons. The units are judged in the parade at the conventions.

In the early '90s, there were the Hambone Award for new innovations, the Sparkles Award for balloons, and the Mitzie Award. In 1995, 2-4 man skits, and 5 or more skits were added to the competition. In 1997, paradeability for all of the make-up categories was also added. The Smile Maker Award was introduced in 1997.

In 2005, unit skits were changed to group skits and 3-5 man skits, in which clowns did not have to belong to the same temple, were added. A new individual category, Clown Extraordinaire, was introduced to the competition at the Mid-Winter for those clowns that had already won 1st or 2nd place in their categories that year. The clown competed in make-up and then later in a skit with an object selected by the education director. The clown extraordinaire winner also received a ring. The balloon competition was only held at the Mid-Winter Convention and not at the Imperial.

In 2011, the best all-around clown category was introduced for any clown that would like to do make-up for the four categories, but the criteria did not allow many participants to qualify in this category at the conventions. In 2012, face painting also became a category for competition at the Mid-Winter. As you can see, the clowns are always working towards innovation, with trial and error efforts to be the best they can be.

Clown of the Year

The Clown of the Year Award was introduced in 1992 and this program is still ongoing in 2013. Clowns of the Year represent the best of the best in the world of shrine clowning.

Since its inception in 1992, the Clown of the Year Committee has been selected from applications submitted by their clown peers a clown that represents the embellishment of all the high standards of a Shrine Clown. Many have been nominated, but in most years, only one outstanding clown would receive this honor. The Clown of the Year is also featured on the cover of the *Clown Alley* magazine.

The outstanding clowns selected for each year are as follows:

1992—Floyd "Creeky" Creekmore, *Al Bedoo*
1993—John "Jocko" Stockham
1994—Elliot "Ellmo the Klown" Moraff
1995—Art "Oscar" Howell, *Ahmed*
1996—Richard "Saxo" Lang, *El Katif*
1997—Bret "Snaptrap" Stahler, *Antioc*, and Gaylord "Zeeby" Thomas, *India*
1998—Bill "Skippy the Klown" Hunter, *Tunis*
1999—Bill "Bluenose" Newcomb, *India*
2001—Gus "Blossom" Butler, *Scimirar*
2002—Derrick "Dusty" Bradley, *Al Shamal*
2003—Robert "Bebunk" Riggs, *Hadi*, and Gary "Bingo" LaMon, *India*
2004—Kenneth "Diamonds" Whigham, *Yaarab*
2005—Arnold "Doc" Murray, *Al Azhar*
2006—Dick "Buttons" Schlecter, *El Riad*
2008—Charles "Buck—E" Parker, *Ararat*
2009—Ken "Dizzy" Gillespie, *KEM*
2010—Bruce "Boo Boo" Long, *Akdar*
2011—Carl "Day Late" Watts, *India*
2012—Michael "Ted E Bear" Ito, *Korein*

Congratulations to all of these outstanding clowns for their hard work and dedication as shrine clowns!

*Note: it was my intent to be accurate with the ISCA history, but I do apologize for any errors and omissions that do occur.

Paul D. Griffin

Buttons, Araba Clowns.

Great skit.

World famous Afifi Shrine Clowns at parade, 2012.

Araba Clowns at parade.

Pickles

Waiting for judges.

ISCA Officers, Fifty Years of Faithful Service
1963-2013

Year	*Position*	*Name*	*Temple*
1963-64	President	Arthur C. Roeber	Medinah
	Vice-President	M.H. Dismukes	Zamora
	Secretary-Treasurer	Joseph F. Sliva	Almas
	Editor	Joseph D. Garner	Almas
	Editor	Joseph F. Sliva	Almas
1964-65	President	M.H. Dismukes	Zamora
	Vice-President	Dr. I. Rutkoski	Kena
	Secretary-Treasurer	Joseph F. Sliva	Almas
	Editor	James E. Moseley	Almas
	Editor	Joseph F. Sliva	Almas
1965-66	President	Dr. I. Rutkoski	Kena
	1st Vice-President	Ralph L. Davis	Sharon
	2nd Vice-President	Thomas Phillips	Zem Zem
	Editor	Ray Spring	Almas
	Editor	Joseph F. Sliva	Almas
1966-67	President	Ralph L. Davis	Sharon
	1st Vice-President	Thomas Phillips	Zem Zem
	2nd Vice-President	Syd Brockman	Nile
	Secretary-Treasurer	Joseph F. Sliva	Almas
	Editor	Joseph F. Sliva	Almas
	Editor	Ray Spring	Almas
1967-68	President	Thomas C. Phillips, Sr.	Zem Zem
	1st Vice-President	Syd Brockman	Nile
	2nd Vice-President	David H. Beatty	Al Sihah
	Secretary-Treasurer	Joseph F. Sliva	Almas
	Editor	Joseph F. Sliva	Almas
	Editor	Hammond H. Hobbs	Almas
1968-69	President	Syd Brockman	Nile
	1st Vice-President	David H. Beatty	Al Sihah
	2nd Vice-President	Jack Cobleigh	Melha
	Secretary-Treasurer	Joseph F. Sliva	Almas
	Editor	Joseph F. Sliva	Almas
	Editor	Hammond H. Hobbs	Almas
1969-70	President	David H. Beatty	Al Sihah
	1st Vice-President	Jack Cobleigh	Melha
	2nd Vice-President	Otto C. Miller	Moolah
	Secretary-Treasurer	Joseph F. Sliva	Almas
	Editor	Joseph F. Sliva	Almas
	Editor	Hammond H. Hobbs	Almas
1970-71	President	G.L. Cobleigh	Melha
	1st Vice-President	Otto C. Miller	Moolah
	2nd Vice-President	Mendel Sackstein	Khedive
	3rd Vice-President	Lloyd F. Brace	Araba
	Secretary-Treasurer	Joseph F. Sliva	Almas
	Editor	Joseph F. Sliva	Almas
	Editor	Hammond H. Hobbs	Almas

Year	*Position*	*Name*	*Temple*
1971-72	President	Otto C. Miller	Moolah
	1st Vice-President	Lloyd F. Brace	Araba
	2nd Vice-President	Glen Wheeler	Zor
	3rd Vice-President	James L. Russell	Alcazar
	Secretary-Treasurer	Joseph F. Sliva	Almas
	Editor	Josph F. Silva	Almas
	Editor	Hammond H. Hobbs	Almas
1972-73	President	Glen W. Wheeler	Zor
	1st Vice-President	James L. Russell	Alcazar
	2nd Vice-President	Cal Druxman	Moslah
	3rd Vice-President	Leroy E. Canada	Melha
	Secretary-Treasurer	Joseph F. Sliva	Almas
	Editor	Joseph F. Sliva	Almas
	Editor	Hammond H. Hobbs	Almas
1973-74	President	James L. Russell	Alcazar
	1st Vice-President	LeRoy Canada	Melha
	2nd Vice-President	Robert Johnson	
	3rd Vice-President	Floyd B. Rinker	
	Secretary-Treasurer	David H. Beatty	
	Asst. Secretary-Treasurer	Lloyd E. Webb (COL)	
1974-75	President	LeRoy Canada	Melha
	1st Vice-President	Floyd Rinker	Syria
	2nd Vice-President	Bob Bannister	
	3rd Vice-President	Dave Bridges	
	Secretary	Dave Beatty	Al Sihah
	Treasurer	Lloyd Webb	Aloha
1975-76	President	Floyd Riner (Uncle Mike)	Syria
	1st Vice-President	Lloyd Webb (Muggs)	Aloha
	2nd Vice-President	Robert Lloyd (Bob-O)	Kosair
	3rd Vice-President	Wayne McDowell (Korky)	El Kahir
	Secretary-Jewelry Salesman	Joseph Paonessa (Jo-Pa)	Zomora
	Treasurer	Samuel Huffman (Sad Sam)	
	Clown Alley Editor	Bud Lindquist (Hi-Pockets)	Yaarab
	Sneaker Fund Chairman	Abe Flaks (Cooky)	Pyramid
1976-77	President	Lloyd Webb (Muggs)	Aloha
	1st Vice-President	Robert Lloyd (Bob-O)	Kosair
	2nd Vice-President	Wayne McDowell (Korkey)	El Kahir
	3rd Vice-President	L. Troy Woerner	Hella
	Secretary	Loren W. Beutler	Moslem
	Treasurer	Samuel Huffman (Samos)	Murat
	Clown Alley Editor	Bud Lindquist	Yaarah
	Sneaker Fund Chairman	Abe Flaks (Cooky)	Pyramid
1977-79	President	Robert L. Lloyd	Kosair
	1st Vice-President	Wayne McDowell	El Kahir
	2nd Vice-President	Loren W. Beutler	Moslem
	3rd Vice-President	Richard Lavin	Aleppo
	Secretary	Ken Barrett	
	Treasurer	Samuel Huffman	Murat
	Sneaker Fund Chairman	Abe Flaks	Pyramid
	Sergeant-At-Arms	Ted M. Funk	Kosair
	Clown Alley Editor	Bud Lindquist	Yaarab
	Clown Alley Assistant Editor	Jim Russell	Al Sihah
	Chaplain	Joseph R. Workman	Kosair

Year	*Position*	*Name*	*Temple*
1979-80	President	Wayne McDowell	El Kahir
	1st Vice-President	Loren W. Beutler	Moslem
	2nd Vice-President	Richard Lavin	Aleppo
	3rd Vice-President	Jack Anderson	Morocco
	Secretary	Kenneth Barrett	
	Treasurer	John Mills	
1980-81	President	Loren W. Beutler	Moslem
	1st Vice-President	Richard B. Lavin	Aleppo
	2nd Vice-President	Jack E. Anderson	Morocco
	3rd Vice-President	Kenneth Barrett	
	Secretary	E.C. Mitzel	
	Treasurer	John Mills	
1981-82	President	Richard B. Lavin	Aleppo
	1st Vice-President	Jack E. Anderson	Morocco
	2nd Vice-President	Kenneth Barrett	
	3rd Vice-President	W.C. Watts	El Mina
	Secretary	E.C. Mitzel	Zurah
	Treasurer	John Mills	
1982-83	President	Jack E. Anderson	Morocco
	1st Vice-President	K. Barrett	
	2nd Vice-President	W.C. Watts	El Mina
	3rd Vice-President	Jim Fankhanel	Beni Kedem
	Secretary	E.C. Mitzel	Zurah
	Treasurer	John Mills	
1983-84	President	Ken Barrett	El Kahir
	1st Vice-President	W.C. Watts	El Mina
	2nd Vice-President	Jim Fankhanel	Beni Kedem
	3rd Vice-President	E.C. Mitzel	Zurah
	4th Vice-President	Chris Johnson	Tebala
	Secretary	David Barnett	El Mina
	Treasurer	Lloyd Webb	Aloha
1984-85	President	W.C. Watts	El Mina
	1st Vice-President	Jim Fankhanel	Beni Kedem
	2nd Vice-President	E.C. Mitzel	Zurah
	3rd Vice-President	Chris Johnson	Tebala
	4th Vice-President	Charles Beumler	Crescent
	Secretary	David Barnett	El Mina
	Treasurer	Lloyd Webb	Aloha
1985-86	President	Jim Fankhanel	Beni Kedem
	1st Vice-President	E.C. Mitzel (Mitzie)	Zurah
	2nd Vice-President & Asst. Editor	Chris K. Johnson	Tebala
	3rd Vice-President	Charles W. Beumler	Crescent
	4th Vice-President	Randolph Holt	Melha
	Secretary	David Barnett	El Mina
	Treasurer	Dr. Paul D. Griffin	Osman
	Sneaker Chairman	W.C. Watts	El Mina
	Chaplain	Robert Swale	El Kahir
	Historian	Glen Wheeler	Zor
	Imperial Liaison	Gordon H. Harris	Bahia
	Executive Editor	Loren W. Beutler	Moslem
1986-87	President	E.C. Mitzel (Mitzie)	Zurah
	1st Vice-President & Asst. Editor	Chris K. Johnson	Tebala

Year	*Position*	*Name*	*Temple*
1986-87	2nd Vice-President	Charles W. Beumler	Crescent
Cont'd	3rd Vice-President	Randolph Holt	Melha
	4th Vice-President	David Barnett	El Mina
	Secretary	William D. Ralph	Aladdin
	Treasurer	Dr. Paul D. Griffin	Osman
	Sneaker Chairman	W.C. Watts	El Mina
	Chaplain	Robert Swale	El Kahir
	Historian	Glen Wheeler	Zor
	Sergeant-at-Arms	Ross A. Scott	Gizeh
	Parliamentarian	Fred Lugar	Sahib
	Executive Editor	Loren W. Beutler	Moslem
1987-88	President	Chris K. Johnson	Tebala
	1st Vice-President	Charles W. Beumler	Crescent
	2nd Vice-President	Randolph Holt	Melha
	3rd Vice-President	David Barnett	El Mina
	4th Vice-President	John Whipple	Afifi
	Secretary	William D. Ralph	Aladdin
	Treasurer	Dr. Paul D. Griffin	Osman
	Sneaker Chairman	W.C. Watts	El Mina
	Chaplain	Robert Swale	El Kahir
	Historian	Glen Wheeler	Zor
	Sergeant-at-Arms - West	Ross A. Scott	Gizeh
	Sergeant-at-Arms - East	Gene Harris	Tebala
	Parliamentarian	Fred Lugar	Sahib
	Executive Editor	Loren W. Beutler	Moslem
1988-89	President	Charles Beumler (PeeWee)	Beumler
	1st Vice-President	Randolph Holt (Tinker)	Melha
	2nd Vice-President	David Barnett (Shorty)	El Mina
	3rd Vice-President	John Whipple (Applejack)	Afifi
	4th Vice-President	Paul Griffin (Griffie)	Osman
	Secretary	William Ralph (Ralph)	Aladdin
	Treasurer	Fred Lugar (Spanky)	Sahib
	Clown Alley Editor	Chris Johnson (Sparkles)	Tebala
1989-90	President	Randolph Holt (Tinker)	Melha
	1st Vice President	David Barnett (Shorty)	El Mina
	2nd Vice President	John Whipple (Applejack)	Afifi
	3rd Vice President	Paul Griffin (Griffie)	Osman
	4th Vice President	William Ralph (Ralph)	Aladdin
	Secretary	Dr. Robert Rychman	
	Treasurer	Fred Lugar (Spanky)	Sahib
	Clown Alley Editor	Chris Johnson (Sparkles)	Tebala
1990-91	President	David Barnett (Shorty)	El Mina
	1st Vice President	John Whipple (Applejack)	Afifi
	2nd Vice President	Paul Griffin (Griffie)	Osman
	3rd Vice President	William Ralph (Ralph)	Aladdin
	4th Vice President	William Knowles (Patches)	Rameses
	Secretary	Dale Bieber (Bago)	Mohammed
	Treasurer	Fred Lugar (Spanky)	Sahib
	Clown Alley Editor	Chris Johnson (Sparkles)	Tebala
1991-92	President	John Whipple (Applejack)	Afifi
	1st Vice President	Paul Griffin (Griffie)	Osman
	2nd Vice President	William Ralph (Ralph)	Aladdin
	3rd Vice President	William Knowles (Patches)	Rameses
	4th Vice President	Ernest Pearlstein (Rollo)	Aleppo
	Secretary	Dale Bieber (Bago)	Mohammed

Year	Position	Name	Temple
1991-92	Treasurer	Mickey Kiefer	Osman
Cont'd	*Clown Alley* Editor	Chris Johnson (Sparkles)	Tebala
1992-93	President	Paul Griffin (Griffie)	Osman
	1st Vice President	William Ralph (Ralph)	Aladdin
	2nd Vice President	William Knowles (Patches)	Rameses
	3rd Vice President	Ernest Pearlstein (Rollo)	Aleppo
	4th Vice President	Lyle Boyd (Oppo)	Afifi
	Secretary	Dr. Robert Rychman	
	Treasurer	Loren Beulter (Blinky)	Moslem
	Clown Alley Editor	Chris Johnson (Sparkles)	Tebala
1993-94	President	William Ralph (Ralph)	Aladdin
	1st Vice President	William Knowles (Patches)	Rameses
	2nd Vice President	Ernest Pearlstein (Rollo)	Aleppo
	3rd Vice President	Lyle Boyd (Oppo)	Afifi
	4th Vice President	Walter Kendell (Troubles)	Moolah
	Secretary	Dale Bieber (Bago)	Mohammed
	Treasurer	Loren Beulter (Blinky)	Moslem
	Clown Alley Editor	Chris Johnson (Sparkles)	Tebala
1994-95	President	William Knowles (Patches)	Rameses
	1st Vice President	Ernest Pearlstein (Rollo)	Aleppo
	2nd Vice President	Lyle E. Boyd (Oppo)	Afifi
	3rd Vice President	Walter Kendall (Troubles)	Moolah
	4th Vice President	Dale Bieber (Bago)	Mohammed
	Secretary	David Mathis (Duck)	Alinad
	Treasurer	Chris K. Johnson (Sparkles)	Tebala
	Sneaker Chairman	Charles Beumler (Pee Wee)	Crescent
	Education Director	Bill Lozon (Billy)	Mosslem
	Clown Alley Editor	Richard W. Burgess (Salty)	Aleppo
	Asst. Editor	Chester Paris (Tux)	Aleppo
1995-96	President	Ernest Pearlstein (Rollo)	Aleppo
	1st Vice President	Lyle E. Boyd (Oppo)	Afifi
	2nd Vice President	Walter Kendall (Troubles)	Moolah
	3rd Vice President	Dale Bieber (Bago)	Mohammed
	4th Vice President	Jim Gill (Jimmy)	Al Malaikah
	Secretary	Frank Yetner (Pinky)	Palestine
	Treasurer	Walter Ulrich (Dandylion)	KOR
	Sneaker Chairman	Carles Beumler (Pee Wee)	Crescent
	Education/Competition Director	Bill Lozon (Billy)	Moselm
	Asst. Education/Competition Director	Dion Cole	
	Historian	Freeman Smith	
	Presidential Marshall	Oscar Cloutier	
1996-97	President	Lyle E. Boyd (Oppo)	Afifi
	1st Vice President	Walter Kendall (Troubles)	Moolah
	2nd Vice President	Dale Bieber (Bago)	Mohammed
	3rd Vice President	Oscar Cloutier (Clyde)	Kora
	Secretary	David Barnett (Shorty)	El Mina
	Treasurer	Walter Ulrich (Dandylion)	Hadi
	Sneaker Chairman USA	Chris Johnson (Sparkles)	Tebala
	Sneaker Chairman Canada	Herb Grills	Al Shamal
	Education/Competition Director	Bill Lozon (Billy)	Moslem
	Asst. Education/Competition Director	Dion Cole	
	Historians	Chris Johnson & Jack Whipple	
	Chaplain	Ernie Pearlstein (Rollo)	Aleppo
	Clown Alley Editor	Bill Knowles (Patches)	

1997-98	President	Walter Kendall (Troubles)	Moolah
	1st Vice President	Dale Bieber (Bago)	Egypt
	2nd Vice President	Oscar Cloutier (Clyde)	Kora
	3rd Vice President	Walter Ulrich (Dandylion)	Hadi
	Secretary	David Barnett (Shorty)	El Mina
	Treasurer	Don Gillman (Tinker)	El Mina
	Sneaker Chairman USA	Chris Johnson (Sparkles)	Tebala
	Sneaker Chairman Canada	Herb Grills (Herbie)	Al Shamal
	Education/Competition Director	Walter Seavey (Skeeter)	Mohammed
	Asst. Education/Competition Director	Jim Richardson (BoBo)	
	Membership Chairman	Gaylord Thomas (Zeeby)	
	Historian	Jack Whipple (Applejack)	
	Chaplain	Ernie Pearlstein (Rollo)	Aleppo
	Clown Alley Editor	Bill Knowles (Patches)	
1998-99	President	Dale Bieber (Bago)	Egypt
	1st Vice President	Oscar Cloutier (Clyde)	Kora
	2nd Vice President	Walter Ulrich (Dandylion)	Hadi
	3rd Vice President	Joe Cole (Ol Coach)	Ben Hur
	Secretary	David Barnett (Shorty)	El Mina
	Treasurer	Don Gillman (Tinker)	El Mina
	Sneaker Chairman USA	Chris Johnson (Sparkles)	Tebala
	Sneaker Chairman Canada	Herb Grills (Herbie)	Al Shamal
	Education/Competition Director	Walter Seavey (Skeeter)	Mohammed
	Membership Chairman	Gaylord Thomas	
	Historian	Jack Whipple (Applejack)	
	Chaplain	Bud Garrison	
	Clown Alley Editor	Gene Harris (Geno)	Tebala
1999-2000	President	Oscar Cloutier (Clyde)	Kora
	1st Vice President	Walt Ulrich (Dandylion)	Hadi
	2nd Vice President	Joe Cole (Ol Coach)	Ben Hur
	3rd Vice President	Richard Cain (RC)	Yaarab
	Secretary	Don Kinyon (Bowzo)	Mohammed
	Treasurer	Don Gillman (Tinker)	El Mina
	Sneaker Chairman USA	Dale Bieber (Bago)	Egypt
	Sneaker Chairman Canada	Herb Grills (Herbie)	Al Shamal
	Sneaker Chairman Mexico	Enrique Finkler (Cisco)	Anazeh
	Education Director	Walter Seavey (Skeeter)	Mohammed
	Membership Chairman	Gaylord Thomas	India
	Historian	John Whipple (Applejack)	Afifi
	Chaplain	Roland Kearley	Kora
	Sergeant at Arms	Harvey Weiss (Ice Cream)	Kora
	Clown Alley Editor	Gene Harris (Geno)	Tebala
2000-01	President	Walt Ulrich (Dandylion)	Hadi
	1st Vice President	Joe Cole (Ol Coach)	Ben Hur
	2nd Vice President	Richard Cain (RC)	Yaarab
	3rd Vice President	Larry Stringer (Foooey)	Moolah
	Secretary	Don Kinyon (Bowzo)	Mohammed
	Treasurer	Chris Johnson (Sparkles)	Tebala
	Sneaker Chairman USA	Dale Bieber (Bago)	Egypt
	Sneaker Chairman Canada	Ed Whitenett (Stripes)	Al Shamal
	Sneaker Chairman Mexico	Enrique Finkler (Cisco)	Anazeh
	Education Director	Walter Seavey (Skeeter)	Mohammed
	Membership Chairman & Webmaster	Gaylord Thomas (Zeeby)	Ainad
	Historian	John Whipple (Applejack)	Afifi
	Chaplain & Parliamentarian	Ernest Pearlstein (Rollo)	Aleppo
	Sergeant at Arms	Edward Heffner	Tripoli
	Sergeant at Arms	Ken Mitz (Mitzo)	Hadi
	Clown Alley Editor	Gene Harris (Geno)	Tebala

Year	Office	Name	Temple
2001-02	President	Joe Cole (Ol Coach)	Ben Hur
	1st Vice President	Richard Cain (RC)	Yaarab
	2nd Vice President	Larry Stringer (Foooey)	Moolah
	3rd Vice President	Walter Seavey (Skeeter)	Mohammed
	Secretary	Don Kinyon (Bowzo)	Mohammed
	Treasurer	Chris Johnson (Sparkles)	Tebala
	Sneaker Chairman USA	Dale Bieber (Bago)	Egypt
	Sneaker Chairman Canada	Ed Whitenett (Stripes)	Alazhar
	Sneaker Chairman Mexico	Enrique Finkler (Cisco)	Anazeh
	Education Director	Oscar Cloutier (Clyde)	Kora
	Membership Chairman & Webmaster	Gaylord Thomas (Zeeby)	Ainad
	Historian	John Whipple (Applejack)	Afifi
	Public Relations Chairman	Ernest Pearlstein (Rollo)	Aleppo
	Clown Alley Editor	Gene Harris (Geno)	Tebala
	Chaplain	Stan Kedzierski (Fuzzy)	Syria
	Parliamentarian	Walter Kendall (Troubles)	Moolah
	Sergeant at Arms	Mike Coffey (U-Who)	Alzafar
		Jerry Correll (YoYo)	Ainad
2002-03	President	Richard Cain (RC)	Yaarab
	1st Vice President	Larry Stringer (Foooey)	Moolah
	2nd Vice President	Walter Seavey (Skeeter)	Mohammed
	3rd Vice President	Ed Whitenett (Stripes)	Al Azhar
	Secretary	Don Kinyon (Bowzo)	Mohammed
	Treasurer	Chris Johnson (Sparkles)	Tebala
	Sneaker Chairman USA	Dale Bieber (Bago)	Egypt
	Sneaker Chairman Canada	Alan Bell (Ding Dong)	
	Sneaker Chairman Mexico	Enrique Finkler (Cisco)	Anazeh
	Education Director	Oscar Cloutier (Clyde)	Kora
	Quartermaster	Sanford A. Morris (Ootz)	Zuhrah
	Membership Chairman & Webmaster	Gaylord Thomas (Zeeby)	Ainad
	Assistant Webmaster	Chris Cheeck (Cheeko)	Yaarab
	Historian	John Whipple (Applejack)	Afifi
	Public Relations Chairman	Ernest Pearlstein (Rollo)	Aleppo
	Clown Alley Editor	Gene Harris (Geno)	Tebala
	Chaplain	Ken Whigham (Diamond)	Yaarab
	Parliamentarian	Jerry Fields (Mr. Smokey)	Yaarab
	Sergeant at Arms	John Thomas (Chatterbox)	Hejaz
		Dennis Lawrence (Baffles)	Yaarab
		Thomas Ledford (Squeaky)	Yaarab
2003-04	President	Larry Stringer (Foooey)	Moolah
	1st Vice President	Walter Seavey (Skeeter)	Mohammed
	2nd Vice President	Ed Whitenett (Stripes)	Al Azhar
	3rd Vice President	Sanford A. Morris (Ootz)	Zuhrah
	Secretary	Don Kinyon (Bowzo)	Mohammed
	Treasurer	Chris Johnson (Sparkles)	Tebala
	Sneaker Chairman USA	Dale Bieber (Bago)	Egypt
	Sneaker Chairman Canada	Alan Bell (Ding Dong)	
	Sneaker Chairman Mexico	Enrique Finkler (Cicso)	Anazeh
	Education Director	Oscar Cloutier (Clyde)	Kora
	Quartermaster	Gordon Keene (Gordo)	Cahaba
	Membership Chairman & Webmaster	Gaylord Thomas (Zeeby)	Ainad
	Historian	John Whipple (Applejack)	Afifi
	Public Relations Chairman	Ernest Pearlstein (Rollo)	Aleppo
	Clown Alley Editor	Gene Harris (Geno)	Tebala
	Chaplain	Michael Howard (Howiee)	Moolah
	Parliamentarian	Walter Kendall (Troubles)	Moolah
	Sergeant at Arms	Mike Coffey (U-Who)	Alzafar
		Bill Howard (Billy)	Moolah
		Charlie Rieder (Tuna)	Moolah

Year	*Position*	*Name*	*Temple*
2003-04 *Cont'd*	Chairman Pins/Patches	Joe Cole (Ol Coach)	Ben Hur
2004-05	President	Walter Seavey (Skeeter)	Mohammed
	1st Vice President	Ed Whitenett (Stripes)	Al Azhar
	2nd Vice President	Sandford A. Morris (Ootz)	Zuhrah
	3rd Vice President	Ken Taylor (Grimee)	Abou Ben Adhem
	Secretary	Don Kinyon (Bowzo)	Mohammed
	Treasurer	Ernest Pearlstein (Rollo)	Aleppo
	Sneaker Chairman US/Mexico	Dale Bieber (Bago)	Egypt
	Assistant Sneaker Chairman USA	Mel Cooper (Happy)	El Bekal
	Sneaker Chairman Canada	Alan Bell (Ding Dong)	Al Shamal
	Assistant Sneaker Chairman Canada	Neil McNeilage (Ho! Ho!)	Rameses
	Education Director	Randy Weldon (Wuzzles)	Za Ga Zig
	Assistant Education Director	David Newcomb (Do No)	Aleppo
	Clown Alley Editor	Gene Harris (Geno)	Tebala
	Pins/Patches Chairman	Joe Cole (Ol Coach)	Ben Hur
	Quartermaster	Robert Bassett (Peaches)	Ainad
	Chaplain	Michael Howard (Howiee)	Moolah
	Parliamentarian	Walter Kendall (Troubles)	Moolah
	Public Releations	Gordon Keene (Gordo)	Cahaba
	Historian	John Whipple (Applejack)	Afifi
	Sergeant at Arms	Bobby Riggs (Bebunk)	Hadi
		Fred Sandall (Yo Yo)	Mohammed
		Richard Burgess (Salty)	Aleppo
		Ron Zappone (Skittles)	Sphinx
	Official Photographer	Richard Cain (RC)	Yaarab
	Marshall	Michael Blais (Bow)	Kora
2005-06	President	Ed Whitenett (Stripes)	Al Azhar
	1st Vice President	Sanford A. Morris (Ootz)	Zuhrah
	2nd Vice President	Ken Taylor (Grimee)	Abou Ben Adhem
	3rd Vice President	Bill London (10 Can)	Moslah
	Secretary	Don Kinyon (Bowzo)	Mohammed
	Treasurer	Ernest Pearlstein (Rollo)	Aleppo
	Sneaker Chairman US/Mexico	Joe Cole (Ol Coach)	Ben Hur
	Assistant Sneaker Chairman USA	Mel Cooper (Happy)	El Bekal
	Sneaker Chairman Canada	Alan Bell (Ding Dong)	Al Shamal
	Assistant Sneaker Chairman Canada	Neil McNeilage (Ho! Ho!)	Rameses
	Education Director	Randy Weldon (Wuzzles)	Za Ga Zig
	Assistant Education Director	David Newcomb (Do No)	Aleppo
	Clown Alley Editor	Gene Harris (Geno)	Tebala
	Pins/Patches Chairman	Bill London (10 Can)	Moslah
	Quartermaster	Robert Bassett (Peaches)	Ainad
	Chaplain	Michael Howard (Howiee)	Moolah
	Parliamentarian	Walter Kendall (Troubles)	Moolah
	Public Releations	Gordon Keene (Gordo)	Zamora
	Historian	John Whipple (Applejack)	Afifi
	Sergeant at Arms	Bobby Riggs (Bebunk)	Hadi
		Fred Sandali (Yo Yo)	Mohammed
		Richard Burgess (Salty)	Aleppo
		Ron Zappone (Skittles)	Sphinx
	Official Photographer	Richard Cain (RC)	Yaarab
	Marshall	Michael Blais (Bow)	Kora
2006-07	President	Sanford Morris (Ootz)	Zuhrah
	1st Vice President	Ken Taylor (Grimee)	Abou Ben Adhem
	2nd Vice President	Bill London (10 Can)	Moslah
	3rd Vice President	John Wilbanks (Hambone)	Yaarab
	Secretary	Robert Bassett (Peaches)	Ainad

Year	*Position*	*Name*	*Temple*
2006-07	Treasurer & Imperial Liaison	Ernest Pearlstein (Rollo)	Aleppo
Cont'd	Junior Past President	Ed Whitenett (Stripes)	Al Azhar
	Public Relations	Mark Burgad (Buzzy)	Naja
	Sneaker Chairman USA	Joe Cole (Ol Coach)	Ben Hur
	Assistant Sneaker Chairman USA	Mel Cooper (Happy 2)	El Bekal
	Sneaker Fund Chairman Canada	Alan Bell (Ding Dong)	Al Shamal
	Assistant Sneaker Fund Chairman Canada	Neil McNeilage (Ho Ho)	Rameses
	Sneaker Fund Chairman Mexico	Leon Portman (Joy)	Anezeh
	By-Laws Committee	Ed Whitenett (Stripes)	Al Azhar
		Larry Stinger (Foooey)	
		Richard Cain (RC)	Yaarab
	Education Director & Webmaster	Randy Weldon (Wuzzles)	Za Ga Zig
	Assistant Education Director	Ed Cox (Fire Plug)	Hella
	Clown Alley Editor	Gene Harris (Geno)	Tebala
	Parliamentarian	Larry Stringer (Foooey)	
	Historian	Richard Cain (RC)	Yaarab
	President's Personal Aides	Ed Mitzel (Mitzie)	
		Mike O'Neil (Crackers)	Zuhrah
	Pin & Patches Chairman	Ed Romine (Tiny)	Kosair
	East Coast Education Director & *Clown Alley* Contributor	David Newcomb (Do No)	Aleppo
2007-08	President	Ken Taylor (Grimee)	Abou Ben Adhem
	1st Vice President	Bill London (10 Can)	Moslah
	2nd Vice President	John Wilbanks (Hambone)	Yaarab
	3rd Vice President		
	Secretary	Robert Bassett (Peaches)	Ainad
	Treasurer & Imperial Liaison	Michael Howard (Howiee)	Moolah
	Junior Past President	Sanford Morris (Ootz)	Zuhrah
	Chaplain	John Hull (Homie)	Abou Ben Adhem
	Quartermaster	Dan Elmore (Cravin)	Abou Ben Adhem
	Sneaker Chairman USA	Mark Burgad (Buzzy)	Naja
	Co-Sneaker Chairman USA	Joe Cole (Ol Coach)	Ben Hur
	Sneaker Fund Chairman Canada	Donald Hamilton (Milty)	Gizeh
	Assistant Sneaker Fund Chairman Canada	Neil McNeilage (HoHo)	Rameses
	Sneaker Fund Chairman Mexico	Leon Portman (Joy)	Anezeh
	By-Laws Committee	Sanford Morris (Ootz)	Zuhrah
		Ed Whitenett (Stripes)	Al Azhar
		Larry Stringer (Foooey)	
	Education Director & Webmaster	Randy Weldon (Wuzzles)	Za Ga Zig
	Assistant Education Director	Ed Cox (Fire Plug)	Hella
	Canadian Education Director	Ed Whitenett (Stripes)	Al Azhar
	Clown Alley Editor	Gene Harris (Geno)	Tebala
	Parliamentarian	Larry Stringer (Foooey)	
	Historian	Richard Cain (RC)	Yaarab
	Pins & Patches Chairman	Ed Romine (Tiny)	Kosair
	Imperial Liaison	Ernest Pearlstein (Rollo)	Aleppo
	ISCA Clown of the Year Committee	Larry Stringer (Foooey)	
		Joe Cole (Ol Coach)	Ben Hur
		Sanford Morris (Ootz)	Zuhrah
	President's Personal Aide	Larry Taylor (Tater)	Kokomo/Murat
	President's Personal Aide	Bret Stahler (Snaptrap)	Antioch
	President's Personal Aide	Greg Keeling (Weezer)	Abou Ben Adhem
	Ambassadors	Don Henson (Lil Bit)	
		Ted Reed (Razzle)	
		Bob Johnson (Bubbos)	
		Mike Nelson (Tickets)	
		Bobby Riggs (Bebunk)	
		Tom Johnson (U-No)	El Riad
	Sergeant-at-Arms	Danny Anderson (Meatball)	Kosair

Year	*Position*	*Name*	*Temple*
2007-08 *Cont'd*		Rex Mitchell (Candy)	India
		Randy Jones (Spazz)	Abou Ben Adhem
2008-09	President	Bill London (10 Can)	Moslah
	1st Vice President	John Wilbanks (Hambone)	Yaarab
	2nd Vice President		
	3rd Vice President	Randy Weldon (Wuzzles)	Za Ga Zig
	Secretary	Bob Bassett (Peaches)	Ainad
	Treasurer	Michael Howard (Howiee)	Moolah
	Junior Past President	Ken Taylor (Grimme)	Abou Ben Adhem
	Chaplain	Gene Bowie (Bow Wow)	Moslah
	Quartermaster & Historian	Dan Elmore (Cravin)	Abou Ben Adhem
	Sneaker Chairman USA	Joe Cole (Ol Coach)	Ben Hur
	Sneaker Fund Chairman Canada	Donald Hamilton (Milty)	Gizeh
	Co-Sneaker Fund Chairman Canada	Neil McNeilage (HoHo)	Rameses
	Sneaker Fund Chairman Mexico	Leon Portman (Joy)	Anezah
	Education Director & Webmaster	Richard Cain (RC)	Yaarab
	Assistant Education Director	Ken Whigham (Diamonds)	Yaarab
	Assistant Education Director	David Newcomb (Do No)	Aleppo
	Assistant Education Director	Eddie Cox (Fire Plug)	Hella
	Webmaster	Gaylord Thomas (Zeeby)	India
	Clown Alley Editor	Gene Harris (Geno)	Tebala
	Sergeant-at-Arms	Mike Coffey (U-Who)	Alzafar
	Public Relations & Photographer	Brian R. Kennedy	Antioch
	Parliamentarian	Larry Stringer (Foooey)	Moolah
	Marshal, Master of Ceremonies & Imperial Liaison	Ernest Pearlstein (Rollo)	Aleppo
2009-10	President	John Wilbanks (Hambone)	Yaarab
	1st Vice President		
	2nd Vice President	Randy Weldon (Wuzzles)	Za Ga Zig
	3rd Vice President	Mark Burgad (Buzzy)	Naja
	Secretary	Bob Bassett (Peaches)	Ainad
	Treasurer	Michael Howard (Howiee)	Moolah
	Junior Past President	Bill London (10 Can)	Moslah
	Chaplain	Randy Young (Toot Roar)	Ainad
	Historian	Dan Elmore (Cravin)	Abou Ben Adhem
	Sneaker Fund Chairman USA	Bil London (10 Can)	Moslah
	Sneaker Fund Chairman Canada	Donald Hamilton (Milty)	Gizeh
	Sneaker Fund Co-Chairman Canada	Neil McNeilage (HoHo)	Rameses
	Sneaker Fund Chairman Mexico	Leon Portman (Joy)	Anezeh
	Sneaker Fund Ambassador at Large	Rex Mitchell (Candy)	India
	Education Director	Richard Cain (RC)	Yaarab
	Assistant Education Director	Ken Whigham (Diamonds)	Yaarab
	Assistant Education Director	David Whigham (Do No)	Aleppo
	Webmaster	Clayton Robertson (Pabo)	Abou
	Clown Alley Editor	Gene Harris (Geno)	Tebala
	Sergeant At Arms	Mike Coffey (U-Who)	Alzafar
	Sergeant At Arms	John Thomas (Chatterbox)	Hejaz
	Public Relations & Photographer	Brian Kennedy (Flatfoot)	Antioch
	Parliamentarian	Larry Stringer (Foooey)	Moolah
	Marshal, Master of Ceremonies & Imperial Liaison	Ernest Pearlstein (Rollo)	Aleppo
2010-11	President		
	1st Vice President	Randy Weldon (Wuzzles)	Za Ga Zig
	2nd Vice President	Mark Burgad (Buzzy)	Naja
	3rd Vice President	George Pipes (Patches)	Cahaba
	Secretary	Bob Bassett (Peaches)	Ainad
	Treasurer	Rob Plummer	Murat
	Junior Past President	John Wilbanks (Hambone)	Yaarab
	Chaplain	Ellis McCormick	Murat

Year	Position	Name	Temple
2010-11	Historian	Richard Cain (RC)	Yaarab
Cont'd	Sneaker Fund Chairman USA	Bill London (10 Can)	Moslah
	Asst. Sneaker Fund Chairman USA	Bobby Byers (BooBoo)	Asiya
	Sneaker Ambassador at Large Western States	Rex Mitchell (Candy)	India
	Sneaker Ambassador at Large Eastern States	Thomas Ross (Tommy Duck)	Medinah
	Sneaker Fund Chairman Canada	Don Hamilton (Milty)	Gizeh
	Sneaker Fund Chairman Mexico	Leon Portman (Joy)	Anezeh
	Education Director	Lon Burke (Cactus)	Ansar
	Education Ambassador	David Newcomb (Do No)	Aleppo
	Education Director Canada	Ed Whitenett (Stripes)	Al Azhar
	Webmaster	Clayton Robertson (Pabo)	Abou Ben Adhem
	Clown Alley Editor	Gene Harris (Geno)	Tebala
	Sergeant At Arms	Bob Fitch (Bingo)	Medina
	Public Relations & Photographer	Brian Kennedy (Flatfoot)	Antioch
	Parliamentarian	Joe Cole (Ol' Coach)	Ben Hur
	Marshal, Master of Ceremonies & Imperial Liaison	Ernest Pearlstein (Rollo)	Aleppo
2011-12	President	Randy Weldon (Wuzzles)	Za Ga Zig
	1st Vice President	Mark Burgad (Buzzy)	Naja
	2nd Vice President	George Pipes (Patches)	Cahaba
	3rd Vice President	Robert Bassett (Peaches)	Ainad
	Secretary	Rupert Solis	Medinah
	Treasurer	Lon Burke (Cactus)	Arab
	Junior Past President	James Kaufman (Koppo)	Murat
	Chaplain	Ray Modisette (Tootsie)	India
	Education Director Canada	Ed Whitenett (Stripes)	Al Azhar
	Webmaster	Clayton Robertson (Pabo)	Abdallah
	Clown Alley Editor	Mark Burgad (Buzzy)	Naja
	Sergeant-At-Arms	Bob Fitch (Bingo)	
	Sergeant-At-Arms	Andy Mellman (Chille)	
	Sergeant-At-Arms	Mike O'Neil (Crackers)	Zuhrah
	Marshall & Master of Ceremonies	Tom Johnson (Uno)	El Riad
	Sneaker Fund Chairman USA	Bill London (10 Can)	Moslah
	Asst. Sneaker Fund Chairman USA	Nick Clausen (Pooky)	El Riad
	Sneaker Fund Chairman Canada	Don Hamilton (Milty)	Gizeh
	Asst. Sneaker Fund Chairman Canada	Bob Gordon (BuzzB)	Rameses
	Sneaker Fund Chairman Mexico	Leon Portman (Joy)	Anezeh
2012-13	President	Mark Burgad (Buzzy)	Al Bedoo & Naja
	1st Vice President	George Pipes (Patches)	Cahaba
	2nd Vice President	Robert Bassett (Peaches)	Ainad
	3rd Vice President	Lon Burke (Cactus)	Arab
	Secretary	Rupert Solis (Cy-Lo)	Medinah
	Treasurer	Nick Clausen (Pooky)	El Riad
	Junior Past President	Randy Welson (Wuzzles)	Za Ga Zig
	Education Director U.S.	David Newcomb (Do No)	Aleppo
	Education Director Canada	Ed Whitenett (Stripes)	Al Azhar
	Webmaster	Clayton Robertson (Pabo)	Abdallah
	Clown Alley Editor	Mark Burgad (Buzzy)	Al Bedoo & Naja
	Sergeant-At-Arms	Mike O'Neil (Crackers)	Zuhrah
	Sergeant-At-Arms	Steven Uttecht (Billy)	Naja
	Imperial Liaison & Master of Ceremonies	Ernest Pearlstein (Rollo)	Aleppo
	Imperial Liaison & Master of Ceremonies	Tom Johnson (Uno)	El Riad
	Photographer & Public Relations	Cliff Hartmier (Mr. Stripes)	Khartum
	Sneaker Fund Chairman USA	Bill London (10 Can)	Moslah
	Sneaker Fund Chairman Canada	Don Hamilton (Milty)	Gizeh
	Asst. Sneaker Fund Chairman Canada	Bob Gordon (BuzzB)	Rameses
	Sneaker Fund Chairman Mexico	Leon Portman (Joy)	Anezeh
	Sneaker Ambassadors	Ed Whitenett (Stripes)	Al Azhar
		Bill London (10 Can)	Moslah

Year	*Position*	*Name*	*Temple*
2012-13 *Cont'd*		Joel Stephens (Ketchup)	Naja
		Ken Whigham (Diamonds)	Yaarab
		Agustin Martinez Sibaja (Windies)	Anezah
		Al Vogele (Whistles)	Naja
	Historian	Richard Cain (RC)	Yaarab

ISCA Sneaker Fund

The ISCA Sneaker Fund is a philanthropy inside Shriners Hospitals for Children. The Sneaker Fund is a fund raising activity for Shriners Hospitals for Children Burn Research and operated only during Shrine events. ISCA operates this activity under the annual permission of the Imperial Council, which it gets from each Imperial Potentate.

An early plaster sneaker.

The Story of the Sneaker

The sneaker shown in this picture is 25" long, weighs 6 1/2 lbs. And the shoe lace is 80" long. This was made by the Uniroyal Co. of Naugatuck, Conn. For us, the Klown Unit of Pyramid Temple to collect funds for the "SNEAKER FUND". The purpose of this fund is to purchase sneakers for the children in the Burns Hospital in Boston, Mass., as the patients there are not allowed to wear shoes; they must wear only sneakers as they start to recuperate and walk around.

The Sneaker Fund is a North East Shrine Clown Assoc. project. At the Imperial Session in Georgia during July 1st to 6th this sneaker was put on display at the National Shrine Clown Association's Planning and Goal Committee for 1973 – 1974. It was then decided by the National Shrine Clown Association Committee to accept this as a national project and thereby provide sneakers for other two Burns Hospitals that are in the United States.

The original idea originated from Bob Andrews, of Manchester, New Hampshire, who is our present President of the North East Shrine Clown Assoc. I discussed this large sneaker with him during a trip to Montreal Shrine Hospital for Crippled Children. He was wholeheartedly in favor of the idea that this Sneaker Fund become a national project.

Now our aim is to get a large sneaker, like this for each of the areas, like North East, Middle Atlantic, South East, etc. so that each area can rotate the sneaker to each of their clown units, so this is how it will become a national project.

The idea of this large sneaker from Uniroyal Co. was the brainstorm of Abe Flaks, of Pyramid Temple. This sneaker will be displayed in all Shrine Klown events and parades. Look for it – help fill it.

This is the largest sneaker that the Uniroyal Co. has ever made.

More information will be available in the next issue on where to obtain shoes if your unit wants to get in on this project.

"Buzz-A-Roo" at fundraiser for children at Waco, Texas, 1986.

NSCA President Glen Wheeler presenting the first sneaker check to Imperial Potentate Wingerter at the 1974 Imperial Session in Atlanta.

Shriners Hospitals for Children

Shriners Hospitals for Children is a network of 22 non-profit hospitals across North America. Children with orthopedic conditions, burns, spinal cord injuries, and cleft lip and palate are eligible for care and receive all services in a family-centered environment, regardless of the patients' ability to pay.

Headquartered in Tampa, Florida, the hospitals are owned and operated by Shriners International. Patients must be minors under the age of 18 and are not required to have any familial affiliation with the Shriners order nor Freemasonry.

History

In 1920, the Imperial Session of the Shriners was held in Portland, Oregon. During that session the membership unanimously passed a resolution to establish the hospital system.

The first hospital in the system opened in 1922 in Shreveport, Louisiana. It provided pediatric orthopedic care. In 1962, the Shriners of North America allocated $10 million dollars to establish three hospitals that specialized in the treatment and rehabilitation of burned children. After visiting 21 university-based medical institutions, the decision was made to build their first pediatric burn hospital on the campus of the University of Texas Medical Branch in Galveston, Texas.

Today, treatment areas cover a wide range of pediatric orthopedics, including scoliosis, limb discrepancies, clubfoot, hip dysplasia, and juvenile idiopathic arthritis, as well as cerebral palsy, spina bifida, and other neurological conditions that affect ambulation and movement.

Three of the hospitals provide spinal cord injury rehabilitation that is developmentally appropriate for children and adolescents, with adventure and adapted sports programs, activity-based rehabilitation, aquatherapy, animal-assisted therapy, and other innovative programs.

Four of the hospitals (Boston, Galveston, Cincinnati, and Sacramento) provide world-famous care for children with burns, as well as treating a variety of skin conditions such as epidermolysis bullosa and toxic epidermal necrolysis. The Boston, Chicago, and Portland hospitals also provide treatment for children with craniofacial conditions, especially facial clefts.

This marker notes the site of the world's first Shriners Hopsital, located in Shreveport, Louisiana.

The hospital in Sacramento is the only hospital in the Shriners' system that focuses on all three areas of treatment (burns, orthopedics, and spinal cord injuries), as well as research. The Sacramento hospital also houses its own orthotics and prosthetics lab and development facilities.

Transportation to the hospitals is often provided free of charge by Shriner-drivers across the country. Children accepted for treatment become part of the Shriners Hospital system until their 18th or, sometimes, their 21st, birthday, eligible for both inpatient and outpatient treatment for all facets of their disability.

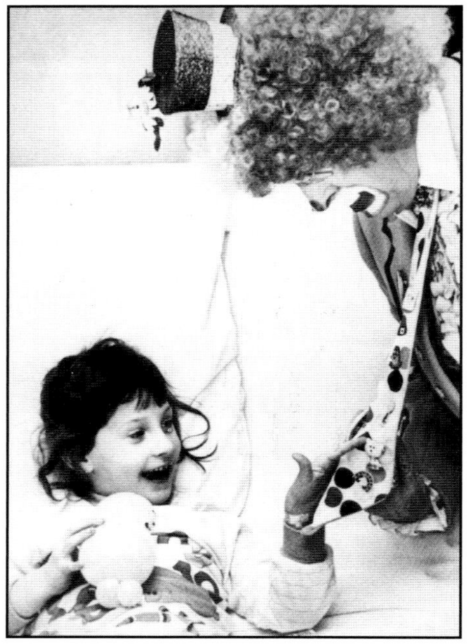

"Jif" at a headstart Christmas party, 1971.

While the overwhelming emphasis of the hospitals is to provide medical care to children regardless of the family's ability to pay, the mission of the hospitals also includes research on the conditions treated and the education of medical professionals, including medical residents and fellows, nurses, physical, recreation, and occupational therapists, speech and language pathology, psychologists, social workers, and child life specialists.

In September 2008, the Shriners Hospital in Galveston sustained significant damage from Hurricane Ike. The hospital was closed for renovation at that time, and care for children with acute burns was provided at other Shriners Hospitals for Children.

On Dec. 13, 2009, the Shriners Hospital in Galveston reopened with a grand reopening celebration and plans to continue to be able to provide excellent care for burn patients in the area.

Mission

Shriners Hospitals for Children has a mission to:

Provide the highest quality care to children with neuromusculoskeletal conditions, burn injuries and other special healthcare needs within a compassionate, family-centered and collaborative care environment.

Provide for the education of physicians and other healthcare professionals.

Conduct research to discover new knowledge that improves the quality of care and quality of life of children and families.

This mission is carried out without regard to race, color, creed, sex or sect, disability, national origin or ability of a patient or family to pay.

Orthopedic Care

Boston, Massachusetts
Chicago, Illinois
Erie, Pennsylvania
Greenville, South Carolina
Honolulu, Hawaii

Houston, Texas
Lexington, Kentucky
Los Angeles, California
Mexico City, Mexico
Minneapolis, Minnesota (Twin Cities)
Montreal, Canada
Philadelphia, Pennsylvania
Portland, Oregon
Sacramento, California (Northern California)
Salt Lake City, Utah
Shreveport, Louisiana
Spokane, Washington
Springfield, Massachusetts
St. Louis, Missouri
Tampa, Florida

Burn Care

Boston, Massachusetts
Cincinnati, Ohio
Galveston, Texas
Sacramento, California (Northern California)

Spinal Cord Injury Rehabilitation

Chicago, Illinois
Sacramento, California (Northern California)
Philadelphia, Pennsylvania

Cleft Lip and Palate

Chicago, Illinois
Cincinnati, Ohio
Houston, Texas
Los Angeles, California
Portland, Oregon
Sacramento, California (Northern California)
Shreveport, Louisiana
Springfield, Massachusetts

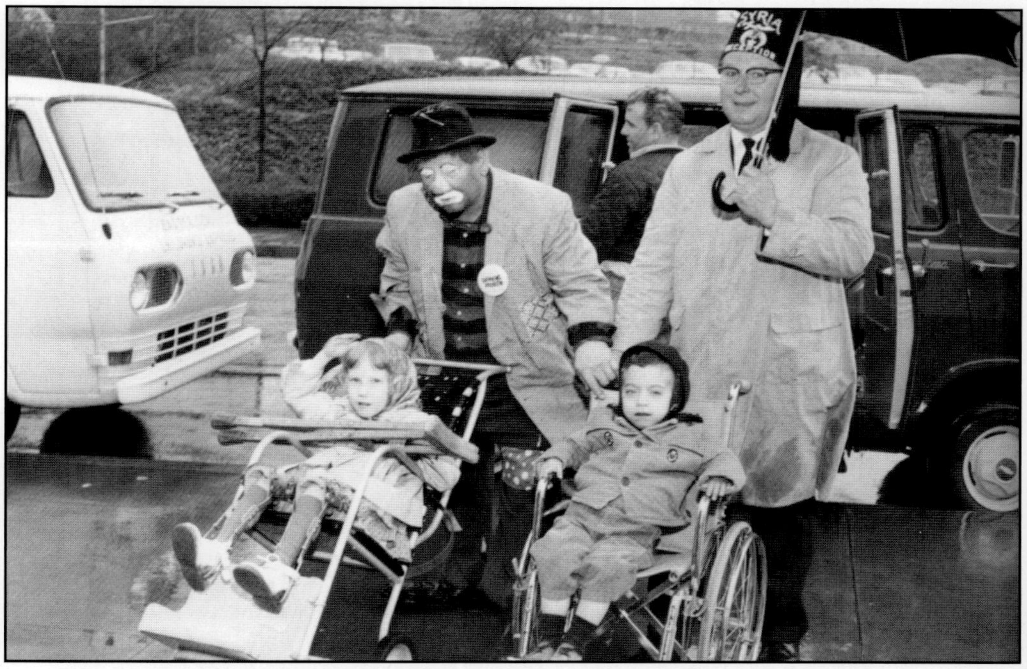

"Dumplin" taking children to the Shrine Circus.

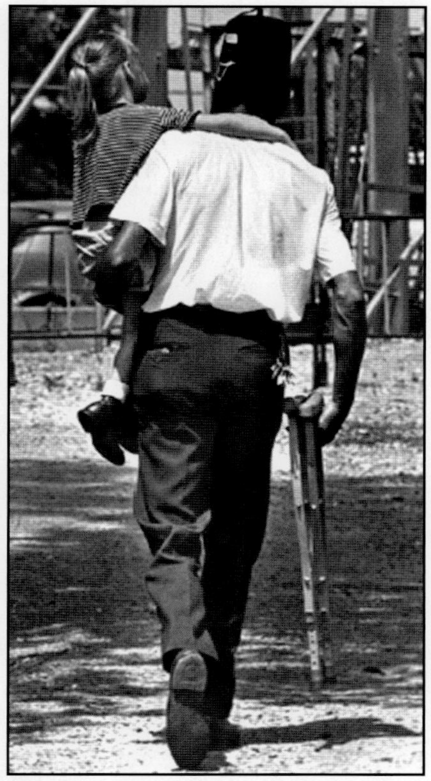

This photo of a Shriner carrying a child served as the first logo for Shriners Hospitals.

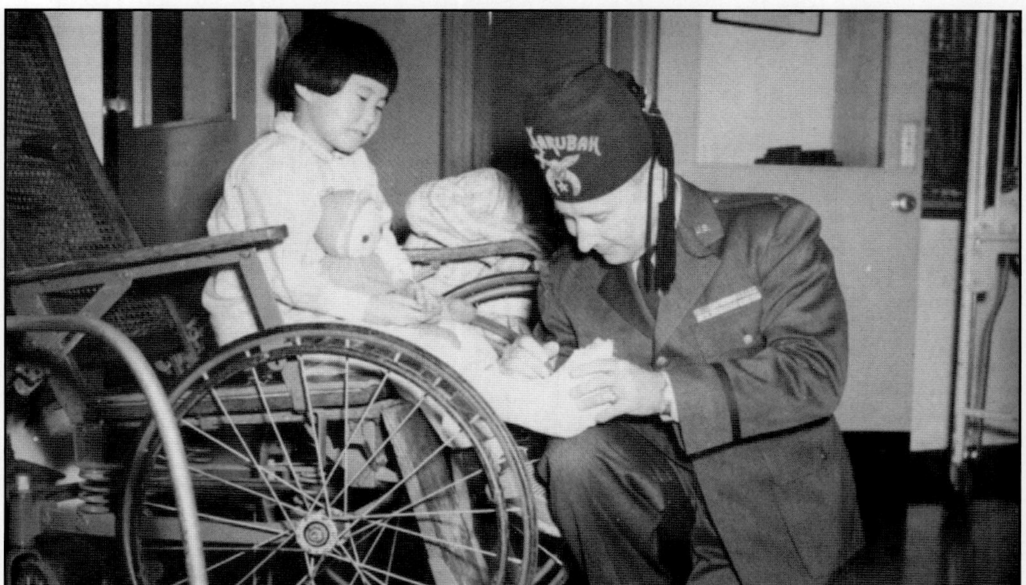

"Jimbo" Chastain autographs the cast of a Japanese crippled girl who is in the Shriner's Orthopedic Ward of the Tokyo Seventh Day Adventist Hospital, Nov. 1957.

The Shriners Hospitals logo

SHRINE
CLOWN
ASSOCIATION

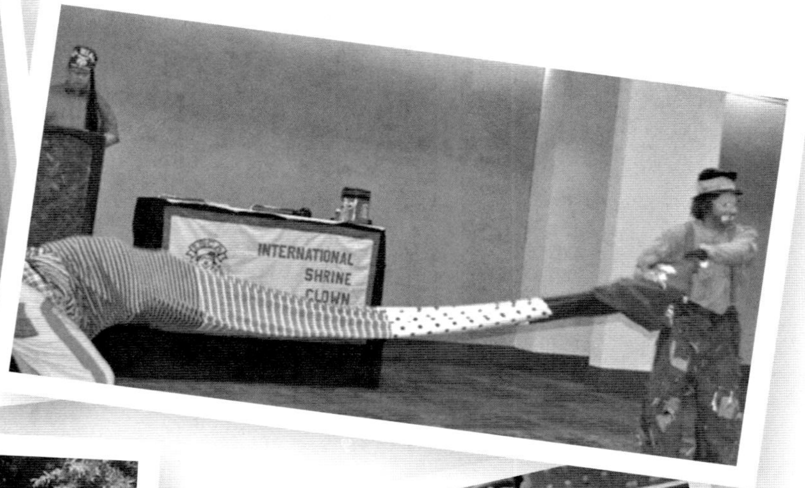
INTERNATIONAL
SHRINE
CLOWN

Shriners
Having Fun &
Helping Kids

The NESCA Road Trip for Hospitals and Kids

By David P. Newcomb, NESCA President, 2007-2008

For three days in July 2008, members of the North East Shrine Clowns Association (NESCA) came together for a very special road trip to benefit the three hospitals in the northeast region and the kids who are patients there. The trip covered over a thousand miles and when it was all over, there were a lot of smiling faces, colorful pictures and happy memories.

The idea for this road trip was actually born back in January at a NESCA meeting in Massachusetts. The meeting was fairly standard, as far as meetings are concerned. Several issues were dealt with, decisions were made and reports were read and accepted. One lively topic of discussion was an idea to make a donation from our NESCA organization to support our causes of Shrine Clowns. A committee was formed to investigate the possibilities and to act accordingly under the restrictive guidelines in place.

A great deal of research was done to find an appropriate donation that would honor the NESCA clowns for their efforts over the years. There were phone calls and emails to hospital administrators, equipment manufacturers, product development personnel and others to find a solution to a reasonably simple request. How can we make use of the NESCA treasury in a special way that supports the three hospitals in our northeast region, supports the Sneaker Fund, gives joy to all concerned and helps our kids?

During a call with an executive at Shriners Hospital in Boston, the idea of a pediatric utility transporter was brought up. This is a versatile and fun kind of wheelchair that allows for pediatric patients to be transported from place to place while enjoying safety and comfort. These colorful BearWagon transporters replace gurneys or stretchers in a non-intimidating, encouraging and "kid-friendly" manner. They are also designed to provide for easy operation with IV pole mounts and equipment holders. Steelcraft Inc., which manufactures the BearWagon transporter, is in Millbury, Massachusetts, and having a local business involved was well accepted by all parties. Doug Backman, President of Steelcraft Inc. was easily accessible, knowledgeable and very enthusiastic about the opportunity to have his equipment in the Shriners hospitals. Without hesitation, Mr. Backman offered to donate a pediatric IV stand with each transporter purchased for a Shriners Hospital. Valued at $300 each, these colorful stands have been specifically designed for pediatric patients. They have roller blade-type wheels with sealed axle bearings, which allow for smooth and silent operation, even over carpeting or elevator door gaps. Armed with this information, the plans began to fall into place and the road trip began to take shape.

The officers of NESCA worked together, making a flurry of further calls and e-mails. Calendars were checked and a plan for deliveries and presentations was put into place, with July 8th as the starting point. Ill. Peter Stone, P.P. and Recorder at Aleppo Shrine Center offered the Aleppo Shrine hospital van to NESCA, to be used for the three-day road trip. NESCA officers and Nobles Dave Newcomb, Ed Dowling and Ernest Pearlstein along with Aleppo Clown Dave "High Tower" Sullivan first traveled to Millbury to pick up the equipment.

We met with Mr. Backman who greeted us with excitement in his voice and a bounce in his step, inviting us into his office and sharing with us some history and background of his manufacturing plant. Our team brought the equipment to the van, secured it inside and continued on to the Springfield hospital.

Arriving right on time, we brought the first transport into the Springfield hospital lobby where we met Mark Niederpruem, the Springfield Hospital Administrator. Also present was Kirk Burkins P.P. and a member of the Board of Governors. Additionally, in attendance there were Melha clown Jim "NitWit" Allard and Anah clown Andrew "Iggy" Matlins, who drove from Bangor, ME to join in the presentation. ("Iggy" left Bangor at 3:00am. Whoever said, "You can't get there from here" doesn't know NESCA Clowns.) A patient was chosen to be the first

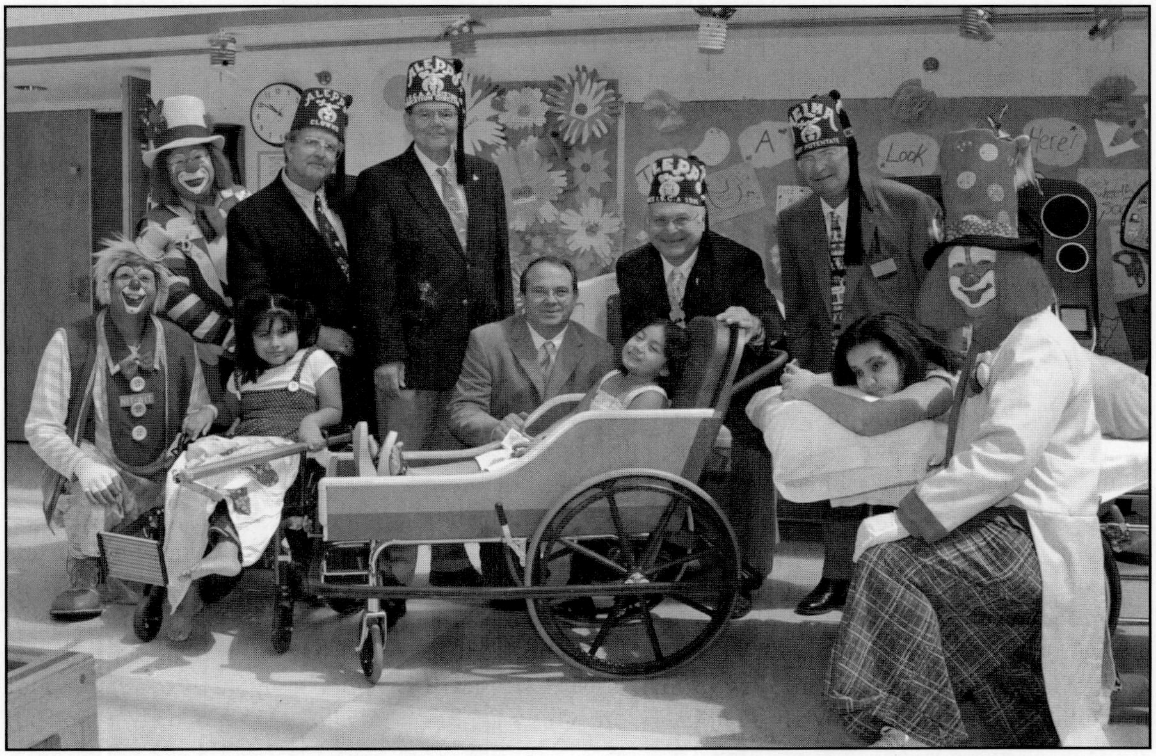

Pictured l-r around the new BearWagon Pediatric Transporter and some of the Springfield patients: "Nit-Wit," "Iggy," Ed Dowling, Dave Newcomb, Springfield Hospital Administrator Mark Niederpruem, Ernest Pearlstein, Kirk Burkins and "High Tower."

to try out the new BearWagon Transporter and her smile told us that this was an excellent gift for the hospital and the kids. "High Tower," "Iggy" and "NitWit" took their opportunity and visited the kids in the playroom and a few pictures were taken there. After the pictures were taken, the NESCA team continued on to the Boston hospital to make the next presentation that afternoon.

Back row, l-r: Ed Dowling, Dave Newcomb, Boston Hospital Administrator C. Thomas D'Esmond, Ernest Pearlstein, David Faulkner. Front, l-r: "Iggy," The new BearWagon Pediatric Transporter with hospital patient and "High Tower."

We arrived in Boston shortly after 1:00 p.m. and were greeted by the Boston Hospital Administrator C. Thomas D'Esmond and David Faulkner, Director of Development. (Mr. Faulkner was instrumental in our donation research and his knowledge of hospital equipment originally led us to Steelcraft Inc. and the pediatric transport.) As in Springfield, the clowns visited the playroom and Iggy and High Tower took the opportunity to spend more time with the kids. A child was chosen to take the first ride, and again, her smile gave them the confirmation we were waiting for. The BearWagon pediatric transporter is a winner and the kids are finding it irresistible.

Our Boston patient was helped out of a similar type of transporter that is more commonly found in many pediatric hospitals. The older version is much plainer looking and without the bright colors and safety rails.

L-r: Karnak Clowns "Squid," "Pi-vous," Ernest Pearlstein, Montreal Hospital Administrator Celine Doray, Dave Newcomb, "MacFEZstir" and Mark Laxer, Karnak Ambassador.

A brief conversation with the staff at the Boston hospital gave us additional confirmation regarding the safety features, specifically the bumper rail. This difference should alleviate many minor accidents associated with the older equipment. Also, the new BearWagon Pediatric Transporters are made with superior materials and should give many more years of service than the currently used models.

With two BearWagon pediatric transporters safely delivered to the two Massachusetts hospitals, the NESCA team called it a day and each member went home. On Wednesday, Nobles Newcomb and Pearlstein would make the trip to Montreal. The travel plans were checked and contacts were made with counterparts in Canada. With passports in hand, we started off at 8:00 a.m. on the 325-mile journey to Montreal.

The weather cooperated for most of the ride, with the only exception being the downpour that happened around lunchtime. While the skies looked threatening when we stopped for something to eat, it was still dry. Unfortunately, coming out of the restaurant, we discovered that the skies had opened and our van was receiving a refreshing rinse. Unfortunately, we received a complete rinse as well. But we still had a few more hours of northbound road-trip remaining, and we still had plenty of time to dry off.

We crossed the border into Canada and checked the directions we had from MapQuest. Our copy gave specific instructions and yet the road signs were not cooperating with our MapQuest directions. Specifically, the road signs were more French

L-r: David "Do-No" Newcomb and Ernest "Rollo" Pearlstein in Montreal with the kids.

than English so we followed the signs to Montreal and continued on. Without any more problems, we cruised over the bridges and into the City of Saints. Finally, we called the hospital and were easily guided in to our destination. Some simple navigation and some good luck had brought us within a few blocks of the hospital and we were within ten minutes of our planned arrival time.

The Montreal hospital was a busy place as Shrine hospitals usually are. The front entrance area was filled with visitors, patients and hospital personnel along with several clowns from Karnak Shrine. They welcomed us with smiles and hugs and brought us inside to meet Montreal Hospital Administrator Celine Doray and members of her staff. The official presentation was made as we had done previously in the Springfield and Boston hospitals. Ms. Doray expressed her gratitude and appreciation, as well as those of her colleagues and the patients who will use the equipment.

The work of the day was completed. It had been a long, tiring day and it was time for relaxing. For dinner, members of the Karnak Clowns treated their American visitors to a delicious dinner at Le Bifthèque steakhouse. After dinner and the easygoing conversations that accompanied it, we retired to our hotel in Montreal to rest up for Thursday.

Nobles Newcomb and Pearlstein, a.k.a. "Do-No" and "Rollo" simply had to take advantage of our opportunity to do what we do best—to perform for the kids at a Shriners hospital. In anticipation of this, we came prepared with our costumes and make-up and were ready as usual. While many of the patients were French, we simply performed in the universal language of magic, laughter and smiles. Rollo was comfortable with his usage of "merci beaucoup" while Do-No freely used his newfound and universally French expression, "ooh-la-la." In a few hours, we were done.

The seven-hour trek back to our homes in Massachusetts gave us time to reflect on our NESCA Road Trip. We both felt the satisfaction of completing our task and representing NESCA honorably. In conclusion, with one more task at hand, the final donation to the Sneaker Fund for Burns Research was made from NESCA. The kids received visits by the clowns. The hospitals received new equipment. The Sneaker Fund received a nice donation. Friendships were made. And the NESCA Road Trip was a success.

Perhaps now, we should start thinking about planning the next road trip. Ooh-la-la....

NAJA
OASIS

WAYNE

502

302

Shrine Temples & Their Clown Units

Temple	Unit
Aahmes	Alchemist Clowns
Abba	Nomads
Abdallah	Abdallah Clowns
Abou Ben Adhem	Clowns
Abu Bekr	Abu Bekr Clowns
Acacia	Klowns
Acca	Acca Klownz
Afifi	Afifi Shrine Clowns
Afifi	Southwest Washington Clowns
Ahmed	Ahmed Clowns
Ainad	Jefferson County Krzy Klns
Ainad	Krazy Klowns
Ainad	Williamson Co. Krazy Klowns
Akdar	Bartlesville Merri-Makers
Akdar	Enid Shrine Klowns
Akdar	Merri Makers
Al Amin	Al Amin Clown Unit
Al Amin	Nomad Jokers
Al Aska	Anchorage Shrine Clowns
Al Azhar	Clowns
Al Azhar	Medicine Hat Shrine Clowns
Al Azhar	Red Deer Clowns
Al Bahr	Al Bahr Clowns
Al Bedoo	Lewiston Klowns
Al Bedoo	Al Bedoo Clowns
Al Kader	Kader Clowns
Al Kaly	Kaly Klowns
Al Kaly	Clowns of Al Kaly Shrine
Al Koran	Cleveland Clowns
Al Koran	Youngstown Clown Unit
Al Malaikah	Clowns
Al Malaikah	Kern County Shrine Clowns
Al Malaikah	Lompoc Shrine Club
Al Malaikah	Paso Robles Shrine Clowns
Al Malaikah	Woodland Hill SC
Al Menah	Al Menah Clowns
Al Shamal	Al Shamal Clowns
Aladdin	Aladdin Clowns
Aladdin	HSCS Clowns
Aleppo	Aleppo Clowns
Alhambra	Alhambra Clowns
Ali Ghan	Harige
Aloha	Aloha Shrine Clowns
Alzafar	Kerr Klowns
Alzafar	Nemnuf
Amara	Komic Klownz
Anah	Anah Shrine Klowns
Anezeh	Tacos
Ansar	Ansar Clowns
Antioch	Funsters
Arab	Clowns
Araba	Fun & Frolic
Araba	Jokers of Araba
Arabia	Town Clowns

Temple	Unit
Ararat	Ararat Clowns
Asiya	Asiya Shrine Clowns
Bagdad	Bannack Klowns
Bagdad	Gallatin Shrine Clowns
Bahia	Fun & Frolic
Barak	Barak Shrine Temple Clowns
Bedouin	Bedouin Clowns
Beja	Beja Temple Clowns
Bektash	Bektash Clowns
Ben Ali	Ben Ali Clowns
Ben Hur	Srekoj Klowns
Beni Kedem	Clowns
Boumi	Boumi Clowns
Cahaba	Buffoons Clown Unit
Crescent	Crescent Clowns
Cyprus	Capital District Clowns
Damascus	Flour City Clowns
Egypt	Fun-Frolic Clowns
El Bekal	El Bekal Shrine Clowns
El Bekal	High Desert Clowns
El Hasa	El Hasa Clowns
El Jebel	Clowns
El Kahir	Jolly Jokers
El Kahir	Northeast Iowa Motor Clowns
El Kalah	El Kalah Clowns
El Karubah	Buffoons Clown Unit
El Karubah	El Karubah Clowns
El Katif	Columbia Basin SC Clowns
El Katif	Inland NW Shrine Klowns
El Korah	Jokers
El Korah	US Klowns
El Maida	Clowns
El Mina	Braz-Clowns
El Mina	Nem Loof Clowns
El Riad	El Riad Clowns
El Zaribah	El Zaribah Clowns
Elf Khurafeh	Elf Khurafeh Clowns
Gizeh	Okanagan Klowns
Gizeh	Skeena Clown Unit
Gizeh	Vancouver Clowns
Gizeh	Victoria Clowns
Hadi	Funsters
Hadji	Komedians
Hadji	Komics
Hasan	Douglas Hobos
Hejaz	Characters Clown Unit
Hejaz	Joker Unit
Hella	Hella Clowns
Hillah	Hillah Clowns
India	India Temple Clowns
Irem	Irem Clowns
Isis	Isis Clowns
Ismailia	Ismailia Shrine Clowns
Jericho	Jericho Clowns

Temple	Unit
Jerusalem	Clowns
Joppa	Joppa Clowns
Kaaba	Ottumwa Shrine Clowns
Kalurah	Klowns
Karem	Karem Clowns
Karnak	Clowns
Kazim	Central VA
Kazim	Kazim Tramps
Kem	Crookston Shrine Clowns
Kem	Minot Merrymen
Kena	Klowns
Kerak	Klowns
Kerbela	Kerbela Klown Kort
Khartum	Komedians
Khiva	Khiva Amarillo Klowns
Khiva	Lubbock Khiva Clowns
Kismet	Kismet Clown Unit
Kora	Kora Klowns
Korein	Casper Calliope Unit
Korein	Korein Clown Patrol
Kosair	Kosair Shrine Funsters
Lu Lu	Klownz
Mahi	Ft. Lauderdale SC
Maskat	Maskat Clowns
Mazol	Gander Shrine Club Clowns
Medinah	Clowns
Melha	Melha Clowns
Midian	Krazy Klowns
Mirza	C K Clowns
Mizpah	Mizpah Shrine Clowns
Mocha	Bruce Clowns
Mocha	Woodstock SC Clowns
Mohammed	Cornbelt Shrine Club
Mohammed	Funmakers
Moila	El Kadir Klowns
Moolah	3 Rivers Shrine Club
Moolah	ECMO Clowns
Moolah	Moolah Temple Clowns
Moolah	Semo Shrine Clowns
Moolah	Tiger Shrine Club
Morocco	Funsters
Moslah	Moslah Clowns
Moslem	Moslem Temple Clowns
Murat	Kokomo Shrine Clowns
Murat	Murat Shrine Circus Clowns
Murat	Shelby County Shrine Clowns
Naja	Naja Clown Patrol
Naja	Rapid City Clowns
Nile	Nile Clowns
Nur	Nur Clowns
Oasis	Clowns
Omar	Clowns
Orak	Orak Clowns
Oriental	Norco Shrine Clowns
Osman	Merry Medies
Osman	Osman Clowns
Palestine	Rhode Island Shriners
Philae	Cape Breton Shrine Clown Unit
Pyramid	Shriner Klown Unit
Rajah	Rajah Clowns
Rameses	Belleville Shrine Clowns
Rameses	El Shamaly Clowns
Rameses	Guelph Clowns
Rameses	Hamilton SC Clown Unit
Rameses	Kawartha Shrine Club
Rameses	Kingston Limestone Clowns
Rameses	Midland Dist. Shrine Clowns
Rameses	Muskoko Shrine Club
Rameses	Oshawa & Dist. Shrine Club
Rameses	Peel Shrine Club Clowns
Rameses	St. Catherine's Shrine Clowns
Rameses	Tecumseh Shrine Club
Rameses	Timmins Clowns
Rizpah	Owensboro Clowns
Rizpah	Rizpah Loonies
Sabbar	Cochise Clowns
Sahib	Sahib Temple Clowns
Saladin	Muskego Shrine Clown Unit
Scimitar	Scimitar Clowns
Sesostris	Sesostris Clowns
Shaddai	Shaddai Clowns
Sharon	Sharon Temple Clowns
Spinx	Funsters
Sudan	Sudan Dunn Clowns
Suez	3 Rivers Clowns
Suez	Abilene Clowns
Syria	Harige
Tangier	Tangier Clowns
Tebala	Tebala Temple Clowns
Tehran	Tehran Clowns
Tigris	Tigris Clowns
Tripoli	Tripoli Clown Unit
Tunis	Brookville & Dist. Shrine Klown
Tunis	Valley Unit
Wa Wa	Saskatoon Clown Unit
Wahabi	Wahabi Clowns
Yaarab	Kennesaw Mountain Jokers
Yaarab	Tucker SC
Yaarab	Yaarab Red Devils
Yelduz	Yelduz Clowns
Za-Ga-Zig	Za-Ga-Zig Clowns
Zamora	Zamora Clown Unit
Zelzah	Selsah Clowns
Zembo	Zembo Clowns
Zenobia	Zenobia Clowns
Ziyara	Zanies Clown Unit
Zor	Zor Temple Clowns
Zor	Sawdusters
Zuhrah	Funsters

ISCA Shrine Clown Units

Note: All ISCA Clown Units were invited to submit material to be featured in the ISCA 50th Anniversary History Book. The following are those that chose to participate.

ABDALLAH SHRINE CLOWNS HISTORY

The Abdallah Shrine Clowns is the oldest unit in the Abdallah Shrine today. The Clown Unit was originally organized in 1948 as the "Stunzts Club". Our early members performed without the formality of being clowns, but that never stopped them. In 1960 the "Stunzts Club" changed its name to the Abdallah Clown Unit. Since its inception in 1948 to the present, the Clown Unit has dedicated itself to supporting the Shriners Hospitals for Children.

The clown unit performs annually at the Abdallah Shrine Rodeo, held on Memorial Day each year. Add this to the numerous appearances at grand opening, picnics, parties, and parades, it makes the Abdallah Clowns one of the most visible units in our shrine temple.

ABU BEKR CLOWNS – SIOUX CITY, IA

The Abu Bekr Clowns have been making 'em laugh in Sioux City, IA for over 67 years.

It all started in 1945 when some members of the Abu Bekr Oriental Band got tired of tooting horns and instead went into makeup. They were still band members, but they were clowning around instead of making music.

Abu Bekr Shrine Clowns, Sioux City, Iowa.

That went on until 1953 when several band members petitioned the Divan to form a clown unit. The early clown unit only allowed 10 active joeys, with replacements coming from a long list of social members.

A year after the unit was formed they had a 1911 Worthington fire engine, which was featured in clown's parades. The fire truck was retired in 1956 and replaced by a 1929 Model A, which was

Kelly "Whoops" Houts and the clown's Model A.

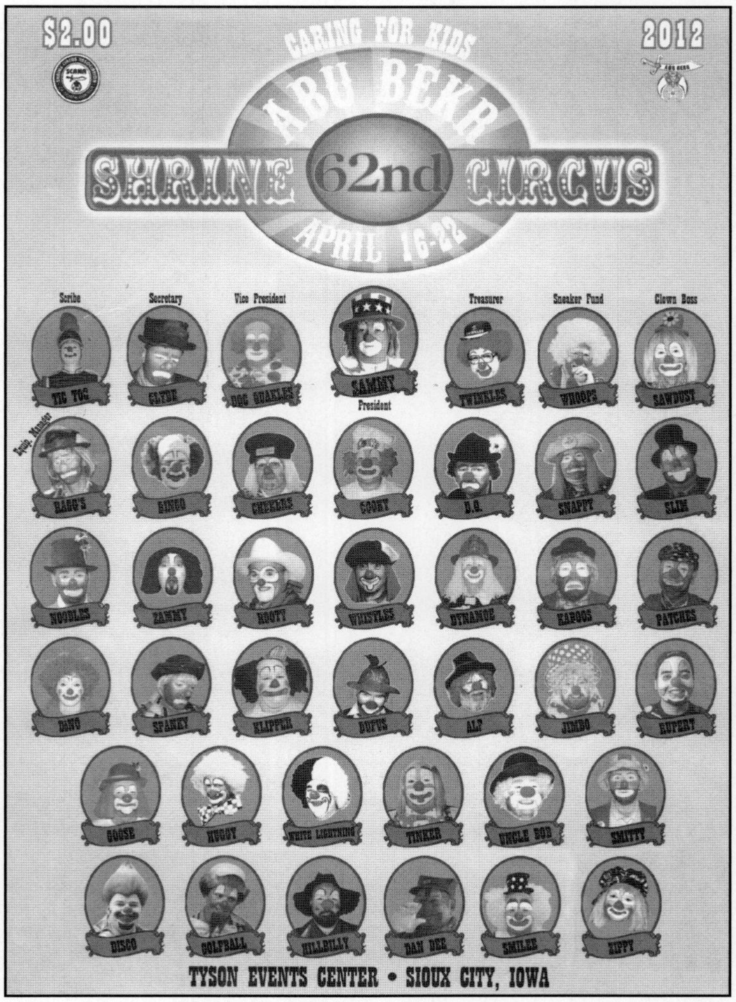

Abu Beker Shrine Circus ad.

transformed into a parade vehicle with a "fringe" on top. It has been maintained yearly and is still running like a wild steer. We also have a golf cart with clowns painted on the sides. Another vehicle is a train. This is pulled by a garden tractor made into a train engine with eight cars following it. We are now a proud owner of a calliope this has been redone and works well and is pulled by the Model A. Some of the clowns have their individual vehicles ranging from small cycles, cars and wagons.

Our clowns work hard at the circus and we are in charge of putting a coloring book together and selling it at the circus. Along with coloring book we give about 38 bicycles away at the circus. We do a lot of parades, Shrine Temple movements, school carnivals and balloon making at various events.

We are proud to work for the Sneaker Fund and have sent in donations every year for the past 20 years. We have a big oversize shoe that we proudly display. We always have Red Nose winners each year and one of our clowns is working on his 3rd Gold Nose. We help the Divan when they hold their hospital screenings. Some of our clowns attend the MSA and Central States Conventions, and have brought home many trophies in individual, skits and balloon making.

Our motto is: WE HAVE FUN SO KIDS CAN RUN.
Written by Kelly "Whoops" Houts

AFIFI SOUTHWEST WASHINGTON SHRINE CLOWN UNIT

The Southwest Washington AFIFI Shrine Clowns have continued to operate as a unit since they were organized in 1988. As members of AFIFI Shrine, we have continued to maintain a very active presence in our area. Our unit was formed as a second clown unit to AFIFI Shrine Clowns and we strive to maintain the reputation of the Tacoma unit, the World Famous AFIFI Shrine Clowns. We participate in local parades with our 1928 Reo fire truck, visits to the Portland unit of Shriners hospital, Christmas parties for the children and assist the local Gateway Shrine club in their activities. These include the annual Freedom Bowl football game and working with the Clark County Youth football league.

Back row, left to right: Pap Paw, Zig Zag, Seaweed and Klutz. Middle row, left to right: Jake, Tugboat and Chipper. Front row, left to right: Bumps and Sparkie.

Our unit currently has a membership of 14 clowns. President David (BUMPS) Bryant is director with Pat (MR STIX) Conroy assistant director and James (KLUTZ) Cobb as secretary-treasurer.

In the past three years we have lost three members to the Black Camel: Gordon (GORDIE) Gray; Clifford (SHOTGUN) Hathaway and William (TUGBOAT) Greene. We hope they are in a place where they can do a little clowning.

Our future looks good as we are receiving applications for membership and any group knows that that is important for survival.

WORLD FAMOUS AFIFI SHRINE CLOWNS

The Afifi Clown unit was formed in 1962 by Illustrious Sir William Brown as Potentate of Afifi Shrine. Illustrious Sir Brown had visited other Temples with Clown Units and decided Afifi should have one.

World Famous Afifi Clowns, 1962. L-r: Phelix "Fatso" Woempner, Bill "Big Bill" Groves, Bill "William" Brown, Lyle "Staff" Stafford, Vic "Tired Blood" Morgan and Wayne "Dude" McAlister.

He contacted Noble Bill Groves, our biggest clown, and asked Noble Bill Groves to form a small unit and act as its Director. Noble William "Big Bill" Groves formed a unit of six members consisting of Nobles William "Big Bill" Groves, Phelix "Fatso" Woempner, Clare Sherrod, Chuck Ellis, Ken Cornell, and Vic Morgan. None of the Nobles had any previous experience, but Phelix "Fatso" Woempner who had transferred from San Diego, CA where he had been in Al Bahr Temples Clown Unit. With much effort and patience on the part of Noble Woempner, they learned to put on make-up and some of the other necessities to

World Famous Afifi Shrine Clowns, 2012. L-r: Tom "Flips" Phillips, Larry "Poppy" Nelson, Daryl "Whut" McGaughlin, Paul "Billy Bob" Evans, Dusty "Sparkey" Rhodes and Randol "Kolohe" Brookshier.

World Famous Afifi Shrine Clowns, Portland Hospital visit.

World Famous Afifi Shrine Clowns, Parade Time.

make a clown. The new unit made their first appearance in the 1962 Daffodil Parade.

Several times during that first year as a unit, they tried to blow up the Temple, disturb the Recorder and generally upset the equilibrium of a stated meeting. This was among many examples of their commitment to keep things light and fun for everyone.

In June of 1962, the unit visited the Shriners Children's Hospital in Portland, OR. This visit alone was worth all the hours of work that this Clown Unit had done to prepare for the visit, as they learned what a privilege it is to be a Shriner.

The Unit later obtained a 1921 Model "T" Ford pick-up to use in parades. Much effort was put into this "T." Their hope was for others to enjoy it as much as they enjoyed fixing it up. The other rolling stock was a BIG RED bus.

During its 50 year history, the World Famous Afifi Shrine Clowns have participated in the annual Daffodil Parade, Junior Daffodil Parade, Toys for Tots, visits to the Shriner's Children's Hospitals in Portland and Spokane, Pacific Northwest Shrine Association, Easter Egg Hunts on the Capitol Grounds in Olympia and many more requests for the Clown services.

During the past 50 years this unit has among its members two Past Potentates; Illustrious Sir Glenn "Henney" Henderson and Illustrious Sir Barry "Speedy" Bede, two past presidents of ISCA; Noble John "Applejack" Whipple and Lyle "Oppo" Boyd, two Ambassadors to the Pacific Northwest; Noble Phelix "Fatso" Woempner and Noble Randol "Kolohe" Brookshier, and one Ambassador to Washington, Noble Dwight "Red" Silspeth.

AINAD KRAZY KLOWNS

The AINAD Klowns was started by Louie Schmulbach in the 1930s. Louie clowned, juggled and was a one man band. He had been with the Drum and Bugle Corp. He was also later joined by the members of the Director Staff. In 1966 these individuals started the Ainad Crazy Klown Unit with the 15 members.

Patch design approved by Red Skelton.

In 1967 they joined the National Clown Association started by Nobel Silva of Almas Temple, Washington, DC.

Members of the Shrine Unit wrote Red Skelton, requesting permission to use his character representation to be used as the patch for the group. He granted our request pending approval of the design. In 1972 Roy Carney and several members of the unit went to the Fox Theatre in St. Louis, MO where Red Skelton was performing. Here the work up of the patch was presented for the comedian's approval. This he graciously granted, and this patch is used to this date.

In the 1970s Adrian Croissant and Harry Collins started the dinner dance with skits and a kitchen band. These continued throughout the 1980s. In 1990 Rags and other members invited Emmett Kelly Jr. to put on a show in Collinsville, IL. The clowns were called upon to save the show and performed many skits to their surprised credit.

From 1966 to 1985 there were approximately 90 engagements per year with 32 parades. We are now doing approximately 35 events per year with 17 being parades.

In 1972 there were 42 clowns participating at the Shrine Parade in Belleville, IL, this being the best participation of this unit in its history. The following members have been recognized at National Conventions: Paul "Tiny" Hoff; Lester "Zippo" Withers; Bob "Peaches" Bassett; Adrian "Fattso" Croissant and Louie Schmulbach receiving many special awards. Special recognition is due to Bob "Peaches" Bassett; years of clowning, sharing his time with the ISCA as secretary for five years—he will be sworn in as ISCA President in 2014.

Other clowns that are active today include: Larry "Taz" Wolsfelt, has been a leader of our group this last several years; John Miller and Nick Miller, our present presidents; and special thanks go to Dave Langford for his insight. *Written by Adrian Croissant (Woowo!).*

AKDAR MERRI-MAKERS

AKDAR Temple has had clowns for a number of years, but the Merri-Makers Unit was actually organized in 1954 by H.L. "June" Moss. Other Charter Members were Hap Parker, Bob Black and Jim Bodelle.

In 1957 the Unit was recognized as a regular Unit by ADKAR and in the same year was received into the Central States Shrine

Association as a recognized body. By the end of 1958 there were 45 members.

In 1959 our Unit Director was Gailard Sartain, who is known for his roles in Hee-Haw and Saturday Night Live. Also, we have had three Potentates who were members of our Unit; H.L. "June" Moss in 1961, Charles Rosenburger in 1965 and Jim Mullins in 2010. Other officers of AKDAR, who are members of the Unit are James "Woody" Woodard, Treasurer for 10 years and our current Recorder, Rick Grubb.

Akdar Merri-Makers. Ron "Wide Track" Leaverton.

Adkar Merri-Makers won the Travel Trophy 12 years in a row, 2000-2011 C.S.S.C.A. Back row, l-r: "Sparky" Steve Carrol, Potentate 2011 David Skaggs, "Wide Track" Ronald Leaverton, "Duffer" Ron Davis, "Repete" Nick Goltra. Front row: "Rascal" Marcus Wilkie, "Boo Boo" Bruce Long, "Gizmo" David May and "Sureshot" Newell Barker.

It has always been the tradition of the Merri-Makers to go to the hospitals and visit children before going to our Children's Christmas Party. In 1992 the clown ladies (Merri-Maids) made Stockings for our "Kids," and the tradition was off and running. With donations from fast food stores, they were able to fill the Stockings during the first years. They cut, painted and filled them with the "goodies" collected. Soon after, other Shrine Ladies wanted to become involved, and the project continues to grow each year. Now, the Stockings are not only filled with goodies, they include stuffed animals and toys.

Our Merri-Makers Unit has become very active and successful through the years at Central States Shrine Clown Association competition, and has won the Traveling Trophy 12 years in a row; 2000-2011. Also, Bruce "Boo-Boo" Long was recognized at International Shrine Clown Association Clown of the Year in 2010.

Lifetime Members include: Robert "Hi I'm Bob" Boucher; Max "LilBit" Leaverton; Ron "Widetrack" Leaverton; H.L. "June" Moss; Bruce Mullins; Harold "Hap" Parker; J.W. "Robby" Robertson; Charlie "Radar" Sewell; Leroy Smith; Sid "Abby" Smithline; Lloyd "Rev" Williams; Rick "Ricky" Wightman and Warren Vandiver. *Written by Ron "Widetrack" Leaverton*

AL SHAMAL SHRINE CLOWNS, Edmonton, Alberta, Canada

The Al Shamal Clowns were organized on October 15, 1985 when 24 clowns of the Al Azhar Temple (Southern Alberta) had their membership transferred to the new Al Shamal Clown Unit of Northern Alberta. Of these clowns, three, Sandy Milligan, (first president of the new unit), Jack McCuaig and Bud Salloum are presently members of Al Shamal Temple. A fourth, George McEwen, was active until his death several years ago.

During the following years the unit has been active in the ISCA and PNSCA (International Shrine Clown Association and Pacific Northwest Shrine Clown Association). The unit has won many ISCA Awards for raising the most donations to the Shrine Hospital, Montreal Unit.

Two of the unit's members, W. Alan "Ding Dong" Bell and associate member Ed "Stripes" Whitenett have been ISCA Sneaker Chairs. In addition, "Stripes has been president of the ISCA.

Others in the unit have held executive positions in the PNSCA. Illustrious Sir Ari "Dr. Sigmund Fraud" Hoeksema has been a Potentate of Al Shamal Shrine Temple.

The unit has been awarded trophies for their outstanding performances in competitions in the ISCA and PNSCA.

Each summer the unit has participated in the parades of many towns in Northern Alberta and in Edmonton's Klondike Parade. In the winter, members have been very active in Christmas programs and the annual indoor Santa Claus Parade,

A highlight of their activities has been their presentation of a "Skit" in the annual Al Shamal Shrine Circus. Other activities have seen the unit performing in the community as they do birthday parties and other performances requested by community organizations. *Submitted by Noble W. Alan Bell*

ALEPPO CLOWN UNIT

Somewhere behind all those Joey's you should find our Cannon, which debuted at the Aleppo Circus this year. That's then Chief Rabban Dennis Reebel leaning out of the mussel.

We trace our roots back to 1961 when the Fitchburg/ Leominster Shrine Club, under President Dr. Phillip Poole, formed a Clown Club with 9 clowns. The following year ('62) Potentate James Bailey formed the Aleppo Unit with Leo Heal as

our first boss and Doc Poole as his assistant. The unit's first tour that year was the Imperial Session in Toronto, Canada.

In '65 Bert Smith took over as boss and in '70 we started initiating each new Potentate as an honorary Clown. In '74 Dick Lavin took over as boss when Bert passed away.

Over our first 20 years we limited our membership to 21 clowns.

In '82 Steve Kapantais became the boss followed by Chuck Setzco in '85. Ernie (Rollo) Pearlstein was the boss in '86 and active ever since. Jim Sickles followed in '87 and was the boss during the ISCA 25th Anniversary.

Over the ensuing 25 years our membership has slowly grown as well as the requests we receive and the total hours spent in face. One constant has been entertaining children and supporting our hospitals.

ANSAR CLOWNS

The "ancestry" of the Ansar Shrine Clowns is Ansar Shrine Center located in Springfield, Illinois. Ansar Temple was granted its charter on July 13, 1915. The word Ansar is of Arabic origin and is translated as "those who gave aid," or "The helpers…title of the believers of Medina who assisted Mohammed after the flight from Mecca."

Ansar Historical Car, 1975.

The Ansar Shrine Clowns began its life during the month of March 1969. Approximately 40 Nobles of Ansar Temple attended an organizational meeting. The Illustrious Potentate Harry R. Kern (1969) ordained Vernon W. "Doc" Powell to organize and establish a Clown Unit. "Doc" became the Clown Unit's first Director. The first By-Laws for the Ansar Shrine Clowns were adopted on May 21, 1969 and were confined to one page. There were no officers, no dues and no regular meetings. At the March 1969 organizational meeting, the charter members voted to purchase a clown car. Each member contributed $10.00 toward the purchase. The car was made from the front ends of two automobiles. One front end was a 1948 Plymouth and the other was a 1949 Plymouth ... both four-door sedans. These were mounted onto a frame fabricated to accommodate both ends. The car was painted red, then lettered and trimmed. At the conclusion of the 1975 parade season the clown car was taken in for major alterations. A 1951 Jeep truck front axle was installed as a rear end in the clown car. With this axle installed, it permitted the clown car to be steered from either end. This feature has brought many laughs from parade spectators and it really has established recognition of the clown car in every parade since that time.

In the years following the beginning of the unit the scheduled activity was usually parades. Occasional functions involved appearances at homecomings, fall festivals, company picnics and parties, and hospital visits.

During 1972, five joeys introduced small engine powered motor scooters to the Unit. The Clown Unit reorganized in 1973 and dues were assessed. At about the same time of the reorganization, a group of nobles were attempting to establish a Motor Clown Unit. When this unit was established, the Ansar Shrine Clowns were authorized only one piece of motorized equipment...the clown car. The joeys with motor scooters were so notified. Now the Unit is known as a "walking unit". The clown car has been refurbished several times over the years. It is the signature recognition piece of the Ansar Clown Unit.

Membership has risen and fallen over the years due to visits from the Black Camel and the general decline in Shrine membership. From 40 members in 1969, it dropped to 29 members in 1973 and rose to 104 members in 1983. Membership now is around 20 members.

The major fund raising activities are appearance donations. The Ansar Shrine Circus consistently brings out the noble joeys in large numbers. Several members have placed in GLSCUA and ISCA competitions. Through the hard work of many of the members and the guidance from some of the "older" joeys, the Ansar Shrine Clowns have become one of the top units in the Ansar Shrine.

ARAB SHRINE CLOWNS HISTORY

Topeka, Kansas

In 1950, Arab Potentate Paul E. Rogers asked Harold Jasperson and Raymond Krueger to assist him and the Shrine Band to entertain the Nobles and their Ladies on a railroad trip to a Central States Shrine Association (CSSA) meeting in St. Louis.

In St. Louis, the group visited the Shriners Hospital. While there, the Band performed circus music. Harold Jasperson and Raymond Krueger clowned around in costume with toy musical instruments entertaining the children. They were the first Arab Shriners to wear clown costumes. A seed had been planted for a clown unit.

The next year in 1951, three clowns marked the beginning of a new Clown Unit. These three clowns were Nelse K. Nelson, Julius Rafflelock, and Harold Jasperson. There was some feelings that clowns should not be permitted to participate in Shriner activities. But, at the CSSA Convention the Imperial Potentate told the clowns, "If you take the Band and the Clowns out of the parade, you might as well cancel the parade. People love Clowns."

During the first years, the Unit primarily participated at Ceremonials. Since that time the Unit has grown both in size and in numbers of activities they participate in. We are now active in the Central States Shrine Clown Association (CSSCA). We have individuals that participate in makeup competition, skit competition, and unit competitions in the yearly CSSA Convention. Since 1981, our Unit has gained respect from larger temples and have brought back numerous trophies. Two members Larry Pressman and Terry Wilson have served as CSSCA Presidents.

Many past members of our Unit have served as Potentates of Arab Shrine. They are Harold Jasperson in 1957, Nelse K. Nelson in 1960, E. Leslie Scrinopskie in 1977, Harlan Whiteley in 1983, Albert Jackson, Jr in 1986, E.I. "Andy" Anderson in 1995, Larry Pressman in 1998, Larry Bryan in 2003, Lynn Holt in 2005, Ron Scrinopskie in 2006, Pat Devlin in 2009, Alan Holt in 2011, and if all goes well, Bob Whitehead in 2013, and Chris Lewis in 2016.

Nick Roach has served as the Treasurer of Arab Shrine for several years. Other Unit members serve the Arab Potentate each year as appointments or serve on committees. Lon Burke has served the International Shrine Clown Association (ISCA) as Education Director, Treasurer, and will be installed as ISCA President in 2015.

Over the past 60 plus years, many members have served as officers of the Arab Shrine Clowns. Doug "Raggs" Jennings served as treasurer for more than 30 years. Current officers are Alan Barrett, Director, Donnie Bohannon, Assistant Director, Jim Blauw, Secretary, and Roger Elsbury, Treasurer.

The clowns are very active in supporting Arab Shrine activities. We participate in Ceremonials, parades, serve as "Bell Hops" at the Potentate's Balls, and run the "Chain Gang" at the annual Kansas Shrine Bowl. We always have good representation at the Shrine Circus. We autograph program books for the kids, and perform in a Unit skit at each performance of the circus. Some members work every performance each year.

Fund raising activities include a Clown's Chili Feed in January and a Clown's Wine Tasting in September. We chaperone kids playing on inflatable bounce games at the Kansas Boy's Wrestling Tournament each year. We raise money by twisting balloons at various organizations parties throughout the year. We enjoy attending the Arab Shrine Mystery Trips a couple of times a year. We have a Unit Picnic each summer for our families that has a large attendance and frequently has most of the members of the Divan and their ladies attending. We have a Unit Christmas Party in December for members and their ladies. At this event, awards are given by the Unit Director for the Clown of the Year, Rookie Clown of the Year, and Clown Lady of the Year.

Unit meetings are usually held monthly. On even numbered months, we invite our ladies to attend a dinner meeting at a local restaurant.

The clowns also take pride in the fact they bring smiles and laughter to people of all ages. One of the most rewarding things is bringing a smile to a child's face.

We are a very active group and have lots of fun. So like they say, if you want to have a good time and lots of laughter - "Be a Clown! Be a Clown!"

ASHLAND EL HASA SHRINE TEMPLE

The idea of a clown unit for the Ashland El Hasa Shrine Temple was formulated in the spring of 1963 with the encouragement and support of Doug Roberts who was in line for Potentate, and Benny Dawson who was then president of the El Hasa uniform units.

I attended the 1963 pilgrimage to the Imperial Council Convention in Chicago, as a clown and was initially assigned to the Director's Staff to see if there would be interest by others in formation of a clown unit, and this would be the first test. In the parade route which went from Wacker Drive to Soldiers Field in Chicago, I paraded in front of the Hillbilly Ford driven by Doug Roberts and Jack Wagoner of Grayson and was bumped from behind by the car as I stooped over with a broom sweeping some imaginary piece of dirt from the street. At the time I was bumped, the radiator was rigged to squirt water, and they would shoot water up in the air and try to hit me with it, which was a crowd pleaser.

That fall, I had a meeting at my home with several potential members, including were Bill Franklin, Don Franklin, Bill Reffit, and Ron Perry on the formation of an official unit. Shortly thereafter, the unit was formally recognized as a separate uniform unit, and I was elected as the first president. The next year, three or four clowns went to the Imperial Council Session in New York City, which was Home of the World's Fair. The following year, nine or 10 clowns attended the Imperial Council in Washington, DC, in which we had a lot of fun giving away funny money printed by Robert's Printing Company of Ironton, OH.

The unit quickly established visitations to the Shriners Crippled Children's Hospital at Lexington, KY, and on one such trip, traveled by way of Ashland Oil's DC-3 airplane. We also participated in many local charity events as preforming clowns as well as Christmas visits to local hospitals. Vera Richey, the wife of L.T. Richey was the first person to donate blood to the Cincinnati Shriners Crippled Children's Burn Unit.

The first clown motor vehicle used in a parade was a 1922 Seagrave fire truck donated from the city of Ashland and restored under the presidency of L.T. Richey Jr. Many of the early founding clown members were on the degree teams for Poage Lodge and Ashland Commandary and did Third Degree Lodge work in many local Kentucky Masonic Lodges. *Written by Charles Donald "Felix" Franklin.*

BOUMI CLOWNS

In January 1967 Potentate Robert Phelps created the Boumi Clown Unit. Thirteen Nobles were charter members and performed at the Potentates Ball, for the first time in early

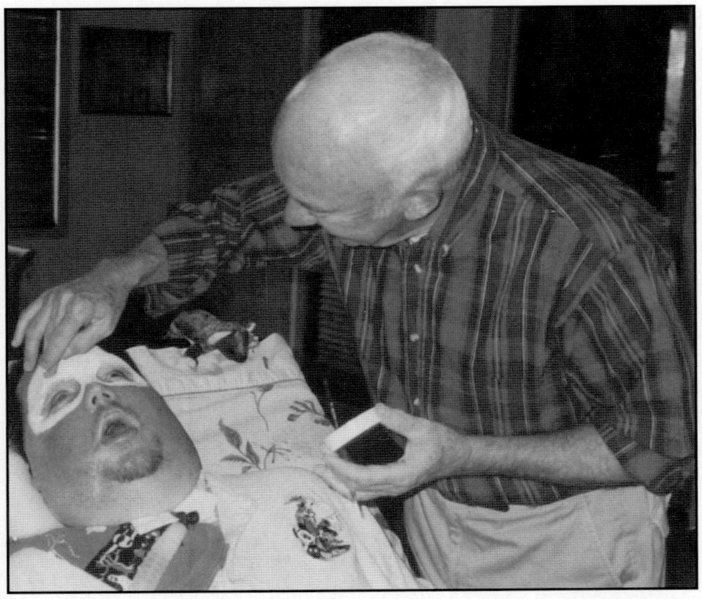

Making up a totally bedridden man for Halloween, 1999.

Homewood Retirement Ceremony

1967 as Hobos, Tramps, White Face, Auguste and Character Clowns.

The Unit continued to grow to a peak of 39 clowns. However, The Black Camel has hit us very hard. In recent years we have lost 10 very hard working, dependable, very seasoned experienced clowns. Our unit has a "Clownette" group of ladies who support us in many ways. Several of their members have passed as well. But the unit continues to have much success in fulfilling its mission:

"Promote the philanthropy of crippled and burned children."

The funds we receive from our "Clown appearances" help support Shrine Hospitals and Boumi's Transportation Fund.

For 14 years a Shrine Clown made a visit to a man who was bedridden and loved clowns and would make him up for Halloween. We made him an honorary member of our unit. His parents never failed to give us several generous donations each year.

Each year at the Mid-Atlantic Shrine Convention we participate in its parade. We use different themes such as: Gone fishing, By the Sea, Clown Babies, Klown Construction, Clowns celebrate Holidays, Race for kids, and Fishing for kids. This means construction of floats, clown dressings for the theme. We have placed 1st seven times, 2nd eight times and four times 3rd, thru a great team effort. We also have participated in several other parades. Solomons Island, Baltimore Mayor Christmas, 4th of July, White Marsh (large community area near us) and a few more. We have a whole "Fist full" of trophies from these efforts.

Visits to Retirement Communities have us doing a lot more than just animal balloons. We ran a mock clown meeting, skits (some with audience participation), we talk about our shrine mission, demonstrate clown completion, clowns rule of conduct. We even put on make-up in front of the audience and explain the cost of our" clown stuff." For those in Care Centers who cannot make it to the auditorium-we visit, blow balloons and give them roses. These visits give us a good feeling of being able to help those less fortunate. Sometimes when doing so little we do so much.

Each year we appear at the IBEW and Steam Fitters Picnics. We receive a very nice donation from each. Our Clownettes show off their face painting skills (about 500) to the delight of both children and adults.

We are also busy on St. Patrick's Day (painting of the green) and several other fundraisers also help to support our Hospitals and Transportation fund. At one time we even worked Oriole Baseball Games.

A visit to Walter Reed Hospital was very eye opening. When one of our clowns got married, he and his new bride were greeted by sword balloons held high over their heads. Easter and Christmas children's parties at Boumi is when the" balloons really fly." We have our own Bunny and Santa give the children presents. We have an Easter egg hunt, the Shrine band plays, the Clownettes prepare food, and it surely puts us in the Holiday Spirit.

In 1992, we concluded since we are so colorful most of the time that we needed something more formal. We decided on white shirts, clown tie, blue blazer, gray pants, dark socks and black shoes. Boy, let me tell you, when we go as a group in our"

Getting ready for the MASCA Competition at Virginia Beach, VA, Sept. 7, 2002. "Clown Construction" won first place!

Boumi Clowns Christmas Party, Dec. 17, 2001. Photos by John E. Clark.

Above and below: These trophies for Clown-A-Rama 2000 were hand painted by Boumi member "Tigger."

dress blues" to weddings, funerals etc....people see us coming and say, "Here come the Shrine Clowns."

Our Clown unit members have included four Potentates, three trustees, three Presidents of Mid-Atlantic Clown Association, three General Chairman-Clown A- Rama, five Masters of their Lodge, and 12 or more Presidents of Shrine Clubs.

For one of our Clown A-Ramas, one of our Clowns had hand-painted 60 trophies.

We are often asked, "What is the difference between a regular clown and a Shrine Clown"?

Simple answer: "A Shrine Clown helps to support the world's greatest philanthropy for the crippled and burned child." *Written by Anton (Rosebud) Endler*

HISTORY OF CASPER CALLIOPE CLOWN UNIT

Many years ago the Oriental Band had a secondary unit called the Calliope. It was essentially made up of band members who were getting older and couldn't walk or couldn't play an instrument. During the 80s the unit was over run with new members who were younger and wanted to do something. These young guys got real active fixing up, cleaning and maintaining the calliope. After a while they decided to add clowns to the mix of members and it became a clown unit. We walk the parade along side of the calliope (1900 National) and Cadillac (1938 Fleetwood V16). To this day the clowns are a main part of the unit.

The calliope is very lucky to have someone who lives in Casper who can fix, tune and help maintain the Calliope (Chuck Ekerson); sad we can't get this gentleman to join the Shrine. He just loves the calliope. His father before him maintained the calliope during the early years of the unit. The calliope has had its ups and downs. A few years ago the calliope was coming home from a parade in another town and the trailer wheels froze up and the whole trailer flipped over and was dragged down the road. It was quite the sight and it looked like a lost cause. Chuck saw the mess and said that he could fix it. Most tubes made it through the accident and were saved. The tubes that didn't make it were remade from scratch. Chuck built a furnace to make the other parts. The internal parts and box were either remade or fixed. It is a labor of love for Chuck and we are lucky to have him taking care of our calliope.

We have lost a few members to death, but the unit still has the most active members of all the other units in the temple. *Written by Michael Ito*

CENTRAL STATES SHRINE ASSOCIATION

The Central States Shrine Association (CSSA) is made up of 24 Shrine Centers in eight states. An Annual business meeting is held each March. A ceremonial session is conducted each August or September and is attended by thousands of Nobles from the member Shrine Centers. These Shrine Centers include:

Adballah, Overland Park, Kansas
Abou Ben Adhem, Springfield, Missouri
Abu Bekr, Sioux City, Iowa
Akdar, Tulsa, Oklahoma
Al Kaly, Pueblo, Colorado
Arab, Topeka, Kansas
Ararat, Kansas City, Missouri
Bedouin, Muskogee, Oklahoma
El Jebel, Denver, Colorado
El Kahir, Cedar Rapids, Iowa
Hella, Garland, Texas
India, Oklahoma City, Oklahoma
Isis, Salina, Kansas
Kaaba, Davenport, Iowa
Midian, Wichita, Kansas
Mirza, Pittsburg, Kansas
Moila, St. Joseph, Missouri
Moolah, St. Louis, Missouri
Sahara, Pine Bluff, Arkansas
Scimitar, Little Rock, Arkansas
Sesostris, Lincoln, Nebraska
Tangier, Omaha, Nebraska
Tehama, Hastings, Nebraska
Za-Ga-Zig, Altoona, Iowa

The Central States Shrine Clown Association (CSSCA) promotes and advances the interest of Shrine Clowning and the Clown Units, which are constituent members of the Shrine Centers of the CSSA.

Clown Units that belong to the CSSCA
Abdallah Shrine Clowns
Abou Ben Adhem Shrine Clowns
Akdar Merri-Makers
Al Kaly Clown Unit
Clowns of Al Kaly
Kaly Klowns
Arab Shrine Clowns

Ararat Shrine Clowns
Bedouin Shrine Clowns
El Jebel Clowns
India Shrine Clowns
Moila Shrine Clowns
Moolah Shrine Clowns
Tangier Shrine Clowns
Za-Ga-Zig Clowns

FUNSTERS

The Funsters are one of the 27 Units and Clubs that represent the Sphinx Shriners of Newington, CT at various Parades and events around the state of Connecticut and throughout New England.

Our primary purpose is to promote fun and laughter to people of **ALL** ages.

The trademark of our Clown Unit is our 1927 Ford Model-T Paddy Wagon. Our members are represented as Keystone Cops at the various parades around Connecticut and as Clowns during our walk-arounds and balloon animal events.

As members of the Shriners, we support the twenty-two (22) hospitals that are owned and operated by Shriners International, for children under the age of 18. The children at our hospitals receive specialized medical care for orthopedic conditions, burns, spinal chord injuries, and cleft lip & pallet regardless of their parents' ability to pay.

Monies received into the unit from the various gigs and parades that we participate in are used to support the unit's operational expenses, the "Sneaker Fund" which supports pediatric burn research at our hospitals, and the Sphinx Shriners' Hospital Transportation Fund which provides transportation of patients and their families to and from their homes to our hospitals for their medical care appointments.

GIZEH SHRINE CLOWNS

Gizeh has such a large geographical area that stretches from Alberta on the East side to the West side of Vancouver Island and from the 49th parallel in the South to the Northern tip of the Yukon which Totals 1,427,178 square kilometres.

We have nine clown units spread over the area putting the color of the Shrine out front, which allows the Units to raise money for *The Red Sneaker Fund.*

The Victoria Clown Unit was formed in 1958 and the Vancouver Clowns were affiliated with the Rajah Club and in 1972 were formed as the Vancouver Clown Unit: the first Presidents were Noble T.W. Thistleton in 1973, Noble C.H. Chamberlain in 1974 and Noble Frank "Copo" Smyth in 1975.

Victoria Clown Units LOCI on parade. Featured are Noble Don "Adorable" Trask and Noble Fred "Freddy" ---.

Noble Richard "Fugi" Kaufman and Noble Grant "Cuddles" Stephens.

Noble "Snuffy"

Some notable members:

• Noble Peter "PeeTee" Thornburn was the longest acting Boss Clown and he was awarded Emeritus status in 2001. He retired as Boss Clown in 2008.

• Gizeh Clowns have had three members become Potentates:

Illustrious Sirs Ross "Rossco" Scott (1995), Ed "Fuzzz" Wilson (1999), Lorne "Chaps" Donaldson (2008) and Dick "Pepper" Gauer (2011).

• Also Noble Isaac "Brokli" or "What" Bower-Berkhoven served as Grand Master of B.C. and the Yukon from June 22, 2006 to June 22, 2007.

• We also have a member V.W. Bro. Norman "Danny Boy" McEvoy who writes **The Educator** articles that he sends out to the brethren by Email.

Noble David "Laffter" Rafter

Within ISCA, Gizeh has been given the following appointments: Illustrious Sir Ross Scott was (Sergeant of Arms 1986 and Canadian Sneaker Chairman 1988), Noble David "Laffter" Rafter (Ambassador 2002), Jim Ferguson (Ambassador 2003), R.D. "Happy" Michaels (Ambassador 2003) and Noble Don "Milty" Hamilton (Canadian Sneaker Chairman 2007 to date).

The late Noble Rod "Poor Rod" McKay.

The late Ken H. "Jelly Bean" Maddison.

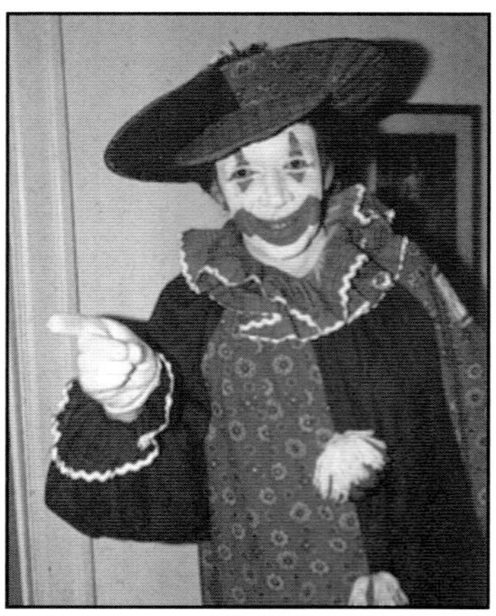

Noble John "Happy" Eveliegh, an early member of the Vancouver Clown Unit.

Noble George "Puddin" Pruden

Noble John "Cupcake" Sands

We have three members that were presidents of the PNSA, Noble Don "Milty" Hamilton, Noble John "Big Foot" Fleming, and Illustrious Sir Ed "Fuzzz" Wilson along with one member currently serving as 4th VP Noble George (Puddin') Pruden. *Submitted by: Vancouver Clown Unit Past President 1998 Noble David "Laffter" Rafter*

GREAT LAKES SHRINE CLOWN UNITS ASSOCIATION

The purpose of the Great Lakes Shrine Clown Units Association (GLSCUA) is to promote and advance the interest of the Shrine Clowning and the Clown Units, which are constituent of the member Shrine Centers of the Great Lakes Shrine Association (GLSA), specifically those in the states of Illinois, Indiana, Michigan, Ohio, Wisconsin, and the Province of Ontario Canada. The objective is to develop fraternal relations with the Member Units in GLSA by promoting better understanding and cooperation; to afford opportunities for exchanging ideas and experiences; to advance the tradition of Shrine Clowning and, the excellent reputation of Shriners International and its philanthropy.

GLSA is made up of 23 Shrine Centers in five states and the Canadian Province of Ontario. An Annual business meeting is held each February. A ceremonial session is conducted each September and is attended by thousands of Nobles from the member Shrine Centers.

The following is a list of GLSA member Shrine Centers, and their home cities: Ainad (East St. Louis, IL), Aladdin (Columbus, OH), Al Koran (Cleveland, OH), Ansar (Springfield, IL), Antioch (Dayton, OH), Elf Kurafeh (Saginaw, MI), Hadi (Evansville, IN); Medinah (Addison, IL), Mizpah (Fort Wayne, IN), Mocha (London, Ontario), Mohammed (Peoria, IL), Moslem (Detroit, MI), Murat (Indianapolis, IN), Orak (Hammond, IN), Saladin (Grand Rapids, MI), Syrian (Cincinnati, OH), Tadmor (Akron, OH), Tebala (Rockford, IL), Tripoli (Milwaukee, WI), Zenobia (Toledo, OH), and Zorah (Terre Haute, IN).

KAREM CLOWNS

Karem Clown unit was organized in January 1961; there is no record of the original number of members. The first function was Karem Temple Family Variety and Talent Show. There was

KAREM CLOWNS

a large body of members to begin because of the large territory of Karem. Aug. 17, 1962 Sharon Temple in Tyler, TX, some 90 miles away, got their own charter and the Karem unit lost about half its members from Tyler. In 1962 a local wrecking yard gave the unit two 1950 and 1951 Chevrolet sedans and they were converted into a topless parade car with two hoods, one facing in each direction with two steering wheels and drivers. For the rear-facing driver to take over, the car was simply shifted into reverse. It was named "Undecided" and has been a hit until the present day. It has two offsetting wheels welded off center and it rocks up and down while in motion. In the early years we had a smoke producing system, which we had to remove because of the pollution it produced. It has been overhauled and repainted several times over the years and has thousands of miles on it. It was hauled with a towing hitch until 1973 when we had a trailer built to haul it. We also had a four-horse merry-go-round on a trailer for several years. About the same time the unit got a cotton candy machine and it is used to make cotton candy at schools, churches and other such organizations splitting the profit with them. It is still working today, although we do not go to as many schools as we did for several years.

Karem clowns are a charter member of the Texas Shrine Clown Association and hosted the first midwinter meeting in Waco in 1964. We have hosted three other Midwinters since then. We became members of the National Shrine Clown Association in 1964, which became the International Shrine Clown Association with our members joining on a voluntary basis and most do become members. We have had three TSCA Presidents, three potentates, several other divan members and committee chairmen, and our current Assistant Rabban is a former clown.

Our membership fluctuates up and down from about 10 or 11 to about 25 or so. Right now we are on an upswing with several new members in the last few months. Almost all our members are past masters of their lodges and several have been Grand Lodge District Deputies

In the early years we had to go to Dallas for make-up because there was none in Waco. One of our later member's mother-in-law had a barber and beauty supply business and she stocked our supplies.

Our members have always been very active in support of the Shrine Hospitals and the Sneaker Fund. Several of our members have been on the Hospital Transportation Committee taking our area patients to Dallas Scottish Rite Hospital, about 100 miles away; Shrine Orthopedic Hospital in Houston, 180 miles and to the Shrine Burns Hospital in Galveston, about 220 miles. Since the Grand Lodge of Texas is in Waco, most of the work in the lodge coffee shop, tilers, etc. is done by members of the local lodges and some of our members have worked several hours volunteering there in support of the Lodge when in session. When our new Temple was being built, the members were asked to do most of the labor and one of our clowns worked in maintenance in a local glass manufacturing plant and offered to help with the electrical wiring and the potentate immediately said the clowns would do the wiring, which we did. We are proud to be members of this fabulous organization!!

Karem Shrine Clowns Black Camel Roster

Alton Abernathey "Buzz-A-Roo"
Elmer Armstrong "Elmo"
Howard Brown "Brownie"
James Chism "Jingles"
Clarence Cobb "Ole Blue"
D. K. Dickens "Deke"
Robert "Bob" Griffin "Buffo"
Bill Howard "Slick"
Burl Hunt "Bo"
Hal March
Joseph Maxwell "O' Jo"
Clint Mckethan
Bill Mosley "Big Mo"
Frank Pirello "Poochie"
Porter Ridlehuber "Nuts'
C. Smith "Hobo"
Dempsey Welch
Bob Westwood "Deadwood"
Kenneth Williams "Kenny"
Honorary Clown Members
Cliff Howard
James "Buddy" Hunt
Dub Garner
Bobby Graham
Bill Griffin

Submitted by Harvey L. Woodard

KHARTUM KOMEDIANS

Khartum Komedians, the clown unit of Khartum was formed in 1962 and since its inaugural meeting has been dedicated to bringing laughter to children of all ages. The early years of the unit were led by dynamic Nobles who included Paul Hunter, Sydney Scott, George Goodrick, Joseph Kerr, Gordon Harris, William Wade, William Thompson and Douglas Adams. These eight nobles established the unit which has now grown to over sixty members, all who have the same dedication to bring laughter to children.

As times changed our focus expanded to include the philanthropy of Shriners, our hospitals and burn units. While memories of the Shrine Hospital in Winnipeg and the care given there is carried on today by the Winnipeg Regional Health Authority we continue to support the hospital in Montreal, the various Shrine Burn Units across North America and the special Sneaker Fund that is unique to the Clown Units of the Shrine. This special fund originally set up to provide running shoes or "sneakers" to all the patients, so they might be able to walk on those shiny hospital floors, now includes support of the burn units and advanced research and development.

Komedians are pleased to have had the opportunity to bring laughter by participating in Shrine Parades, local parades, hospital visits, festivals, parties and circuses. From the first appearance of the Komedians at the Princess Elizabeth Hospital (now the Riverview Health Centre) with the friendly Komedian Donkeys in 1968 to the introduction of the Volkswagon with its unlimited number of clowns, which continues to be a part of every Winnipeg performance of the circus, to the extravaganzas of the International Shrine Clown Association five hour parades hosted in Winnipeg in 1977 and 1986 Winnipegers have been entertained.

On the bumper are Nobles Constante "Chibu" Uson Past Grand Master for the Grand Lodge of Manitoba and (Ill) Harry "Fphooozziye" Rosenbaum Potentate 2012 for Khartum Shriners. 2nd Row are Nobles James "Klik" Krokosh, Dennis "Todo" McQuade, Gerry "Popkorn" Derhak, Al "Bundy" Romani, Kevin "Bobo" Davis, Ernest "Squeeky" Smith, Guy Gigglzz" Arbez and, Gordon "Lumpy" Williams. 3rd Row are Nobles (Ill) Jack "Hoops" Hooper, Reginald "Reggie" Hall, Sidney "Sparky" Denby, Clifford "Mister Stripes" Hartmier and, (Ill) Don "Red" Thomson. Missing members are Nobles Johann "Joey" Arnason, Paul "Wingo" Bayda, Murray "Tag" Botterill, Robert "Bonzo" Brock, Archie "Jello" Davidson, Don "Dee Cee" Fournier, Robert "Pop Top" Gardiner, Herb "Herbie" Hein, Doug "Klod" Hill, Al "Jumbo" Johnston, Ted "Tee Jay" Jones, Murray "Specs" Knazan, Ron "Butts" Ledingham, , Rick "Chewski" Malczewski, Don "Flip Flop" McLachlan, Dennis " Dinty" McLean, Robert "Dozey" McLeod, John "Noodles" Nordal, (Ill) Darcy "Dipper" Pagan, Bill "Quincee" Quinn, Robert "Sunshine" Robinson, Doug "Smitty" Smith, Barry "Willie" Unsworth, Steve "Kit Kat" Urias, Rudy "Orville" Weidenbacher and, Thor "Junior" Weidenbacher.

We are pleased to be a part of Khartums 100th Anniversary Celebration this year and hope that in the years to come Winnipegers will continue to support us in our endeavours.

Past Presidents

1962-1964	Paul W. Hunter*
1965	Sidney Scott*
1966	George C. Goodrick*
1967	Arthur G Teskey*
1968	Alan J. Grundy*
1969	William G. Moody*
1970	Gordon F. Collins*
1971	Ben E. Boylan*
1972	Joseph S. Reynolds*
1973	Noel F. Brown*
1974	Kenneth G. Collins#
1975	Charles Brown PP*
1976	George A. Thompson#
1977	Albert A. Martin#
1978	Raymond A. Beaque*
1979	Monty Flom
1980	George J. Forzley*
1981	Kenneth J. Whiteside+
1982	Joseph Samalack#
1983	Harry A. Martin*
1984	Richard O. Brown#
1985	Alexander H. Shiels*
1986	Earnest H. Barker*
1987	Douglas J. Smith
1988	William J. Quinn
1989	Dennis J. McQuade
1990	Gerald D. Derhak
1991	David A. Deally*
1992	Gerald E. Bennett+
1993	Murray B. Knazan
1994	Douglas C. Hill
1995	Richard A. Malczewski
1996	Robert A. McLeod
1997	James R. Krokosh
1998	Robert J. Robinson
1999-2000	Murray G. Botterill
2000	John P. Czarnecki PP+
2001	Reginald J. Hall
2002	Edward H. Jones
2003	Rudolph F. Weidenbacher
2004	Kevin J. Davis
2005	Constante S. Uson
2006	Steve Urias
2007	James R. Krokosh
2008	Kevin J. Davis
2010	Clifford C. Hartmier
2011-2012	Reginald J. Hall

Past Secretaries

1962-1963	Gordon C. Harris*
1964-1965	Douglas Adams*
1966-1967	John J. Mortimer*
1968	Njall O. Bardal*
1969-1970	George C. Goodrick*
1970-1973	George J. Forzley*
1974	Ben E. Boylan*
1975-1976	George J. Forzley*
1977-1978	John G. Emmons*
1979	Edward Chambers+
1980-1984	Ben E. Boylan*
1985-1986	Raymond A. Beaque*
1987-1988	Donald K. McLachlan
1989-1991	Richard W. Taylor+
1991-1993	George J. Forzley*
1994-1995	Hugh Magill*
1996-1997	Gerald D. Derhak
1998-2003	Harry J. Rosenbaum
2004	George J. Forzley*
2005-2008	Rudolph F. Weidenbacher
2009	Gerald D. Derhak
2010	William J. Quinn
2011-2012	Clifford C. Hartmier

KLOWN of the YEAR
Award Winners

1999	Dennis "Todo" McQuade
2000	John "Glok" Czarnecki PP+
2001	Kevin "Bobo" Davis
2002	Dennis "Todo" McQuade
2003	Archie "Jello" Davidson

2004 Edward "Tee Jay" Jones
2005 Ernest "Squeeky" Smith
2006 Gerald "Popkorn" Derhak
2007 Brian "Nooofee" Hurley #
2008 Rudy "Orville" Weidenbacher
2009 Donatien "Dee Cee" Fournier
2010 Allan "Jumbo" Johnston
2011 Al "Bundy" Romani

Honorary Members

Nobles Richard "Joey" Bloom, Gil "Fragile" Fraser, (Ill) Jack "Hoops" Hooper PP, (Ill) Tom "Rainbow" Johnstone PP, (Ill) Ken "Kaptain Krunch" Kristjanson PP, (Ill) Don "Santa Claus"Kunderman PP, (Ill) Gary "Jukebox" Saunders PP, (Ill) Bob "Joey" Spear PP, Brian "Socks" Terin, (Ill) Don "Red" Thomson PP and, (Ill) Fraser "Woody" Woodward PP

Honoured Ladies

Aileen Barker, Lauraine Brown, Hilda Collins, Arlene Crone, Margaret Deally, Wendy Dowle, Ruby Harper, Shirley Hawryshyn, Hazel Hill, Berith MacKenzie, Merl Mac|Pherson, Nanette Magill, Dorothy Martin, Shirley McGregor, Dorothy Schwabe, Judy Shields, Betty Surtees and, Doris Woodward.

**Deceased / # Demitted* *+Suspended / PP Past Potentate*

LAKE COUNTY SHRINE CLOWN UNIT

OASIS CLOWNS

Group photo of Oasis Clowns. Courtesy of French Harvey, Captain.

JOKERS
SOUTHEAST IDAHO SHRINE CLOWNS

In 1972, a member of the Radiant Chapter, Order of Eastern Star, by the name of Bob Briggs, wrote a "clown" skit and, for a little fun in their meetings, some of Bob's friends, i.e., Emmette Spraker, Arcealous Wike, Robert Elderkin and Jack Stanturf, participated in "acting out" the skit. Bob continued writing skits, narrating them while his friends continued acting.

In 1975, during a Shrine meeting, a Shriner by the name of Elmer Steinlicht, gathered Bob Briggs and his "actors" together and asked them if they would be interested in forming a clown unit. Of course they were excited about the idea so, as a result, an application to create a unit by the name of the "Jokers" was submitted to El Korah Shrine, in Boise, ID, and the Unit was chartered that same year.

Get ready for the circus.

The Jokers with their golf cart.

A few of the original members, Jack Rucker, Dewey Doss and Elmer Steinlicht, began "clowning" for the Cub Scouts and grade school classes by performing a few magic tricks, blowing balloons and tying them into animal shapes. The Jokers became an instant hit in the Pocatello, ID Community.

1981 brought three new members on board. Johnny Lynch, Larry Oram and Jerry Lynch joined the group. By now, it was a growing organization clowning for many large company picnics, parties and even small birthday parties for children.

Johnny Lynch (Jrel)

David Pianezzi (Sunshine)

Jim Birdwell (Nickel)

Stan Wallerstedt (Scrubby)

Ralph Huntington (Wheels)

Larry Oram (Bubba)

The many faces of Jerry Lynch.

In 1997, a formal set of bylaws were submitted to El Korah for approval and, in 1998, they were approved by Potentate Chuck Turner. From the very beginning, our dues have only been membership in the International Shrine Clown Association and from the donations made to our Unit for our "Clown Jobs," we donate to the International Shrine Clown Association Sneaker Fund, the JOKERS Million Dollar Club and the Travel Fund.

At the end of each year, we hold a Holiday luncheon where we install our officers for the coming year. Our Officers Elect for 2013 are: James M. Birdwell, President; Stanley A. Wallerstedt, Vice President and Herb F. Petersen, Secretary/Treasurer. Our current members are: Jim Birdwell; Bob Bitton; Ralph Huntington; Roger Larkins; Jerry Lynch; Johnny Lynch; Larry Oram; Joe Parkton; Herb Petersen; David Pianezzi; Stan Wallerstedt and John Williams.

SREKOJ CLOWN UNIT

"SREKOJ" is "JOKERS" spelled backwards. Members of Ben Hur Temple belonging to other Units, especially the Directors' Staff and the Band would don make-up and clown before the Unit was formed in 1957. Max O. Slade and Barney Koepp were the founders. Max was the ramrod and 1st president.

This is one of the hardest working Units of the Temple, because everybody especially kids from 2 to 92 love clowns.

In addition to donning make-up and being a vital part of every parade and circus performance, members of the Unit visit the children's wards of many hospitals and happily respond to many, many other requests for these joy dispensers. Former members of Ben Hur Clown Unit, Max O. Slade & Barney Koepp were instrumental in organizing and leading the Texas Shrine Clown Association, one of the outstanding organizations of its kind in the world. Max Slade appointed Barney Koepp President the first year of TSCA in 1960-1961 then he headed it up in 1961-1962.

To become a member of the Srekoj Unit you need submit an application, and then if approved, spend a term as a novice before you are deemed qualified to be a full fledged clown.

The unit participates in the Texas Shrine Association Convention (All-State) and competes in several categories for trophies. Ben Hur Srekoj has made its mark and has delivered its share of trophies to Ben Hur's well stocked. Trophy case. Recently the State organization has held a mid-winter meeting where competition is also held. We have made our presence known at those meetings also.

We think there is no better way to advertise Shrinedom and to get real satisfaction from the smile of a child than to be a clown. If you love hard work and can spend many hours of your time entertaining young and old, then: the Srekoj Unit may be the one for you. Those smiles you put on a person's face give you a wonderful feeling that can last you a lifetime.

Submitted by Joe C. Cole, TSCA President, 1989 – Potentate, 1994 – ISCA President, 2001

HISTORY OF THE YAARAB RED DEVIL CLOWNS

The Yaarab Red Devil Clowns almost didn't come to be. The Potentate in 1944, was diametrically opposed to forming the organization. It was his personal feeling that clowning and being a Shriner was unbecoming to Shrinedom. So as they say in Shrinedom, if you not happy with the current Potentate, just remember, he is only in office for one year! Of course, that is what we did, we waited.

The clowns were eager to hit the streets for the first time in the spring of 1945. Like a sleeping giant, the clowns were already organized and ready to go and show their stuff to the public and were an instant hit. We believe that we are the oldest clown unit in Shrinedom. Since 1945, Yaarab Red Devil Clowns have been instrumental in a number of projects. During WW II, they were busy selling war bonds for the war effort. When they were not parading, they were going to the local hospitals and entertaining youngsters of all ages.

The Red Devil Clowns were a reckoning force, organizing the first Southeastern Shrine Clown Association in 1957. As you can guess, a Red Devil Clown stepped up to the plate and served as President and his name was Noble Charlie Parker, with his personal friend, Potentate J.C. Reary, who served as secretary. Many others have also served as President of SESCA over the years. The Red Devil Clowns have always provided leadership on all levels of clowning. Our most recent leadership was placing two Red Devil Past Presidents in leadership roles for the ISCA. We also have elected three clowns as Potentates at Yaarab. So you can see that our clowning roots are deep rooted and continue to aspire our members toward leadership positions. It is our mission to provide good leadership with youthful replacements of our own.

Most weekends, our clowns are represented at our Potentate sanctioned parades around North Georgia, sometimes two to three a day. We have a 10-day circus billed as the largest shrine circus in the nation with 28 performances by our Red Devil Clowns. Each year, we sponsor a golf tournament in memory of our own, Jerry "Mr. Smokey" Fields, as a fundraiser to raise monies for the Sneaker Fund for the hospitals. I can truly say that we are the goodwill ambassadors of Yaarab Shrine Temple. *Written by Richard "RC" Cain, Red Devil Clowns Historian*

THE ZOR SAWDUSTERS

This unit may well be a lesson to others who think one try at success is enough. It was back in 1974 and early 1975 that about four or five of the now charter members got together to try and put a clown unit together. The big item then lacking was how to get off the ground and be recognized. The idea just sort of got "back burnered." Those Nobles were Bob Dawson, Howard Bowers, J. Kevin Johnson, Tom Target and Bob Wilkenson, to name a few.

1976, however, was when Gordon Marx, former President and a charter "Fire House Jester," came to Eau Claire with his son Dick, and had the spark and answer as to how to get rolling as a unit.

Our first official meeting was called in February of 1976. In April of 1976 with an ambitious schedule of over 20 parades and Zor functions planned, we were in a position to seek sanctions of Zor. By October of 1976 we were a recognized unit.

We had 35 charter members, of these 29 have dressed at one time or another. We have big clowns, small clowns, fat clowns and a few thin but our biggest of all was our 1929 REO Speed Wagon.

The "old" REO was found by one of our charter members, Tom Target, in running condition, and with a lot of total unit help was completely restored. The candy apple green and gold paint job was supplied by our member Eugene L. Johnson, a body shop owner.

We normally participate in over 20 parades in a 100 mile area of Eau Claire. We also participate in our local circus and a Christmas raffle was held to benefit Shriners Hospital for many years.

An added attraction the Sawdusters have brought to each community, is a visit to all of the nursing homes and any hospital serving the area. We have also in route spotted a nursery school or two and watched young as well as old faces light up with joy.

Due to age, condition and cost of upkeep, like some of our older members, the REO has been retired to a modern pick-up decorated much as the original truck. In 2007 a calliope was added to the unit on a bright red trailer. Many trophies have been won but none is as important as a smile! *By J. Kevin Johnson.*

UTAH

ISCA BIOGRAPHIES

The Antioch Funsters about 1965. Pictured l-r: W. Jackson, J. Askren, R. Schuler, J. Costin, Al Fink, Ed Broaddus, R. Wilson, L. Shick, and H. Hofmann.

ACKERMANN, STEVEN G. (Bubbles) was born in Belleville, IL October 5th, 1948. Graduated high school 1966, enlisted in the U.S. Navy 1968, served four years and attained the rank of Second Class Petty Officer, Aviation Machinist Mate (JET) ADJ2 and Honorably discharged. Worked for the U.S Air Force, Scott AFB IL for twelve years as a flight line supervisor. Transferred to the U.S. Army for twenty-two years and retired from U.S. Army Engineering, Research and Development Command with 38 years with the U.S. Government.

Has been blessed to be married to Sharon, who supports him in all his Masonic endeavors. Have been together since 1978 and now live in Harvest, Alabama.

Raised to the degree of Master Mason (June 25th 1987) in East Lodge AF & AM Masonic Lodge #504, Fairview Heights, IL. Conferred to the Consistory of the Valley of Southern Illinois, Belleville, IL October 24 1987. Crossed the hot sands of Cahaba Shrine September 2nd 2000. Became a member of Masonic Lodge # 24, Ardmore, TN. Had the privilege and honor to be installed as Worshipful Master of Masonic Lodge #24, Ardmore, TN, on December 12, 2011. Attained the Title of Knights Templar York Rite, June 2010.

Member Cahaba Buffoon Clown Unit, September 2000, Dixie Shrine Clown Association, Southeastern Shrine Clown Association and International Shrine Clown Association in January 2001. Elected Director of Cahaba Buffoon Unit 2004 and again in 2005. Elected Treasurer of Cahaba Buffoon Unit 2012. Elected President of Dixie Shrine Clown Association in 2007. Certified as an ISCA Judge October 2009. Has earned a Red Nose Award every year since becoming a clown and in 2006 and 2012 received Gold Nose Awards.

BABBERT, ERVIN C. (Ears) was born May 18, 1933 in Columbus, OH. On Aug. 31, 1952 he and Bonnie were married. They have two children, Chuck and Ronald, and two grandchildren, Logan and Jacob. They reside in Hebron, OH. In 1960, he decided to start his own business as E.C. Babbert, Inc. installing water softeners and water pumps. His wife and both sons are in the company. He was also a square dance caller for many years and had his own band for a while.

In 1965, he was raised in Ralph R. Rickley Lodge #670. He was initiated at Aladdin Temple, where he walked the hot sands in 1970. In 1975 he joined Aladdin Clown Unit. He has won many ISCA Awards, individually and along with his clown parade partner, Gerald Staiger (Stretch). His most memorable moments were when he got to meet Red Skelton and visits to the Shrine Hospitals.

BAHMER, DAVID (Tic Toc) was born in Sioux City, IA, November 25, 1966, ninth of 11 children. When he's not clowning around, "Tic Toc" owns and operates David's Watch and Clock Repair in Sioux City, IA.

In 2011, David served as Worshipful Master of Morningside Masonic Lodge 615, Sioux City, IA. He is a 32nd degree Scottish Rite Freemason having served as Venerable Master of The Knights of St. Andrew, Valley of Sioux City, Orient of Iowa, a member of Morningside Rose Croix Chapter No. 502, Order of The Eastern Star, and a Noble of The Mystic Shrine, Abu Bekr Temple, Sioux City, IA.

"Tic Toc" is Past President 2011 of the Abu Bekr Shrine Clown Unit. He was awarded 1st Place, Character Division, at the Central States Shrine Clown Association (CSSCA), held in Overland Park, KS, 2011, and 2nd Place, Character Division, at an International Shrine Clown Association (ISCA), Mid Winter Session, in Des Moines, IA, 2011.

As her last wish, David was encouraged to become a Shrine Clown by his loving mother, Mary Ellen.

"Tic Toc" was Abu Bekr Clown of The Year in 2009.

BANKA, ROBERT S. (Huggy) was born Nov. 2, 1927 in Manitoba, Canada. In 1955 he was married to Joyce Suzanne (deceased) and they had two children, Andrew and Katherine, and two grandchildren, Dustin and Erica. He was an auto body technician and auto damage appraiser until retiring in June, 1993 and presently resides in Utah.

"Huggy" was raised in Tyrian Lodge #508 on Feb. 24, 1966. He was initiated at Abu Bekr Temple and on June 6, 1966 he walked the hot sands. He joined the Abu Bekr Clowns in September 1966. He served as Secretary from 1979 – 2010. "Huggy" has been a member of ISCA since 1969.

BARKER, NEWELL 33° (Sureshot) was born in Vandalia, IL, in 1937, and has lived in places from Canada to Venezuela, South America. He received a BS degree in Petroleum Engineering from Texas Tech University in Lubbock, TX. Barker is a registered professional engineer in Oklahoma and Texas.

His Masonic and Akdar Shrine (Tulsa, OK) career began in 1975. Newell was Worshipful Master of Wah-Shah-She #110, Pawhuska, OK in 1979 and 1992. Barker has presided in the East in Bartlesville (OK) Chapter #55, Bartlesville Council #41, Calvary Commandry #26, Past High Priest Association, Wise Master of Rose Corix in Scottish Rite, Osage County Scottish Rite Society, Bartlesville (OK) Merri-Maker Shrine Clowns, Wasono Shrine Club, Kara Grotto, also golf and social clubs in Venezuela.

Barker was President of Central States Shrine Clown Association in 1992 and Grand High Priest of Royal Arch Masons of Oklahoma in 2002-03. He is a 33° Scottish Rite Mason. Barker is a member of KYCH, Red Cross of Constantine, Royal Order of Scotland, Grotto and the following clown organizations — ISCA, CSSCA, SCSCA, COAI, WCA and TCA.

"Sureshot" began clowning as "Babblin Barker", the mobile news reporter for "Silly1" in 1976 and received his first award (1st place) in 3-5 man skit with two friends in 1978 at the Central States Shrine Clown Convention in Tulsa, OK. Barker has been fortunate to have received clown awards in ISCA, CSSCA, SCSCA, COAI and Supreme Grotto. He has also been very fortunate to have received over 250 awards in boxing, bowling, golf, costume design, drag racing and clowning over the years. He was a torch bearer in the 1996 Olympics. Newell was Akdar's Shriner of the Month in October 2012. He was Tulsa Scottish Rite Membership Man of the Year in 2012.

He attributes *all* of his success to the grace of God, his mother and dad, his family, his many friends, employers and co-workers.

BASSETT, ROBERT "BOB" (Peaches) is a lifelong resident of Marine, IL. He married his wife, Beverly, on Friday, July 13, 1979. They have two daughters, Amanda and Hanna, and two grandchildren, Cheyenne and Wyatt. He has been employed at Boeing, St. Louis since 1986.

"Peaches" is an active member of Marine Masonic Lodge #355 and the Scottish Rite of Southern Illinois, and Ainad Shriner's. He is serving as a Temple Ambassador.

In 1991, Bassett became a Noble of the Ainad Shriners, East St. Louis, IL. In 1994 he became a member of Ainad Krazy Klowns, the GLSCUA and the ISCA.

In his years of clowning, he has been fortunate to receive many awards: Great Lake Shrine Clown of the year, 2000; President of the Ainad Krazy Klowns in 2000 and 1st recipient of the ISCA Clown Etraordinaire in 2006. He has placed many times in make-up and competition.

In 2004 "Peaches" was appointed to serve as the ISCA Quarter Master. In 2006 he was elected to the position of ISCA Secretary, serving five years. In 2011 he was elected as the 3rd Vice President of the ISCA. He will serve as the ISCA President in 2014.

BAXTER, JIM(BO) has been an Aleppo clown since 1990. He has been the unit secretary on and off for many years. He is from Reading, Mass., where he is a Past Master of Good Samaritan Lodge. He has been married to his wife Sheila for 42 years. They have three children and ten grandchildren.

Jim(bo)'s grandfather was the professional Clown 'Doc Campbell'. He traveled the world performing. Prior to WWI he held the record of nine performances at the Palace Theater in London.

BELL, WILLIAM N. (Ding Dong) was born in Indiana, PA on Nov. 9, 1930. He and Rose were married in 1956. They have four children: John; Michael; Bill and Sara. Their grandchildren are: Kristy Starnes; Justin Bell; Alicia Bell; Adria Bell; Brianna Bell and step-grandchildren Sarah Hice; Madison Hice and Tyler Hice. Logan Starnes is their great-grandchild. He has owned and operated an Automotive Tire Dealership and service and repair shop that opened Nov. 1, 1962. They celebrated 50 years of service in November 2012.

"Ding Dong" has been a member of Syria Heritage Unit since November 1979. In 1983 he won first place August Clown at MASCA Spring Convention in Zembo Shrine Center. In 1984 he won 2nd place in a two-man skit and 2nd place as an August clown with a gimmick at the ISCA competition at the Imperial Session in Boston, MA. He was appointed to Syria Shriners seven year line as 2nd Ceremonial Master in 1984. Then in 1986 he was elected Oriental Guide and was elected to the office of Potentate, Syria Shriners in January 1990.

In January 1992 he was appointed to the Board of Governors at Shriners Hospitals for Children-Philadelphia and served for nine years on that Board of Governors. He was elected President of the Mid-Atlantic Shrine Association in 1995 and served as President in 1995-1996.

He clowned on many occasions during those years, but the past few years he has not been as active as he had been up until 1990. He is a member of ISCA and MASCA clowns.

BELL, WILLIAM ALAN (Ding Dong) was born in Edmonton, Alberta, Canada, on Sept. 5, 1931. After completing his public schooling he enrolled at the University of Alberta where he graduated with degrees in Fine Arts, Education and Graduate Studies. He began his studies as a violinist at the age of 10 years. He is married to Lady Alice McGirr, a retired school administrator. They have three "chosen" children who are Vietnamese Refugees.

He began his teaching career with the Edmonton Public Schools in 1955. During his 31 years as a teacher he taught Band, String Orchestra, Choral Music and Art in the secondary schools. In 2004 he was elected President of the Canadian College of Teachers and was awarded the designation of "Fellow of the College" (FCCT). In 2003 he was honored by Phi Delta Kappa, an Education Fraternity, as "Kappan of the Year" He has also been honored by the "Medal of Merit" from Scouts Canada.

His father and grandfather were Masons. In 1981 he joined his father's lodge, Norwood Lodge #90, and in 1993 became its Master. In 2007 he was elected the District Deputy Grandmaster of the Lakeland District of the Grand Lodge of Alberta.

In 1984 he became a member of the

Edmonton Valley of the Scottish Rite and has been active in the choir and degrees.

"Ding Dong" was the first member of Al Shamal Shrine Temple at a ceremony in Red Deer, Alberta in October of 1985.

In Al Shamal he has served as Vice president, Secretary, Treasurer, Sneaker Chair and Sneaker Ambassador of the Clown Unit. He received numerous awards at PNSCA and ISCA competitions. In 2002 he was appointed to the ISCA Board and served as Sneaker Chair, Canada, Montreal Unit, until his retirement in 2007. During those years he attended International meetings and visited numerous hospitals. He became a Life Member of the Al Shamal Shrine Clown Unit in 2007.

BIRDWELL, JAMES M. (Nickel) was born Aug. 26, 1926 in Detroit, MO. A veteran of WW II, he always dreamed of being a Shrine Clown. Towards that goals, Aug. 19, 1995, he was raised a Master Mason by Mt. Kinport Masonic Lodge #95. He became a member of El Korah Shrine Temple May 1997, a Permanent Contributing Member May 2010, and joined the Jokers, southeast Idaho's clowns, in November 1997.

Jim has held an office in the Jokers every year he's been a member; 2002, he was also President of the local Shrine Club and Worshipful Master of his Blue Lodge. He continues to be active in Mt. Kinport Lodge serving as Worshipful Master in 2002, 2003, 2007 and 2010.

In 2004, as Hospital Committee Chairman, Jim began collecting stuffed animals and medical equipment to be donated to the Intermountain Shriner Hospital. Thanks to his perseverance, over 10,000 items have been delivered.

BOWIE, GENE (Bow-Wow) was born Oct. 23, 1931 in Dayton, OH. He and wife, Linda, have three children: Tim Bowie; Lynn Bowie and Cindy Taylor. Grandchildren are: Tara; Taylor; Travis; Trevor; Melanie and Armando. Gene is retired from employment.

Bowie was raised in 1989 at Arlington Heights Lodge 1187. He was initiated at Moslah Temple and walked the hot sands in 1990. He joined the Moslah Clowns Unit in April 1991.

"Bow-Wow" served as President in 2000.

BRADLEY, DERRICK AND JOHN ALEXANDER (Dusty and Tiny, Al Shamal Clowns) - John has been clowning since 1994 and Derrick since 1998. Both are accredited clown judges and both are active in their unit. They are past Presidents of Al Shamal Clown Unit, John in 2004 and Derrick in 2003. They are also past presidents of Pacific Northwest Shrine Clown Association, (John 2007 and Derrick in 2011). Derrick was I.S.C.A. Clown Of The Year in 2002 and John was I.S.C.A.'s first Smile Maker (2005). They are frequent competitors at Midwinter and Imperial Conference competitions. Their version of the "Stagecoach" 2-man skit has won many international awards.

Dusty and Tiny first started competing at ISCA Mid-Winter and Imperials in 2000. As John was the Worthy Grand Patron of the Eastern Star in 2000 and he designated Derrick as the chief of his assistant sentinels we couldn't attend our district PNSCA competition so we required another event to qualify for our Red Nose awards. We decided to do Las Vegas Imperial session and thus the first performance of the Stage Coach.

BRADT, MARTIN (Shuffels) was born Dec. 19, 1931 in Johnstown, NY. He and Susan were married in 1967. They have two children, Michelle and Deborah and one grandchild, Danielle Osborne. Martin

retired on Sept. 30, 1991 from Beech-Nut Life Savers, Inc.

On March 29, 1979 Martin was raised in St. Johnsville Lodge #611, New York. On June 6, 1981 he walked the hot sands at St. Johnsville Temple #611. On Jan. 1, 2001, "Shuffels" joined the Zanies Clown Unit.

From 2001-2011, he was associated with N.E.C.I. From the Clown School he has received 11 Red Noses and one Gold Nose. From NYOSA, he received the Master of Fun and Laughter in 2009; the Funniest Clown in 2009 and Craftsman Clown in 2007. He also has served as Treasurer of Zanies.

BRAEUEL, CHRISTOPHER HANS (Teddy Bear) was born in Kanata, ON, December 27, 1968. After completing high school in 1988 he joined the international Up With People troupe for one year, representing Canada among over one

hundred international students providing community service and performing worldwide. Upon earning a Master's degree in Public Administration in 2000, Chris joined the Canadian government and has devoted his career to public service at the local, national and international levels ever since. In August of 2012, he married his lady, Evisa Abolina, in Riga, Latvia. Chris joined Doric Lodge 58 in Ottawa, ON on November 7, 1996 and was raised on April 18, 1997. He was initiated to Ottawa Tunis Shriners 179 on June 1, 2011 and soon after fused his love for entertainment and charity by joining the Tunis Clown Unit in August 2011. As an active clown, Chris also served as Secretary for his local Clown Unit for 2012.

BRODEUR, MATTHEW (Dusty) was born June 30, 1983 at Brockton. He is a student at the University of Massachusetts, Dartmouth.

"Dusty" was raised at George H. Taber Lodge; walked the hot sands at Aleppo Temple and joined the Aleppo Clown Unit. Matt started clowning in 2003 but before that he used to follow his dad on foot at all his parades, keeping up with the clown unit and he knew he wanted to be out there with them some day.

Local clowns Richard "Hoppy" Brodeur and Matt "Dusty" Brodeur.

He earned Clown of the Year in 2007 and Craftsman Clown in 2009. In 2012 Matt became the youngest person to earn Master Clown after having gone to the Northeast Clown Institute and has since attended Bubba Sikes University and several other training programs. He does pocket magic, balloons and walk around, and slits. He and his dad often perform together and enjoy entertaining the crowd with their silly gags and crazy antics.

BRODEUR, RICHARD (Hoppy) was born June 2, 1948 in New Bedford, MA. He has one son, Matthew. Richard retired in 2008 from Massachusetts Highway Department, where he served as an engineer from 1971-2008.

"Hoppy" was raised at George H. Taber Lodge and walked the hot sands at Aleppo Temple. Richard started clowning in 2002 at the Rhode Island Shrine but moved to the Aleppo Shrine in 2006.

He was named Clown of the Year in 2007; a member of ISCA in 2007-2011, and Regional in 2003 and 2011. He was named Craftsman Clown in 2009 and Master Clown in 2012.

He and his son, Matt, perform as a team and have a lot of fun together. They were the first father-son team to earn their master clown and are very proud of that. Richard has attended the Northeast Clown Institute as well as Bubba Sikes University and the Hearts and Noses hospital training. Richard's specialty is props and he is constantly building new ones for the duo.

When they go to a parade, thanks to Dad, they have a box load of props to choose from and there is always something new in the collection.

BROOKSHIER, RANDOL K. (Kolohe) was born in Healdton, OK, April 9, 1929. After attending school, he served in the US Army during WW II, Korea, and Vietnam. He married the late Akiko Sawada of Tokyo, Japan and they had one child, Desiree, and two grandchildren, Rachel and Tara. They resided in Japan, Okinawa, California and Oklahoma. Retiring from the US Army after 25 years, as a Chief Warrant Officer, they set up residence in Tacoma, WA, where he went to work for a public utility owned short line railroad. He worked for the railroad for 20 years, retiring as Chief Clerk.

Randol came into Freemasonry in Sendai, Japan, was raised to the sublime degree of Master Mason on May 3, 1956. He was initiated into the York Rites in 1968 and initiated into Aloha Shrine, walking the hot sands in 1968, and then joined the Aloha Shrine Club of Okinawa in 1968. He was also initiated into the Okinawa Shrine Clowns.

"Kolohe" brought to the ISCA a long career of leadership which included, Worshipful Master of Royal A. Gove Lodge F&AM#230, Worshipful Master of Cedar Lodge F&AM #104, District Deputy of the Grand Master for District #14 of the Grand Lodge of Washington, First Ceremonial Master, Second Ceremonial Master, Treasurer, Director of the Divan, and Captain of the Guard, all of the Afifi Shrine Center, Tacoma, WA. He was Ambassador to the Northwest for ISCA.

He was Captain of the First Veil of York Rites, Director of the World Famous Afifi Shrine Clowns and was on the Twelfth and Twenty-Fifth Degree Team of the Scottish Rite. He is a member of the Royal Order of Scotland.

BROWN, DONALD R. (Snooz-O) was born July 2, 1937 in Providence, RI, graduating in 1955 from Providence High School. He served four years active duty with USMC, two years in Active Reserves, being honorably discharged in 1960. On April 8, 1961 he married Nancy Davis. After retiring in 1995 from Benny's, Inc. they moved to North Fort Myers, FL. He is a lifetime member of the Church of the Master (Baptist). Donald has received countless awards and honors in his private and professional life.

Donald was raised on May 11, 1963 at Roger Williams Lodge #32. He served as Master in 1971 and 1981. He is a 49-year member of Grand Lodge of Rhode Island; a 46 year, life member, Scottish Rite and a 21 year member of Tall Cedars of North America. He has served in several capacities in Masonic affiliations and has received numerous awards and honors.

Brown joined Araba Shrine in October 2001 and the Araba Clowns Fun and Frolic in January 2002. He currently is a Senior Aide (five years); Co-Chairman Sanbaggers Golf Comm. (nine years); Chairman Sunshine Comm. (10 years). He has also been a hospital driver, making 85 trips of 22,350 miles.

On Oct. 23, 2010 he was a Fall Ceremonial Honoree. He is a Certified Craftsman/Master Clown, has received nine Red Nose and four Gold Nose awards and 100 plus 1st, 2nd, 3rd, and Top Tens awards.

BURGAD, MARK G. (Buzzy, Checkers, Wilbur) was born in Bismarck, ND in 1953. After completing high school, he served three years in the U.S. Army from 1972 thru 1975. He is married to Lynn and has one son Derrick. He completed college receiving a B.S. degree from North Dakota State University. Most of his working career was spent as a Light Fixture Manufacturers Rep.

He was Master of his Lodge. He is a member of the York Rite. He began his clowning career in Billings, MT. He was President and also Secretary/Treasurer of the Northern Hills Shrine Club. He was President and also Secretary/Treasurer of the Midwest Shrine Clown Association. He served two terms as Public Relations Director for ISCA and one term as Assistant Sneaker Fund Chairman. In 2009, he became the 3rd VP for ISCA and in 2012, he became the President of ISCA.

BURKE, LON (Cactus) was born in Herrin, IL, April 25, 1951. After receiving his M.S. degree from Southern Illinois University, he married Barbara Rapp in 1979. He joined Polk Lodge AF & AM #137, McLeansboro, IL in 1980. He began working for the USDA, Risk Management Agency and they moved to Springfield, IL. He joined the Scottish Rite, AASR, Valley of Springfield in 1983. A few months later, he joined the Ansar Shrine in Springfield, IL and became a member of the Clown Unit in February 1984. He chose "Cactus" as his clown name and for many years clowned as a character cowboy. "Cactus" and Barbara's daughter, Susan, was born in 1984 and their son, Sean, was born in 1987. They only know their dad as being a Shrine clown.

"Cactus" first appearance in both makeup and costume was at the Great Lakes Shrine Clown Units' Association (GLSCUA) Mid-Year Convention competition held April 1984 in Springfield, IL. He did not place in that competition, but over the years, competed in many GLSCUA and ISCA competitions and won or placed in several categories. Cactus listened to advice from his mentors and made changes to improve.

Cactus served the Valley of Springfield as Director of Makeup for over 15 years and received the Meritorious Service Award (MSA) in June 1991 from the Illinois Council of Deliberation, Northern Masonic Jurisdiction, Scottish Rite Freemasonry.

After serving in various officer positions, in 1996-1997 he was elected and installed as President of GLSCUA. In 1997, he began competing again in GLSCUA, and was awarded the "Bob Jones All-Around Clown Award". In 2005, he received the designation of "Emeritus Clown" with GLSCUA.

In October 2008, he transferred with USDA to Topeka, KS, joined the Arab Shrine and became a member of the Clown Unit. He is now a member of the Central States Shrine Clown Association and has competed and placed the last two years in CSSCA.

Cactus was appointed in 2010 to serve as the ISCA Education Director. In 2011, he was elected and served as the ISCA Treasurer. In 2012, Cactus was elected ISCA 3rd Vice-President. In February 2015, Cactus will be installed as President of ISCA.

BURKHOLDER, DENNIS (Skooter) and wife Cindy have a daughter, Isabel "Bella." They live in St. Peters, MO. He is employed in National Sales for Epic Solutions.

Dennis is a Lifetime Member of St. Charles Lodge #241, St. Charles, MO. He was raised as a Master Mason in January 1999. In January 1999 became a 32 degree member of Scottish Rite (Lifetime Member). He joined Moolah Shriners in January 1999 (Lifetime Member) and joined the Moolah Clowns in January 1999. He is a member of the Royal Order of Scotland - knighted in 2004; Reenactor for F&I events - Masonic Beaver Degree - 2004; PR Chairman for Moolah St. Louis and Past Membership - Retention - Chairman for Moolah St. Louis.

"Skooter" is a multiyear recipient of the "Red Nose" Award from the International Shrine Clown Association.

"Skooter" is a member of the International Shrine Clown Association, Clowns of America, Local Alley #128, World Clown Association, International Clown Hall of Fame, and the Puppeteers Of America. He was the founder of "Clowns for the Cause," a national program to help charitable groups throughout the United States and Canada through clowning.

He has been clowning since 1974.

"Skooter" "attempts" magic, balloons, puppets, and silly jokes. He appears in parades, corporate events, parties, picnics, grand openings and other big happenings throughout St. Louis and the Midwest. He has entertained kids in Kansas, Tennessee, Kentucky, Indiana, Ohio, Colorado, Mississippi, Georgia, Illinois, Kentucky, Iowa, Missouri and even in Canada.

All proceeds from his appearances benefit the Shrine Hospitals for Children and other charitable groups.

Motto: The clowns are witnesses to the passing of centuries, the social commentators. The clowns reflect the eternal spirit of mankind. They are grounded and realistic, telling little stories of everyday life - where everyone is a hero, where anyone can fall in love and suffer a broken heart. The clowns are visionaries - philosophers of absurdity. Endearing, comical and child-like, they turn the world into a circus.

CADDICK, DAVID W. (Digger) was born in Philadelphia, PA May 30, 1947. After graduating from Frankford High School he enlisted in the Navy at 17. He attended school in the Great Lakes for electronic technology and was sent to Alaska for his first tour of duty. He was eventually assigned to the *USS Forrestal* OE division. On July 29, 1967, while in the Gulf of Tonkin, an explosion and fire occurred on the *Forrestal* considered the worst naval disaster since WW II. A total of 134 young men lost their lives that day, many while sleeping under the flight deck. On July 29, 2002 Dave participated in a memorial service and wreath laying at the Vietnam Veteran's Wall in Washington, DC, representing his OE Division. He will never forget them!

Dave attended Penn State University and graduated with a degree in transportation engineering. He married Donna Dunn, a PGH nurse in 1970; a son and daughter followed and eventually five grandchildren. Dave worked for SEPTA in their transportation-engineering department for several years, left to work for a paving and utility contractor and started his own construction company in 1975.

Dave was raised as a member of Jerusalem Lodge 506 in November 1974. He walked the hot sands June 20, 1984 as a member of LuLu Temple and joined the LuLu Klownz unit in 1998. He has been Noble of the year, received his red and gold clown noses, helps with all construction and maintenance needs for the circus, rodeo and haunted house. He continues to visit the Shriner's Hospital in Philadelphia and participates in local parades including the Boscov's Thanksgiving Day parade in Philadelphia and the St Patrick's Day parade in Savannah along with the Alee Clown Unit.

He has been active in many other organizations throughout his career including: Penn State Alumni Society Board, awarded Heart of the Lion, 2008, Scoutmaster, (awarded the Celtic Cross by Boy Scout Troop #542) Indian Princesses, (YMCA), President of LuLu Country Club and long time board member, Republican Committee Man, a coordinator of youth group projects at church, sponsors several youth baseball teams, Citizen of the week Ambler Gazette, ABC (Associated Builders and Contractors), (NRTW) National Right to Work, Pa Right to Work, lifetime member of Vietnam Veterans, and after his wife's diagnosis of breast cancer endowed the "Donna Caddick Health and Wellness Fund" which offers students and faculty screenings and programs for health education.

CAIN, RICHARD (RC) was born and raised in Atlanta, GA. "RC" has been an active Shrine Clown since 1973.

He has won top awards and has placed first in the tramp category in the SESCA, GA Shrine, Yaarab Temple, SE Clown Association, the International Shrine Clown Association, and Northeast Clown Institute. "RC" has served as President of the Yaarab Red Devil Clowns, Yaarab Clown Association, Georgia Shrine Clowns, SESCA, ISCA as well as the Peachtree Clown Alley. He was inducted into the Red Devil Clown Hall of Fame in 2004 and received the ISCA Lifetime Achievement Award in 2011. He was recognized at NCI as a Master Clown for his achievements in clowning after many years in attendance and where he currently is an instructor. He served as ISCA Educational Director for two years and was also appointed as Historian for many years. "RC" is a member of COAI and the World Clown Association and has served on the Board of the International Clown Hall of Fame. "RC" is also a lifetime member of Anezeh Temple in Mexico City.

CANAVAN, PATRICK J. (Dr. Cuddles) was born March 18, 1949 in Braddock, PA. He was married to Christine in August 1972 and they have two children, Melanie Canavan Henninger and Patrick Joseph Canavan. Grandchildren are: Molly Belle Henninger, Murphy Jane Henninger and Mason Patrick Canavan. His employment has been: 1972 USX - Millwright; 1985 Sales Representative - Garlock Inc.; 1991 Clairton Municipal Authority - Lab Technician; 2004 Clairton Municipal Authority - Plant Superintendent. His family lives in West Mifflin, PA.

Patrick has been a member of Homestead-Amity McCandles Lodge #582 since 1987. He belongs to Syria Shrine Temple and has held the following positions: Past President of Caravan 24; Past President of Caravan 4; Aide for various Potentates; Ambassador for Syria Shrine; Executive Assistant to Potentate Rev. David L. Kinsey, 2006; Deputy Director General of Mid Atlantic Shrine Association (M.A.S.A.), 2011; and Executive Assistant to Potentate Gary Helander, 2011.

"Dr. Cuddles" joined the Syria Harige Clown Unit in 2000 and has been an active member. In 2001 he was a member of the Executive Board; Treasurer; Secretary and Captain of the Unit in 2009.

From 2009-2010 he was an Officer for Mid-Atlantic Shrine Clown Association (M.A.S.C.A.) and will be President in 2013-2014. He has been a M.A.S.C.A. Life Member since 2011.

"Dr. Cuddles" participated in competitions before getting in line for M.A.S.C.A. and received various 1st, 2nd, and 3rd place awards for costume/make-up and skits.

He has been an ISCA member since 2002.

CANTRELL, GENE (Sawdust) was born on Sept. 25, 1930 in Shawnee, OK. Gene served in the US Army in Korea from 1953-1955. Gene is a retired teacher of 38 years and has been married to his wife, Elaine, for 56 years. They have four children and numerous grandchildren.

Sawdust belongs to Omadi Lodge in South Sioux City, NE. He was raised to a Master Mason in 1968, joined Abu Bekr Shrine in 1987, and the Clown Unit in 1992. He has participated in many parades, school carnivals, picnics and entertaining with balloon sculpturing. He has been Clown Boss and Scribe several times.

Sawdust has attended 10 MSA and CSSA conventions. He has won numerous awards for individual makeup, Skits, balloon sculpture and paradeability. Sawdust has received 12 red noses, two gold noses and Clown of the Year in 2000 and 2012.

His biggest joy, next to his family, is "Clowning Around."

COBB, JAMES ARNOLD (KLUTZ (the magnificent)) was born April 25, 1929 in Portland, OR. He and wife, Lois, have five children and five grandchildren. He retired from USAR after 31 years and from Teamster Union, June 1980. His hobbies include building remote control airplanes, fishing, and shooting sports. He has volunteered at Clark County Juvenile court system for 27 years and Two Rivers Heritage Museum, Washougal, WA for four years.

He was raised in Washington Lodge # 20, Sacramento, CA in February 1965. In 1980, he demitted to North Bank Lodge # 182, Washougal, WA. He served as Worshipful Master in 1985 and Secretary of North Bank Lodge 182 since 1998. He joined Scottish Rite, Vancouver Valley in 1980.

Cobb joined AFIFI Shrine, Tacoma, WA on June 7, 1980 and ISCA in 1980.

He became an AFIFI Shrine Clown in 1980 and a member of South West Washington AFIFI Shrine Clowns in 1995. He took 1st place White Face in 1987, 1988 and 1989. He has been a member of Clowns of America since 1997.

"Klutz" received Silver in 1997, Gold in 1998, People's Choice Spokane. He has been treasurer/secretary of SW Shrine Clowns since 1995.

COBB, THOMAS J. was a member of First AbouBenAdhem in Springfield, MO, Moslah Shrine in Fort Worth, TX, and the Mansfield Shrine Club, which is a unit of Moslah Temple. He held lifetime memberships in the Hadi Temple of Evansville, Indiana, and the Tri-County Shrine Club. His memberships also included the Maple Leaf Clan No. 59 of Grand and Glorious Order of Hill Billy Degree of Canada, The Hoosier Clan No. 14, the Ancient Order of Turtles Inc., Cowtown Stable No.23 of Fort Worth, the Artisan Order of Quetzacoatl of North Amaerica, Kokopelli Teocalli No. 33 Garland, Grand Order of the Sword of Bunker Hill Falls of Ohio Order 11. He also held the Commission of Colonel in the Honorable Order of Kentucky Colonels and a member of the International Order of the Odd Fellows.

Above all he was a clown in Moslah Clown Unit of which he was the past president and a lifetime member. He was awarded the Louis Stamm Award for Improvement in makeup and the J. Tom Shelton Clown of the Year Award. He was the only clown to win back to back International First Places in 1994 and 1995. He also took first place in Texas Shrine Clown Association 1994-1996 in makeup and costume. He placed in the top ten at TSCA and International for the last seven years and took second place in the two-man skit competition. He received Red Nose Awards in 1997 and 1998. He was a member of the Texas Shrine Clown Association, Clowns of America International, and International Shrine Clown Association.

His motto was "Always leave them smiling".

COFFEY, GARY MIKE (U-WHO) was born at 11:54, February 29, 1944, at San Antonio, Texas. After attending school, he served in the U.S. Coast Guard as an electronic technician. He married Claire Christilles (Little Bit). They are retired and reside in La Coste, Texas, where he was an accountant and then a teacher.

"U-WHO" has been president of Alzafar Nemnuf and Kerr Klowns, president of Texas Shrine Clown Association, twice Sergeant of Arms of International Shrine Clown Association, member of Alzafar Finance Committee, Ambassador to Alzafar, president of Boerne Shrine club, and is a member of Boerne Lodge #897.

"U-WHO" has won numerous awards for his skits but is always trying to keep winning first place.

COLE, JOE C. (Ol' Coach) was born November 28, 1938 in Brady, Texas. Graduated in 1957 from Brady High School where he was an All-State football player. He received a football scholarship to Texas Christian University. He graduated from T.C.U. in 1962 with BS degree in Physical Education and Science.

Joe married Starr Harrison on June 11, 1960 while at T.C.U. They have three children. Curt, Brad and Courtenay. They have six grandchildren. Curt has a daughter Madison and a son Mason. Brad has a daughter Kendyl. Courtenay has a son Chase and two daughters Kristen and Amy. They are members of the Episcopal Church.

After graduating from T.C.U., Joe coached and taught high school for the next 32 years.

Joe's Masonic relationship started while he was in high school. He became a De Molay in 1953. Texas. Raised as a Master Mason on June 27, 1967 in Hill City Lodge #456 of Austin, Texas. Traveled the Hot Sands at the Spring Ceremonial at Ben Hur Shrine Temple 1980. This is when he joined the SREKOJ Clown Unit as "Ol' Coach" - President '84. He has won numerous awards & three Gold Nose Awards. I.S.C.A.- Sneaker Fund Ambassador '84-'88 and I.S.C.A. Sneaker Fund Board Councilman '88-'93, Texas Shrine Clown Association - President '89-'90. Potentate of Ben Hur Shrine Temple in '94. As Potentate, he started the Hillbilly Club. Served as Raban of the Clan (President) in '94-'95 and '96. A member of the 100 Million Dollar Club, Permanent Contributing Member, Life Member of the SREKOJ Clown Unit, Ben Hur Shrine Temple, I.S.C.A. and the Cabiri. Joe was appointed to the Imperial Athletic Committee '95 - ! and as the Texas General Chairman for the California/Texas Shrine High School Football All-Star Classic '95 – '97! Joe was appointed to be an Aide to the Imperial Outer Guard '96. Joe was elected to serve as Parliamentarian for the Texas Shrine Clown Association in '96. President ISCA 2001-2002. Appointed Sneaker Fund Chairman – USA '04 – 09'.

CORBIN, NELSON K. (Baby Face Nelson) was born July 31, 1934 in St. Louis, MO.

He was raised on June 30, 1958 at Woodriver, IL Lodge 1062 AF&AM. He demitted to Service Lodge #327 F&AM, Long Beach, CA in 1968; demitted to Palmdale Lodge #769 F&AM, Palmdale, CA and joined Lancaster Lodge #437 F&AM, Lancaster, CA in 2005. Nelson walked the hot sands in May 1963, Al Menah Shrine, Nashville, TN. In 1964 he transferred to Al Chymia Shrine, Memphis, TN and then to El Bekal Shrine, Long Beach, CA in 1968.

Nelson was on weekend reserve duty at Bakalar AFB in Columbus, IN on Oct. 3 and 4, 1961. On Oct. 4, the whole unit was activated for the Cuban Missile Crisis. Nelson was sent to Seward AFB in Smyrna, TN. Two Masons in the dental clinic were the dental surgeon and Dr. Ramsey. Later Nelson found out Dr. Ramsey was past president of Al Chamia Clown Unit. Ramsey was responsible for Nelson being "Baby Face Nelson."

The El Bekal Clown unit was invited to attend the 1972 Santa Claus Christmas Lane Parade in Hollywood, CA.

One day during spring maneuvers with South Korea, Nelson dressed as a clown to visit an orphanage. He dressed in the orderly room and stepped outside on the street. A company of Korean army troops was marching up the streets and the leader ordered them to look left. The soldiers broke ranks and scattered all over the street laughing. It took ten minutes for them to get back in formation and continue marching. At the orphanage he blew up a gross amount of balloon animals and hats. Each child was happy to receive a balloon; they were laughing and talking to be in Korean.

Later he was invited to lunch and his host asked him to wear his clown outfit and they went to a restaurant down by the harbor. At the restaurant the workmen at the harbor stopped working as we walked by. The band, waitress cooks, patrons, and cashiers came to a complete stop. Nelson was the first live clown to be seen in this area of Korea. You can say he was the first shrine clown to be seen. Before leaving Korea he attended a Masonic Lodge on base there. The charter was from Scotland and all Officers of the lodge wore Kilts.

CORY, THOMAS L. (Hugger) was born in Alhambra, CA in 1944. He married his wife, Reneise, in 1967 and they settled in Yorba Linda, CA.

Following his graduation from the California State University, Los Angeles in 1973, Thomas began his career as a Speech and Language Pathologist in 1974. He completed his Ph.D., in Education from Claremont Graduate School in 1988.

Thomas became a Mason with the Alhambra Lodge F&AM #322 and was raised to Master Mason in 1983. In 1996, he became a member of the Scottish Rite Valley of Santa Ana and El Bekal Shrine. His work in the Shrine focused upon the El Bekal Clown Unit when "Hugger" took his "hot sands" in the summer of 1996 in Palm Springs.

"Hugger" was Clown President in 2000 and Unit secretary for six years.

Along with his wife, Reneise, they keep busy with the activities within the El Bekal Shrine, LOSNA RAMA COURT and the Daughters of the Nile. "Hugger" served as Rear Commodore for the Shrine Yacht Club from 2010 through 2011.

"Hugger" enjoys the parade activities and focuses upon the Garden Grove "Strawberry Festival," the Indio "Date Festival," and the Capistrano "Swallows' Day Festival." "Hugger" offers yearly support to the Juvenile Diabetes Research Foundation "walk-for-a-cure" at UCI in Irvine. For the past three years, "Hugger" has served as a Screening Clinic Aide and resident clown.

COX, JIM (Frenchee) was born in St. Louis, MO in 1945. He is a member of Pauldingville #11 Lodge (raised in 2003), Moolah Temple, and walked the hot sands in April 2004. He has a member of the Moolah Clowns since May 2004, and was president of the Moolah Clowns in 2009. Jim has competed in both character and Auguste contests.

Jim married Pam in 1968 and they have one child, Angie, two grandchildren, Josh and Matt, and two great-grandchildren, Collin and Olivia. He worked 32 years for the Missouri Department of Transportation, retiring in 1995.

CREEKMORE, FLOYD V. (Creeky) was born July 14, 1916 in Coffee Creek, MT. After attending school in Great Falls, MT, he left home after his freshman year. He them attended school in Arrow Creek, MT and graduated from Denton, MT. schools.

He married Betty Smail and they have three children: Larry, Cheryl and Dave; five grandchildren: Stephen; Scott and Sirl Creekmore and Brent and Thomas McGraw; and 11 great-grandchildren. He operated a cattle ranch and then moved to Stanford, MT, where he was engaged as a contractor. In 1969 he moved to Billings, MT.

Floyd was raised on April 17, 1950 at Palistine Lodge #88, Stanford, MT. In September 1981 he walked the hot stands at Albedoo Temple. He joined the Albedoo Clowns in February 1982 and served as President, Master of Palistine Lodge #88 and three times as Worthy Patron of Eastern Star. He was High Priest, Master, Commander and Red Cross of Constantine of York Rite, and member of the Scottish Rite and Jesters. He joined ISCA in 1983 and won many awards.

He was Clown of the Year in 1993 and Ambassador for 18 years. He made the Guinness World Records as "The Oldest Active Clown" in 2012.

CROISSANT JR., ADRIAN E. (WoWo) was born Dec. 18, 1936 in East St. Louis, IL. Ne married Norma Munro in 1958. Their children are Adrian, Abbey Todd and Terri. Grandchildren are Ian, Austen, Jessie and Drew. Adrian was a school teacher in School District 189 from 1965 to 1995 when he retired. Then he was a substitute teacher until 2006.

"WoWo" was raised at Gothic Lodge #852 in 1958. He joined Ainad Temple and in 1967 joined the Ainad Temple and Ainad Clowns Unit. He was President in 1974 and 1982. Since 2000, he has been P.R. Adrian is a Past Master of Gothic Masonic Lodge and has been Secretary since 1995.

He was awarded Top "10" Clown in 1975 at Toronto. He was in N.S.C.A from 1967 to 1980. Their unit did 90 engagements per year, and now they do around 40.

"WoWo" clowns with large pants and shoes with double soles, so they pop!

DAVIS, CHARLES RONALD (Duffer) was born in Tulsa, Oklahoma, Nov. 14, 1948, where he still resides with his wife, Rosemary. They reside on the same property he was raised on. Physically raised that is...his Masonic raising in 2003 was at Redfork-Brookside Lodge. He joined the Shrine that same year in the fall and began clowning in 2004. He has continued to make the trip to CSSCA supporting Merri-Makers as they continually won the overall trophy through 2011. This included being the Unit's Director in 2005 and 2008.

Ron has supported his family working in the oilfield services industry designing and manufacturing equipment. He did work as a golf instructor for the Nike Learning Center in Boulder, Colorado a couple years. Currently he works for Global Industrial.

Duffer loves to clown up for kids and the Shrine Circus is one of those major events. Duffer always recruits his family to help out during the circus.

Favorite saying: "Sometimes you feel like a nut".

DELLHIME, KENNETH M. (Gold Dust) born in Hartford CT, May 15, 1954. Employment: Electro-Mechanics, now Westinghouse Electric in Windsor, CT as a Spare Parts engineer on CE/ABB Legacy Plants (31+ years). Became Master Mason at Orient Lodge #62, East Hartford, CT on February 20, 1993. Served as Tyler for nine years before becoming a member of Anchor Lodge #112, in East Hampton. Became a Shriner at Sphinx Temple, Newington, CT in December 1993 and joined the Funster Unit in January 1994. Served as Chief in 2003, 2004 & 2009. Became a Life member in March 2005. Serving as Secretary from 2006 to present. Also, involved with the Connecticut Trolley Museum, in East Windsor, "Rails to the Darkside", playing a dead Keystone Cop in 1991, 1993 & 2010 to present. First marriage of 20 years ended in divorce with no children. Second marriage (H. Kim Lour), have four stepsons, 11 grandchildren & one great-grandson. His wife and grandchildren bring him the most happiness, followed by clowning.

DISLER, BOB (Dizzy) joined the Al Shamal Shrine Clowns in 1993 .He developed his character during 1994 as Dizzy the Clown, due to his personality in the old days. He seemed to be in a fog and nothing worked as far as magic and Balloon making, but after a while things got better.

Dizzy has participated in many events from 1994 - 2007. His picture has been in the newspaper and on television. Dizzy has performed at Birthday parties, BBQ's, senior homes, Shrine Circus, parades, Hospitals and Edmonton special events. He also has attended many Northwest Shrine conferences and won various competitions in costume, skits and balloons. "Dizzy" is proud to be a part of the wonderful caring Clowns Hospital Clowning since 1998, which has been very rewarding.

Over the years Dizzy has been influenced by the talents of both the caring Clowns and the Shrine Clowns for their involvement in the community and hospital Clowning. As a final note Dizzy has been ever so grateful for the opportunity of Clowning around with so many talented people.

ENTRICAN, RICHARD (Zero) was born June 7, 1945 in Alameda, CA. He and Darleen have been married 26 years. Richard has been retired for seven very happy years after 21 years with CSUS.

"Zero" was raised in Wash. Lodge #20. In December 1977 he walked the hot sands at Benali Temple and then joined the Benali Clown Unit.

He is Past President (1992), Past Treasurer, Past ISCA Ambassador, and Past Executive Secretary of Western Shrine Clowns Association.

ESTRIN, EDWARD Z. (LoMax) was born in California, September 14, 1949. He is a U.S. Army Vet serving in Vietnam. He graduated from Woodbury University in Los Angeles. He married Leah (Saenz) Rountree. They have three children and three grandchildren. He currently resides in San Diego, CA. He is a CPA and Chief Financial Officer for Private Asset Management, Inc.

Edward joined Oceanside Masonic Lodge, #381, in Oceanside, CA in October, 1988 and was raised to Master Mason April 10, 1989. He served his lodge as Treasurer for three years.

Edward joined Al Bahr Shrine, San Diego, CA on May 6, 2000.

He joined the Al Bahr Clowns soon thereafter as IMAX. In 2003 LoMax, an Auguste, was born and has been the main character for Ed. LoMax served as Secretary/Treasurer, as Director, and as President (2 terms) for Al Bahr Shrine Clowns.

LoMax is a member of ISCA, WCA, COAI and San Diego Clown Conspiracy.

He has been awarded Gold Metals, Silver Metals and Bronze Metals in Make up/Costuming, in single and group Skits, in Balloons and in Paradeability.

LoMax has served World Clown Association as Treasurer, as Chairman of Business Services committee, as Alley Director and as Vice President.

FANKHANEL, JAMES HARRY was born July 14, 1935 in Minneapolis, MN. He attended William Windom Grade School (K-6), Ramsey Junior High School (7), Jefferson Junior High School (8-9), West High School (10-12) and the University of Minnesota (graduating with a BA in 1957).

He worked for Rexnord Inc. of Milwaukee, WI (Sales/Engineer Trainee), 1957-59 and in Pittsburgh, PA (Sales Engineer) 1959-64; Wall Conveyor & Mfg. Co. of Huntington, WV (purchased half-interest), 1964, and by 1976 had become sole owner. He retired and closed the business in 2001.

He is a member of ATO Fraternity, University of Minnesota; Unizar Lodge #347; A.F.&A.M., Roseville, MN; Scottish Rite Bodies & York Rite, Huntington, WV; Beni Kedem Shrine, Charleston, WV.

His hobbies include hunting, fishing, camping, etc., but since 1972 clowning as a Shrine clown has been the most fun. He was president of the Mid-Atlantic Shrine Clown Association in 1980 and President of the International Shrine Clown Association in 1985. In the last few years he has had parts in amateur productions of "The Wizard of Oz", "A Christmas Carol", "Gypsy", "Annie", "It's a Wonderful Life," and a local adaption of the Orson Wells' radio drama "Invasion from Mars". He is very active as treasurer of Christ the King Lutheran Church (ELCA).

He was married first to Arlowyn Jean Thornton (1956-1976) with children Cindy Lynn, Carine Elisa, Christina Lane, James Harry Jr. and Collette Rachel; second to Trudy Marie Lowery (1976-dec. 2011) with one child, Tammy Marie; and in 2012 married Carolyn Rose Breisler.

FORD, MICHAEL LEE (Splatter) was born in Spokane, WA, Sept. 12, 1954. He served three years in the U.S. Army and afterwards in 1980 met his future wife, Betsy. They married in 1982. Alysia and Jason complete this wonderful package. They reside in Austin, Texas where Michael works as a Graphics Artist for the Texas Department of Transportation, designing the artwork that goes on the sides of bridges and retaining walls in the state.

Shortly after joining the Ben Hur Shriners, Mike joined their Srekoj Clown Unit (Jokers backwards). Seemingly to have been born to be a clown, Splatter immediately became active in parades, the Ben Hur Shrine Circus, hospital visits and clown competition. He loved it all. His competitions have included Whiteface, Auguste, and Character. In these categories as well as skits, Splatter had taken home multiple first place awards and two Top Five Clown Extraordinaire titles as well. Skits, performing and parading are actually still his preferences he reports because there is where you have the best opportunity to touch the hearts of all who remain young at heart. Splatter is also proud of his several Red Nose Awards and annual participation in the Mardi Gras Centurion Parade where he earns money for the Sneaker Fund through his participation in the Centurion Parade and Ball.

Splatter currently sports the "Bald" look in real life and often in clown as well. Seems several years back while wife Betsy was attending a conference in Galveston, TX, Splatter decided he'd tag along and visit the Galveston Shrine Hospital children while in town. But, oops, the then whiteface clown had forgotten his skull cap. What's a clown to do – you can't disappoint the children! So, without much of a second thought, out came the razor and off came the hair making his bald whiteface look still possible for that visit and forward. Mike's remained bald ever since.

In 2007 Michael was elected to the Ben Hur Divan and served as their Potentate in 2011. While enjoying his time on the line, Michael was very happy to once again return to Shrine Clowning in 2012 upon completion of his Divan term. Mike's favorite phrases – Good Morning (all day long) and Life just keeps getting better and better! Hope your life is the same. What a gift it is to be a clown!

FORNEY, MICHAEL J. (Wheeelz) was born Jan. 25, 1973 in Racine, WI. He was raised on March 17, 2010 in Charles A. Welch Loge, Maynard, MA and walked the hot sands in Nov. 2010. Michael joined the Aleppo Shrine Clown Unit on March 21, 2012, and is a member of Aleppo Shrine in Wilmington, MA.

Michael is a first-year clown but has been a clown all his life. After joining Aleppo Temple in 2010, he joined the motorcycle unit. After a bad crash in a parade in August 2011, he felt he needed a change of pace and joined the clowns.

He is an accounts payable coordinator handling capital expenditures for a health care company. He enjoys kayaking, especially whitewater, flies stunt kits, rollerblading, his scooter, and now loves to clown around.

Michael is married to Lisa, with children Brett and Eli.

FOX, LYLE (Foxy) was born March 30, 1944 in Richland Center, WI. He and Carol have three children: Kelly; Misty and Joe. Their grandchildren are: Kaitlynn, Kyle, Tyler and Jarrett. Lyle has been barbering for 46 years.

Lyle was raised in Sun Prairie Lodge #143 on May 3, 1982. At ZOR Temple, he walked the hot sands on Dec. 5, 1987. In 1988 he joined the ZOR Clowns Unit.

"Foxy" has served as Past Master and Secretary of Lodge #143. He is Past "Boss Clown" of his Clown Unit. Since 1987, he has been a member of Madison Scottish Rite Bodies; an ISCA member since 1991 and Midwest Clowns.

FRANKLIN, CHARLES DONALD (Felix) was born in Ashland, KY May 1, 1934. After attending school at Ashland Junior College, he served four years in the United States Marine Corps during the Korean War. He married Mary Katherine "Katie" Bailey, April 2, 1956 and had three children: Becky; Charley and Kevin, and five grandchildren: Tyler; Alex; Phillip; Shayna and Shaun.

Felix was raised a Master Mason 1955. He became a York Rite Mason in 1962.

He became an Eastern Star in 1964 and Scottish Rite Mason in 1966. In 1963, Felix joined El Hasa Shrine and in the same year he became a charter member of El Hasa Clown Unit. The unit joined the National Shrine Clown Association, which was later changed to International Shrine Clown Association. They also joined the South Eastern Clown Association. They also joined South Atlantic Clown Association.

Felix is an active clown in all functions from parades, to hospital visits, circuses and children's parties. He has enjoyed working with children throughout his clown career of 49 years.

FRASER, JOHN R. (TEEZ) was born in McLennan, Alberta, August 4th 1939. Married Joyce Tannas July 4th 1964. They have one daughter and one son with two grand daughters. He started his career with the Northern Alberta Railway in 1955 in the locomotive shop and progressed from labourer to a steam locomotive watchman, later becoming a machinist. Further advancements lead to supervisor, inspector and master mechanic. In 1981, CN Rail acquired the NAR and his career went from motive power to car equipment, where he became manager of a large car maintenance and repair facility. On his retirement at 55, he was Senior Manager of Operations Training-west for CN Rail.

He joined Patricia Lodge No. 91 GRA February 27, 1976; Worshipful Master in 1985, 1994 and 2006, and Secretary 1995-2005; elected DDGM for the Northern Lights District in 1997 and District Secretary in 2003; served the Grand Lodge of Alberta on several committees: BGP 3 yrs., Finance 7yrs. and Publications & Forms since 2004.

Edmonton Chapter, Order of DeMolay advisory council 1986-1991. Awarded the DeMolay Cross of Honour November 15, 1991. A member of the AASR, Edmonton Valley since 1978 and active in the 7th and 16th degrees.

Joined Al Shamal Shrine October 16th 1993, and the clowns in 1994. Secretary 1996 to 1998, President 2001 and Event Coordinator 1999, 2003 to 2007. PNSCA Top Banana Award 2008. He is the first member to have 18 consecutive ISCA Red Nose Awards. He was a finalist for ISCA clown of the year 2008, President Clown Association 2000-2008, Secretary 2009-present.

He remains an active member in his church, Chairman of the Official Board 1982-83, serving on several committees over the years.

FRY, DOUGLAS "DOUG" (BB) had always clowned for the children and upon being raised a Master Mason decided to Cross the Hot Sands in May 1998 where he joined the El Zaribah Shrine Clowns. Three days later he was involved in a near fatal traffic accident and because of the grace of the All Mighty and his desire to live he was called the Bionic Bozo. That is when BB Clown became known as The World Famous "BB Clown", but his world is kind of small. Helping children is his passion, understanding their pain is a first hand experience. Educating the novice clown is where he sees his passion continue.

PVST 29 Masonic Lodge; 32° Scottish Rite; York Rite; multiple Past President, El Zaribah Shrine Clown Unit; Past President, WSCA; Past President, Loose Knit Clowns of Phoenix, AZ; Member, ISCA; APS Volunteer Clowns.

GALE, ROBBY got his start as a DeMolay and the Chairman of our Advisory Council, who was his first line signer for Lodge, Scottish Rite, the Shrine and the Clowns was Bob "Winky" Eustace. He even patterned my costume after Winky. He was likely one of the youngest clowns in the Shrine, having joined prior to his 23rd birthday. Back then he joined the NSCA, the predecessor of ISCA, and is still a member of Liverpool-Syracuse No. 501 F&AM and the Valley of Syracuse AASR.

He was only in Tigris Clowns for two years before work took him to Pensacola, Florida and he transferred to Hadji Temple and Clowns. He still retains membership in both, serving as President of the Clowns in 1984 and 1985. He was appointed an Ambassador of Hadji Temple in 1986. In 1990, his work brought me to St. Louis, Missouri and he became a dual member of both Hadji and Moolah Temple and Clowns. He has been active in Moolah Clowns for the past 22 years.

Robby is a Chemical Engineer by trade and worked for Monsanto/Solutia from 1975 through 2001 and from 2001 to present he works for Emerson Process Management, working in the field of Safety & Health.

GALLMAN, JERRY (Buster Brown) is now a member of the Red Devils Clown Unit, Yaarab Temple, Atlanta, GA.

In 1975 he joined the Shrine and joined the Funny Bones Clown Unit in Dalton, GA. "Buster Brown" has clowned at hospitals, nursing homes, birthday parties, school and church Easter Egg hunts. He has enjoyed being a clown for 33 years. "Buster Brown" has been in over 300 Shrine parades all over the country, clowned at fairs and the Shrine Circus.

He placed in Top 10 in New Orleans, LA. In 1987 he won 1st place in paradeability at Georgia Shrine Clown Association. He won 1st place at Yaarab Clown Asst. as a car clown in 1992. He won Clown of the Year from Funny Bones Unit in 1987, 1989 and 1991. He was Captain of the Funny Bones Shrine Clown Unit.

His goal was to be a Shrine Clown so he could visit hospitals, nursing homes and parades to give people pats and have them give him a big smile and say thank you. He has been on TV, radio stations, and on the front page of newspapers.

He has been asked when he is going to retire. His answer: I will clown until my toes turn up.

GISCHLER, FRED L. (Hobo Freddy) was born in Columbus, OH, July 13, 1935. After attending school, he served in the U.S. Air Force during the Korean War. He married B.J. Easterday and has three children and five grandchildren. They reside in Reynoldsburg, OH and are retired, since 2000. They winter in Naples, FL.

Fred was a charter member of Bexley DeMolay, and was raised at Bexley Lodge #704 Bexley, OH in 1956. Currently he is a member of Baltimore Lodge #0475, in Baltimore, OH. He walked the Hot Sands of Aladdin Shrine #67 in 1965.

At Aladdin Shrine, he was appointed Ambassador and received two medals, Meritorious Service and Potentate's Special Award. The latter was for his work as a "Road Runner" for six years, taking children to seven Shrine Hospitals in six states, driving over one hundred thousand miles. He has served five years on the potentate's staff.

He is also active in Royal Order of the Jesters Court #8 and the Ambassadors Club.

"Hobo Freddy" joined the Aladdin Clown unit in 1967, where he has participated in countless parades and other activities plus competitions, including Great Lakes Unit Meets, Florida Shrine Clown Convention and Imperial Sessions. In the winter, he is active with the Araba Shrine Clowns, in Fort Meyers, FL and participates in their parades.

GRIFFIN, PAUL D. was born June 14, 1930 in Sioux City, IA. A graduate of public schools, he attended Morningside College, Iowa State College, Illinois College of Optometry, receiving Doctor of Optometry degree in 1954. He was drafted into the US Army in 1955 and honorably discharged in 1957 as First Lieutenant.

He joined DeMolay in 1945. In 1951 he was raised a Master Mason at Landmark Lodge 103, Sioux City, IA and is still a member. He took the Scottish Rite degrees in the Class of 1954 in the Valley of Sioux City and was a Charter Member of Lebanon Lodge, Egan, MN. Since 1961 he has been an active member of Osman Shrine Temple where he has held many offices.

He has attended all Mid-Winter Conventions of I.S.C.A. since 1975. In 1982-83 he was President of Mid-West Shrine Clown Association. From 1985-1987 he was Treasurer; served as Vice President from 1988-1991 and on Feb. 29, 1992 was installed as President of I.S.C.A.

He was appointed State Representative of C.O.A. in 1975. From 1982-1984 he was President of Alley #19. He has appeared on TV and lectured and judged more 100 meetings and competitions.

He has taken First Place in all three categories (White-Face, Auguste and Tramp) of Make-up and Costume; First Place in Balloons and Large Balloons; and Second and Third Place in numerous other competitions.

HABER, HOWARD (Pappy) was born March 16, 1948 in Cleveland, OH. He was raised on June 2, 1971 at Lyndhurst Lodge #508. He walked the hot sands on June 16, 1983 (Al Koran) and has been affiliated with Yaarab Temple since 2006, joining the Red Devil Clowns in 2009.

Howard was 2010 Rookie of the Year, 2011 Clown of the Year, 2010 SESCA (Greenville) 1st Place Happy Hobo, 2011 SESCA Mid-Winter 1st Place Happy Hobo, 2012 elected Director of Work.

He married Barbara in 1971 and has three children, Howard Jr., Jennifer and Kathleen, and six grandchildren. Howard worked for AT&T for 32 years and British Telecom for 10 years, retiring in 2007.

HARTMIER, NOBLE CLIFF (Mister Stripes) credits his membership with Winnipeg Chapter Order of DeMolay for starting his love of the art of clowning. Cliff was raised by Charleswood Lodge # 163 in May 1985, joined Khartum Shriners in October 2002, Komedians in 2005, and ISCA in 2006.

Cliff was elected unit President in 2010, Secretary in 2011, and also assumed the responsibilities of Treasurer in 2012. Cliff and Deanna with their wedding party walked down the aisle as clowns on April 29th 2000.

They also hold Clowns of America and World Clown Ass'n memberships. At the time of this writing, Deanna has just been elected to the President-Elect of the WCA and is destined to be installed as the President of the WCA in February 2013 for a 2-year term. Noble Cliff is involved in many aspects of the Masonic Family with numerous past presiding and district offices held.

HARVEY, FRENCH B. (Patches) was born in St. Augustine, FL in 1942. He served in the U.S. Navy for 23 years active duty retiring at the rank of Commander. After retiring he spent 17 years teaching NJROTC at a high school in Charlotte, NC. He married Julie Roberts in 1966, they have one son, David.

"Patches" was raised a Master Mason in Flint Lodge No. 15, Flint, Michigan solely so he could become a shrine clown. He "crossed the hot sands" in Honolulu, Hawaii while stationed at Pearl Harbor naval base. He was a member of the Honolulu Scottish Rite Bodies. He is now a member and Past Master of James K. Polk Lodge, No. 759 in Pineville, NC.

"Patches" began his clown hobby while a dramatic arts student in college in 1963. He became a shrine clown with Aloha Temple in 1980 while stationed at Pearl Harbor, HI. After moving to Minneapolis, MN in 1982, he became a member of the Zurah Funsters and was active in Clowns of America, International where he served as 1st vice-president and chief judge for their clown competitions. He now resides in Charlotte, NC and a member of Oasis Temple since 1986. He has served as Circus Boss Clown and ten years as Circus Director. He was appointed by the Potentate as Captain of the Clown Unit for 2012-2013. "Patches" credits his success as a clown to his mentor, Jack "Freckles" Anderson, who became a dear friend and supporter. French says," Jack took me under his wing after my first competition in Las Vegas at a Western Shrine Association convention and gave me pointers on my make-up and costume."

He was installed as the President of SASCA in 1993.

HEIDENBURG, DONALD C. (Kasper) was born in Buffalo, NY, Nov. 13, 1930. He graduated from high school and joined the US Marine Corp in 1950. Donald graduated from Lehigh University in 1957 and went to work for Bethlehem Steel Corporation for 42 years.

In 1960 he was raised a Mason in Fraternal Lodge #627 and received his 50-year pin in 2010. In 1972 he was Worthy Patron of Starlight Chapter #731, OES. In 1975 Donald joined Ismailia Shrine #37 in Buffalo, NY and was adjutant of the patrol for six years.

In 1982 "Kasper" joined the Royal Order of Jesters Court #22 and the same year joined Ismailia Shrine Clown Unit and became Kasper the Clown. In 1985 he attended his first winter meeting and attended the conventions for the next 10 years.

"Kasper" competed in single balloons and in 1989 in Mississippi placed 2nd; 1990 in Texas placed 3rd and in 1994 in Ohio placed 2nd.

HENSLEY, ERVIN 'JAKE' (BUG DUST) born Logan, WV, December 27, 1948. A member of the UMWA Jake retired after 30 years, 15 above ground and 15 underground. Marrying Diane, June 1980, they have two children, Jessica and Patricia and 2 grandchildren, Alec and Phoenix.

He began his Masonic journey in 2001, joining Aracoma Lodge #99 AF&AM, Past Patron of Logan Chapter #60 OES, Logan Chapter #41, Logan Commandry #26, 32 degree KCCH Scottish Rite, and walked the hot sands joining Beni Kedem Shrine.

In 2002, "Bug Dust" was born. Jake is past president of the Logan Shrine Club & Logan Clown Alley. An honorary member of Kazim and Kerbela Klowns, and a Kentucky colonel, Jake is past president of SASCA (2010-2011). Among his awards is included Children's Choice at Fun Fest 2012.

HEROMAN, DORIAN PAUL (Brushes, Marty-Graw, Topper) was born in 1949 in Lake Charles, LA. He was raised in 1989 at Fairfields Lodge #425 (PM, Treasurer) and is a Scottish Rite and York Rite member. He joined the Acacia Shrine Temple of Baton Rouge in 1990 and has served as Chaplain, on the Ways & Means Committee, Building and Maintenance Committee, Imperial Representative, and Potentate in 2012.

He joined Acacia Klowns in 1990 and has served as President, Vice-President and Secretary-Treasurer. He is a member of South Central Shrine Clown Association, serving as Secretary-Treasurer in 1995 and 2005. He was earned awards as the #1 Auguste clown, #1 character clown, and #2 Hobo clown. He is also a clowning instructor and competition judge.

In ISCA has served as Regional Deputy, 1994 and a certified competition judge. Highest awards are #2 character clown and #1 Auguste clown.

He graduated from Louisiana State University in 1970 and became a registered civil engineer in 1974. He is married to Connie Braud Heroman with three sons, Matthew, Timothy and Billy, and one grandson, Ethan.

HINKLE, JASON S. (J-Bird) was born on Feb. 7, 1980 in Charleston, WV. He is employed with the Federal Bureau of Prisons, US Department of Justice. He and his lady Amy share two daughters named Madison and Erin.

On Nov. 14, 2008, Jason was raised to the Degree of Master Mason in Lodge #107 Camden on Gauley, WV. He walked the Hot Sands on Dec. 16, 2008, thus becoming a Beni Kedem Shriner. Jason is an active member of the Nicholas County Shrine Club and subsequently elected Director of the club in 2011. He joined the Beni Kedem Clowns as J-Bird in September 2011. He also joined the International Shrine Clown Association and the South Atlantic Shrine Clown Association. He appears in parades and competitions. By clowning, Jason "J-Bird" is able to promote awareness and spread the message of the World's Greatest Philanthropy, Shriners Hospitals for Children.

HOUCHINS, TOM (Buckshot) was born July 10, 1939 in Beckley, WV and presently lives in Decatur, GA. He and wife, Dee, were married in 1963 and have two children, Kristin and Clint, and four grandchildren: Nicolas; Maria; Grayce and Grant.

Tom was raised on July 12, 1999 at Philologia Lodge #178. On Sept. 11, 2002 he walked the hot sands at Yaarab Temple. He is a member of the Red Devils Clown Unit.

"Buckshot" is a member of Thousandaire Club.

HOUTS, KELLY (Whoops) was born Oct 16, 1928 in Estherville, IA. Raised to a Master Mason on Dec. 29, 1978 at

Morningside Lodge 615, Sioux City IA. He joined the Shrine in 1979, York Rite in 1980. He is Past High Priest, Past Illustrious Master and Past Commander of the York Rite Bodies in Sioux City and a long time member of Eastern Star, HI Twelve, Scottish Rite and York Rite College. He has held several offices in Grand Chapter and Grand Commandery for the State of Iowa.

Whoops joined the Clown unit in 1979 and served as President in 1983. He has been Pres. of the Midwest Clown Assn twice. He is presently Sneaker Fund Chairman, which he has done for 20 years. Kelly has received the Red Nose award several times and has been in charge of the Circus's coloring book for many years Whoops has been chosen "Clown of the Year" for Abu Bekr. He has won several trophies at Midwest and Central State conventions. He is a longtime member of ISCA and has attended many Mid States, Centra States and ISCA Conventions.

Kelly is a retired State Farm Agent, a graduate of the State U of Iowa [1952]. He served with the US Army in Korea from 1946-48. He is Past Commander of American Legion Post 697 in Sioux City, IA. Kelly has eight children, 32 grand kids and 34 great-grand kids. He can often be seen at the Shrine Circus, many parades and special events around Northwest Iowa.

ITO, MICHAEL (Ted E Bear) was born Feb. 20, 1952 at Worland, WY.

He was raised at Pathfinder Lodge #42 in Casper, WY. On May 30, 1981 he walked the hot sands at Korein Temple, Rawlins, WY. He joined the Casper Calliope Clowns unit shortly after joining the Shrine.

Over the years he became President and later became a clown after the unit added clowning as an activity. He got a 3rd place White Face the first time he competed in Calgary in the summer of 1999. He served as Secretary/Treasurer for the Pacific Northwest Shrine Clown Association around 1995. He has been an active member of PNSCA, just finishing a term as trustee. He has on several occasions been a judge at the regional meetings.

JEFFERSON, DELMER L. (Jeffie the Clown) was born in Topeka, KS on July 12, 1925. He left school at age 17 to serve in the Navy on the *USS Ticonderoga* during WW II.

Jeff married Joann Hughes in 1950 and has four children, three grandchildren and two great-grandchildren.

Jeff first joined the Eastgate Masonic Lodge 630 on Jan. 28, 1970, the Consistory on Feb. 26, 1970, the Za-Ga-Zig Shrine on July 20, 1970, and the Walking Clowns on July 30, 1970.

His first Mid-Winter was in Cedar Rapids, IA in 1975. His picture first ran in Clown Alley in 1975, the same picture was in the 2007 Clown Alley (A Blast from the Past).

Jeff was president of the Za-Ga-Zig Walking Clowns in 1975 and president of the CSSCA in 1983. He is a past member of the National Shrine Association in 1972 and Clowns of America.

Jeff is still an active member of the Clowns, and still puts on grease for many parades and events, and at age 84, still does competitions.

JENSEN, PETER (Pete Re Pete) was born July 30, 1959 at Ft. Belvoir, VA. He worked at DC Fire Department for eight years and Children's National Medical Center for 19 years. Peter has one son, Rob, and two grandchildren, Isabella and Olivia.

On May 15, 2010 Peter was raised at Henry Lodge #57. He walked the hot sands on June 14, 2010 at Kena Temple. On March 1, 2011 he joined the Kena Clown Unit. He started as an "under cover" Klown and has progressed to a hobo.

He has been a Junior Warden in Henry Lodge #57, a Senior Deacon in the Patriot Lodge #1957, Captain of the Host at Faulmier RAC #25 and Senior Warden at Piedmont Commandery #26.

JOHNSON, J. KEVIN (Johnny, aka The Old Clown) was born in Baldwin, WI on Jan. 11, 1940. "Johnny" attended a one-room country school for eight years, graduated from Baldwin High School then UW River Falls with a major in Agriculture Education and Economics. Now retired after 46 years in the insurance business and residing in Eau Claire, WI with his wife of 50 years, Janet. Kevin and Janet raised three children, two living in Texas gives them great traveling pleasure along with managing their 120A tree farm north of Eau Claire.

"Johnny" has been very active in his community and church along with serving on many state and national insurance committees. His Masonic journey started in Lodge #109 F&AM in River Falls, WI in 1967, transferring to George B Wheel #151 in Eau Claire (Master 1988), also a member of River Falls Chapter # 45 RAM, Chippewa Council #25, Eau Claire Commandery# 8, Scottish Rite Valley of Eau Claire (33rd degree), Eastern Star, Zor Temple, (Potentate 1997) Red Cross of Constantine (Sovereign 2004), Royal Order of Scotland, Tall Cedars of Lebanon and Cabiri.

"Johnny" is past president of Mehara Shrine Club and current secretary, founder and past Raban of the Northland Badger Hillbilly's of Zor Temple; one of the founding and Charter Members of the Zor Sawduster Clown Unit (1976) of Zor Temple and has held all unit offices. He served nine years on the Board of Governors of Shriners Hospital for Children Twin Cities and is now an Emeritus Member.

Johnny begin his clown adventure in 1976 as a "Tuxedo Clown" by request of a longtime friend who had been a patient at

Shriners Hospital in 1937, and gave "Johnny" the tux he had worn for 22 nights on a trip to Europe he had been able to take after treatment at Shriners. "Johnny's" second daughter felt a sad face with the motto "I'll share your sadness, you share my happiness" made "Johnny the clown" he was looking for. After many years of make-up, skin problems began to be a major issue and "Johnny" became a Hillbilly Clown, still with his friendly Skunk he has had as a partner since 1976. Now as a senior member "Johnny" says "Don't push the river, it flows by itself."

JORDAN, SAMUEL (Happy Sam) was born April 9, 1954 at Washburn, ME. "Happy Sam" resides in Washburn, MI where he owns and operates Jordan's Masonry & Construction Co. and Jordan's Snowmobile Rentals. "Happy" and Jodi have a daughter, Mellisa and two grandchildren, Mikayla and Jadden.

Samuel was raised at Washburn Lodge #193 in March of 1992. He has attended and performed at Amara's Circus 133 times in the Center Ring, representing the Amara Komic Klownz.

"Happy" has found time in his busy schedule to visit these Shrine Children's Hospitals: Greenville, SC; Lexington, KY; Philadelphia, PA; Erie, PA; Boston, MA; Springfield, MA; Cincinnati, OH; St. Louis, MO; Shreveport, LA; Houston, TX, Galveston, TX; Mexico City, Mexico; Minneapolis, MN and Honolulu, HI.

JOSEPH, JOHN (Jay Jay) started with the Medinah Shrine Clown Unit, Chicago, IL, in 1982. He started as a White Face Clown, then a Tramp Clown. He won numerous awards competing both within the Shrine and against professional clowns. Jay Jay is now Goofer, an Auguste lite clown who appears regularly at the Chicago Shrine Hospital as Dr. Goofer.

"Jay Jay" has been a lecturer at numerous clown gatherings around the country. He is Past President of the Great Lakes Shrine Clown Units Association (2010) and Past Chief Joey of the Midwest Clown

Association (2002-04). He was inducted into the MCA Hall of Fame (1998) and received the lifetime Achievement Award from MCA in 2012.

"Jay Jay" and his Lady Judy have four grown children and four grandchildren. "Jay Jay" has been in the insurance industry for over 30 years and also served in the USNR for 28 years.

KELLNER, ALFRED H. (Alfalfa) was born April 23, 1940 at Baltimore, MD. He met Carolyn Trueblood on a blind date in August 1959 and they married on March 23, 1963 after his service in the U.S. Army. He was widowed Dec. 25, 2009 after 47 beautiful years of marriage. They have one daughter, Catherine Jayne and one grandson, Seth. "Alfalfa" retired in 2002 from Bethlehem Steel Corporation after 43 years.

Alfred was raised at Patapsco Lodge #183, Dundalk, MD in December 1970. He walked the hot sands at Boumi Temple in June 1974, joining Boumi Clowns in January 1982.

"Alfalfa" was secretary of Clown Unit in 1984, 1985, 1986, 2011 and 2012; Director of Clowns Unit 1987 and 1990; appointed Director of MASCA 1988 and 1999; joined Mid-Atlantic Shrine Clown Association (MASCA) 1982; joined ISCA 1982; President MASCA 2000; member Boumi Yacht Club and joined Chester River Shrine Club in 2007 serving as Secretary in 2008, 2009, 2011 and 2012.

KENNEDY, RAY (Hobo Joe) was born in Oklahoma City, OK and now lives in Leon, KS. He and wife, Marium Kennedy, have three children: Belinda, Charity and Rye; and four grandchildren: Cade; Autumn; Conner and Cameron. Ray worked for 10 years at Feed Lot Cowby; 10-1/2 years at Inland Container; nine years at Coastal Gas Co.; three years at JW Operations; owned Quality Home Inspection five years and Property Manager for five years, retiring in 2009.

Ray was raised on Oct. 10, 1983 at Joppa Lodge #223, Leon, KS. On May 10, 1986 he walked the hot sands at Midian Temple and joined the Krazy Klowns Unit on Jan. 2, 2009.

"Hobo Joe" was Treasurer in 2010 and Boss Klown in 2011. He was Master at Syracuse 309, Emerald 289 and Joppa 223; and District Deputy, District 39 in 1998.

KNAUSE, ROBERT "ROB" W. (Sinker) was born Dec. 14, 1947 in Brush, CO. He was raised on June 13, 1995, Independence Rock #56 (Past Master). A member of Korein Temple, he walked the hot sands on Nov. 11, 1995. He joined the Colliope Clown Unit on Nov. 12, 1995.

Rob has served as ISCA unit president, competition and awards in Pacific Northwest Shrine Clown Assoc. (PNSCA) – paradeability, character, and skits. He is a third generation Mason, father-in-law Joe A. Dunmire (2nd generation).

He is married to Jolene and they have four children, Zach, Kristen, Adrian, and Amber, and four grandchildren, Katelyn, Carter, Eddie, and Cristopf. He works for NCO Financial Systems.

KROUSKOP, FRITZ C. (Fritzer) was born in Russells Point, OH (Indian Lake) on Jan. 21, 1954. He has had many Lady Friends, but never been married or had a family. He has worked for CSX Railroad for many years.

Fritz is a member of Indian Lake Masonic Lodge #722 where he was Worshipful Master for the years 2008 and 2009.

He is a member of Antioch Shrine Temple, Dayton, OH and is a very active member in The Antioch Funsters Clown Unit where he was voted Clown of the Year, 2009. He has won numerous awards in GLSCUA and ISCA clown competitions, including ISCA Clown Extraordinaire in Atlanta, GA, 2009.

LANG, RICHARD L. (Saxo) was born in Portland, WA, March 12, 1943. By 12, he was directing a 10-piece band, "The Starlighters". Upon graduating from High School in Spokane, WA, he joined the Army for three years. In the service, he married his first wife Judy. They settled in Tri-Cities, WA where he owned and operated a gas station with a fishing and gun trade store. Judy passed away in 1988. After selling the business, he followed his dream to become a jeweler, an owner, and an operator of a jewelry store for the next 20 years. He met his current wife, Rita, in 1990 and they have many grandkids and great grands now.

"Saxo" was raised up as a Master Mason October 9, 1967 at Lodge #283 in Richland, WA, in Scottish Rite in 1993, and as a Shriner at El Katif Temple in 1993. He immediately joined the Columbia Basin Shrine Club, CBS Clowns, El Katif Shrine Clowns, PNSCA, and ISCA, along with the GROTTO in Spokane, WA.

"Saxo" has been President of the CBS Clowns, Director of the CBS Clowns, and the Sec/Treas of the CBS Clowns, newsletter reporter, and Trustee at large for Columbia Basin Shrine Club.

His love for clowning led him to be a Past President of the Pacific Northwest Shrine Clown Association and the fun to be appointed the Personal Ambassador for several past presidents of ISCA. He was inducted at the Clown Hall of Fame in Milwaukee, WI as the ISCA Clown of the Year for 1996.

"Saxo" and Rita in 1998 were presented the Grand Masters Youth Support Award and in 2002 presented the Washington DeMoley Foundation Appreciation Award. "Saxo" was awarded in 2002 the HIRAM Award for outstanding service by the Most Worshipful Grand Lodge of Free and Accepted Masons of Washington. In 2005 he was awarded the Honorary DeMoley Legion of Honor lifetime membership.

He retired from the business due to health problems in 2002. He played the small soprano saxophone where ever he went. Kids of all ages love it. His love for the kids is what keeps him clowning.

LaRUE, JOHN (Long John) was born Nov. 22, 1949 in Chattanooga, TN. He married Mary in 1970, and they have two children, Michelle and Michael. Jonathan, Matthew, Zachary and Mason are their grandchildren. John worked 12 years for Cobb County Fire Department; 25 years as a building contractor and 16 years as an independent insurance adjuster.

"Long John" was raised at Kennesaw Lodge #33, then walked the hot sands on Dec. 10, 1980 at Yaarab Temple. In January 1981 he joined the Red Devil Clowns unit. He served as President of Red Devil Clowns in 1987; Executive Secretary/Treasurer SESCA from 2000 to 2006 and Treasurer of Red Devil Clowns from 1995 to present.

"Long John" has won multiple 1st, 2nd, and 3rd place awards in SESCA and Georgia Clown Association.

LEBOW, JOEL H. (Stitches) has been a member of Aleppo clowns since 2001. His first parade was in Sciuate, MA, St. Patrick's Day, March 17, 2002. He is now in the process of switching to Yaareb "Red Devils" in the Atlanta area.

Joel was born Feb 9, 1939 in Boston, MA in the middle of a blizzard. His mother happened to be in the hospital at the same time. Both survived. He attended grammar school in Brighton, MA, went two years to historic Boston Public Latin School before moving to Newton, MA. He graduated from Newton High in 1956 and went four years to graduate at Brandeis University in Waltham, MA. He did some graduate work in science and history (my majors at Brandeis) before going into U.S. Army reserve program for six years.

In 1963 he permanently joined the family business...Lebow Bros. Clothing Co. Inc., founded in 1928 after 50 years under other names. He inherited the CEO position in 1978 and ran the business until shutting down in June 2009 due to the economic crisis.

He began his Masonic work in 1964, being raised at Garden City Lodge in Newton in June 1964. Soon in Nov. 1964 took all the Scottish Rite degrees, and in January 1965 became a member of Allepo Temple Shriners. He transferred blue lodges to Nehoiden in Needham, where he had moved with wife and two beautiful daughters. About 1997 he was approached to join the Aleppo Adjudants; this turned out to be a fine experience.

At this time he discovered the clown group and approached Nehoidens Master, Rt. Wor. David Newcomb, who was also boss clown at time. He advised him on procedures to join, the work and study involved, etc. After only three times through clown college, he was accepted into the Aleppo clowns. He is most happy with these guys, their antics and dedication, the parades and ceremonials. He would like to publically thank Dave Newcomb and the other boss clowns and officers who guided him over the years.

LOFTIS, KENNY (Sparky) was born in Lafayette, TN, December 14, 1961. He graduated from Tennessee Tech University. On July 22, 2006 he married Helen (P-Nutt) Crawford. They reside in Hendersonville, TN.

Kenny was raised a Master Mason of Hillsdale Lodge #664 in 1985, where he served as Master in 1988. He joined the

Scottish Rite and Al Menah Temple in 1985. He became a member of the Al Menah Clowns in 1988 and won Clown of the Year honors in 1992 & 1994 and the Captain's award in 1995 before going on to serve as Captain in 2000. He then served as President of the Southeastern Shrine Clown Association in 2009-2010. In 2009, he was recognized into the Scottish Rite Knight Commander Court of Honor. He became a member of the Order of the Quetzalcoatl in 2007 and received his OKET in 2011.

"Sparky" has won several awards in regional competitions and is a six-time White Face/Makeup 1st Place winner at Imperial Sessions. "Sparky was the recipient of the Imperial 2012 Smile Maker Award. "Sparky" has a passion for collecting funds for the hospitals and performing at the Shrine Circus.

LONDON, BILL (10 Can) was born Sept. 29, 1941 at Decatur, TX. He was raised on Sept. 7, 1990 at Bowie, TX Lodge #578. He joined Southside Commandry No. 83; Southside Polytechnic #315 R.&S.M.; Scottish Rite Freemasonry SJ U.S.A.; ROJ Court #32, and Moslah Shrine Flying Fez.

Bill walked the hot sands on Sept. 14, 1990 at Maskat Temple and in October 1994 joined Moslah Clown Unit.

He was awarded Moslah Clown of the Year, 1998; President Moslah Shrine Clowns, 2001; Louis Stamm Make up Award, 2004 and Unsung Hero, 2006. Bill served as President of International Shrine Clown Association in 2008.

He has won many Make-up and Costume Awards in various ISCA Mid Winters and Imperial Sessions. He also has won many one-man skit; two man skit awards; Unit Skit and paradability. Bill "10 Can" London won Red Nose Awards in 1997 and a Gold Nose Award in 2002.

Bill "10 Can" London was elected as 3rd Vice President in Louisville, KY in 2005 and served the ISCA for four wonderful years. He was the Sneaker Fund Chairman for Moslah Shrine Clowns for several years prior to going on to the ISCA line and serves as the Sneaker Fund Chairman USA for the ISCA. He traveled to Huntsville, AL the second week of Feb. 2013 for the ISCA Mid-Winter and was presented with two awards he didn't expect to receive: the Lifetime Achievement Award and the Sneaker Fund Emeritus Award.

LONG, BRUCE A. (Boo Boo the Clown) was born in Bartlesville, OK, November 7, 1945. After attending High School he served in the U.S. Air Force Security Service. He married Judith Bellmyer in 1966 and they have two children, Bruce and Jennifer, and two grandchildren, Forrest and Dawson. They resided in Darmstadt, Germany, San Antonio, Texas and now reside in their home town, Bartlesville, Oklahoma.

Bruce is a life member of Bartlesville Lodge 284 AF&AM. In 1977 Bruce crossed the Hot Sands of AKDAR Temple and Boo Boo the Clown was born. He joined the Bartlesville Merri-Makers in 1977 and held all offices. In 1978 Boo Boo, his brother Steve, and Newell Barker entered the 3-5 man skit competition and won first place in their first competition experience. ISCA president that year, BOB-O, invited them to do the skit as an exhibition at the upcoming 1979 ISCA Midwinter convention, which was held in Jackson, Mississippi. That started Boo Boo's long career in clown competition.

The Bartlesville Merri-Makers desolved with two clowns remaining, Bruce Long and Newell Barker, who then joined the Tulsa Merri-Makers in 1996. Boo was director in 2009, and in 1999 was president of the Central States Shrine Clown Association. Boo Boo has won or helped win more than 110 trophies in competition. He also helped the Tulsa Merri-Makers win the traveling trophy at CSSCA 12 years in a row.

Since those early years when Boo looked so shabby and had so much energy, he can now entertain almost any crowd with his crazy juggling, amazing balloon creations, unicycle riding, close-up magic, puppetry, singing his goofy songs, and face painting. Boo has more than 20 years of restaurant clowning. Boo Boo and wife, Judy, AKA Nurse Bubbles, RN, have attended many judging seminars. Boo Boo is a member of the International Shrine Clown Association, the Central States Shrine Clown Association (CSSCA), Clowns of America International, and the World Clown Association. In 1989 Bruce founded the Bartlesville Fun-Addicts clown club in Bartlesville, Oklahoma, COAI Alley #188. The Akdar Shrine Circus is, no doubt, Boo Boo's favorite yearly event. Judy's proudest moment was when Boo was named "Clown of the Year" for 2010.

Boo Boo will never retire, he'll just parade away. Boo Boo's website is at: http://www.boobooclown.com

LYCETT, PHILIP S. (Pete) was born July 26, 1935 at Gloucester, MA. He and Phyllis E. were married in 1965. They have three children: Philip S.; Holly A. and Michael S. and eight grandchildren. "Pete" retired in 1997 after working as a medical laboratory technologist, school teacher and chemical engineer.

Philip was raised on Jan. 21, 1961 in Acacia Lodge. He walked the hot sands at Aleppo Temple on May 3, 1992. On July 26, 1997 he joined the Aleppo Clown Unit.

"Pete" has participated in many events, parades, circuses, skits, etc. He has won a Red Nose award every year, the Funny Bone award, and has been secretary for 50 years.

MARACLE, ROLAND M. (Rollo) was born in Marysville, Ontario, Canada, May 25, 1933. He attended Queen Alexandria, and Queen Mary grade schools. He graduated from Belleville Collegiate High School as a woodworking cabinet maker.

Roland moved to Syracuse, NY and went to work for Stickley Furniture as a Designer. He married Betty Jeanne Fairchild on May 25, 1957. They have two sons, Dorian, Dwain, and daughter-in-law, Terry.

Roland was raised in Cazenovia Lodge #616 on June 21, 1963. They moved to Rochester, NY where I joined the Scottish Rite. On May 25, 1966 he joined Damascus Shriners and the Clown Unit.

"Rollo" retired from 25 years at Kodak and moved to Shannonville, Ontario where he affiliated with Rameses Temple. "Rollo" then joined the clown unit of the Belleville Shrine Club. He also has joined the clown unit of the Kingston Shrine Club. Roland was made Ambassador to Damascus in January 2005.

MARSH, STEPHEN D. (Swampy) was born May 28, 1939 at Bell, CA. In 1964 he and Lorraine L. were married and now live in Billings, MT. Stephen retired from teaching after 35 years.

He was raised in December 1961 at Rimrock Lodge #149. In 1975 he walked the hot sands at Al Bedoo Temple and joined Al Bedoo Clowns Unit the same year.

Stephen is past President, Past Director and Past Master of Lodge #149. He is also Past Potentate (1990), Past Director of Jesters, Past Illustrious Gr. Master of Cryptic Masons of Montana (2010). She is Past V. Master of Sottish Rite-KCCH; Past Gr. Chap. Royal Arch; Past Gr. Prelate, Knights Templar; Past Com. Knight Templar; Past High Priest, Royal Arch and Past Illus. Master of Master Council. He belongs to Red Cross of Constantine.

He has received his 50-year membership in the Masonic Order.

MARTINEZ, REUBEN V. (Boo Boo) [MASCA/ISCA] was born in New York City. He has four children and one grandchild. Reuben became a Mason, Scottish Rite and Shriner while serving on Active Duty in Panama, Central America in 1991 (Army/Air Force - Retired 2000). He is a member of Abou Saad Clowns, Director's Staff & Legion of Honor (Life Member). While serving as Abou Saad Ambassador, he joined the Kena (Fairfax-VA) Klowns (Director 2005-Life Member), and Ritualistic Divan, where he welcomes new Nobles as "The Fez". He has held various Lodge offices, in Panama (Gatun-Massachusetts) & Virginia (Olive Branch 114). Reuben

can be counted on to bring humor to any occasion, particularly in support of the World's Greatest Philanthropy. Boo Boo/ DJ Reuben regularly supports children's charities, church activities, the Veterans of Foreign Wars (Life Member-Past Officer), and others. Clowns equal Smiles and are the Face of the Shrine!

MCDONALD, DREW R. (Duffer) was born in Eston, Saskatchewan, Canada, Jan. 19, 1942. The family lived in Eston, Lloydminster, and Moosomin, Saskatchewan. After graduating from Moosomin High School he became purchasing agent for Beaver Lumber in both Regina, Saskatoon. and Edmonton, Alberta. In 1969, he became manager of the Beaver Lumber Store in Provost, AB. While managing the store he also contracted local projects through Drew McDonald Construction. In 1974, he became an Esso agent for fuel and fertilizer. He sold his business in 1986, retired, and still manages Drew McDonald Holdings Ltd. He married Linda Stewart in Regina in 1962 and they have a son, daughter and five grandchildren.

He joined the Northwest Mounted Police Masonic Order in Regina in 1964 and still maintains that membership. He was Worshipful Master of the Provost Lodge #61 in 1980. In 1990, he moved to Edmonton where he belonged to the Evergreen Lodge #166 and the Scottish Rite. In 1994 he joined the Al Shamal Shrine Temple and became "Duffer" the clown. His clown name was reflective of his love of golf. He lived at Moose Lake by Bonnyville, AB for 10 summers and travelled with the Lloydminster Shrine Club to parades over the summers. During that time, winters were spent in Arizona where he appreciated the number of friends who were Masons and Shriners. He moved to Medicine Hat in 2005 and transferred to Al Azar Temple in 2006. He has been producing clown for the last two years and enjoys working with the local clowns. Drew has collected five red nose awards and is working towards his first gold nose award. He became a director of the Medicine Hat Shrine Club in 2009. He transferred his Scottish Rite membership from Edmonton to Medicine Hat in 2008.

McGOWAN, LLOYD (Yogi) was born Nov. 20, 1942 in Jackson, MS. Lloyd has five children, seven grandchildren and three great-grandchildren. He was employed as an offset printing and dark room technician and then a computer technician.

"Yogi" was raised in 1972 at Forest Hill Lodge and is now at Capitol Lodge #600. In 1972 he walked the hot sands at Wahabi Temple and joined Wahabi Clowns Unit the same year.

In 1980 he was Funster of the Year and was President of Wahabi Funsters in 1985. He has been Worthy of Patron of Radiant OES #120, Jackson, MS four times. "Yogi" was awarded the Exchange Club Book of Golden Deeds in 2005.

MEEKS, DENNIS ARDEN (Bubbles and SKIP) was born Aug. 29, 1949 in Ft. Wayne, IN. He was raised on June 24, 2002 at Cromwill Lodge #705, later a member of Mizpah Temple in Ft. Wayne (Nov. 15, 2002), the Mizpah Clown Unit (Dec. 2002) and the Ocala Shrine Club (2006). He joined ISCA in 2005 and has served as Chief Clown of the Ocala Clown Unit in 2008, 2009 and 2012.

He served in the U.S. Army as Entertainment Director of the 4th Basic Training Brigade (1969-'72) and produced, Unit and Post level, variety shows. He has worked at WLYV Radio, Ft. Wayne as a Newsman, and was News Director of WFDT-FM Columbia City and later Reporter/photographer for the Columbia City Post And Mail, newspaper ('75-'76). He was also Co-chairman of the Bicentennial Committee in Columbia City, and was Asst. Producer of the Home And Garden Show (78-79) in Ft. Wayne and is a Ventriloquist and "Bubbles The Clown". SKIP, his dummy, and he were a fixture at the Ft. Wayne Shrine Circus until he moved in 2005. They have been in many parades, and performed in the Circus at Jacksonville and Ocala, Florida. Although not in the sport any longer, he is a licensed skydiver and an ultralight aircraft pilot.

Dennis was married to Diane (dec. 1999) and has one son, Christopher, a pilot for GoJet who is married to Lisa and has two lovely children, son Arden and daughter, Avery. They live in Ft. Wayne. Dennis retired from the Main Post Office in Ft. Wayne to a farm outside of Albion, IN and Florida, where he lives within the boundaries of Ocala National Forest.

MICHEL, JAMES W., M.D. (Doctor Spot) was born June 19, 1946 in Boulder, CO. He was raised Aug. 8, 2009 at Carmel, CA #680 and is a member of Asiya Shriners International No. 15, walking the hot sands on Nov. 19, 2011. James joined the Asiya Shrine Clowns, ISCA AAONMS on Jan. 12, 2012.

He has supported local clown projects to raise money for the Shriners Hospitals for Children, and has been a doctor for several screening clinics to identify children who would benefit from the hospital's services.

James is married to Lady June Michel (Raggety Ann), Ladies of the Oriental Shrine.

MITCHELL, MERLIN (Magic) was raised in Nebraska; he left in June 1954 to join the US Navy and was assigned to the *James E. Kyes DD787*. After four years in the Navy and then three months as a civilian plumber, he re-enlisted in the US Army, serving for 17 years, with service in Hawaii and MACV, retiring in October 1974 as a Medical Equipment Repair Officer. Merlin was a Senior Instructor and Service Manager for General Electric Medical Systems for 14 years; three years as Regional Manager for Kaiser Hospitals in Southern Calif, and three years as a Service Manager for Philips Medical Systems. He retired from the medical field and bought Mail Box Plus in Yuba City, which he owned for five years before retiring (?) again.

"Magic" was raised to Master Mason in Marysville, CA in 1996. He joined the Sacramento Scottish Rite and Ben Ali Shrine in 1996. In 1997 he joined the Ben Ali Clowns and served as President of the Clowns in 2000. He is still active as "Magic" the Clown at the hospital. Merlin is presently 1st VP for the Central Sacramento Valley Shrine Club and First Officer of the Flying Fez.

"Magic" and Myrna, his first wife who passed away after 47 years, had four children, three girls and a boy, and 12 grandchildren. Vivian and "Magic" were married in October of 2005 and whenever possible they travel in their new motorhome across this great country visiting family, friends, and seeing as many of the national and natural sites as they can. Vivian is a 30-year member of the Fremont Hospital Auxiliary in Yuba City and is still active with that and Merlin is active with the Ben Ali Shrine. They are also active with Ben Ali Bedouin RV Club.

MODISETTE, RAYMOND (Tootsie) was born Nov. 30, 1949 in Oklahoma City, OK. He joined the Masonic lodge in Norman, OK, the Scottish Rite in Guthrie, India Shrine Center in Oklahoma City, and the India Shrine Clown unit all in 1997. He served as Clown Director in 2008. Served as International Shrine Clown Association Chaplain in 2011-12 for ISCA President Randy Weldon. Received many awards during 15 years of local and international competition.

Raymond married Janice in 1986. They have four children: Jay, Jeff, Adam and Amanda. He retired from General Motors Oklahoma City assembly plant in 2009 after 30 years of service. He is thankful for the opportunity to clown for the benefit of children.

MOFFITT, FRED LEVAUGHN (Muffett) born October 29, 1924 in Altoona, PA, grew up in Bellwood, PA. After High school Fred joined the US Navy in May 1943. Achieved the rank of Petty Officer Second Class, Aviation Metalsmith (AM2). Awarded the American Campaign medal, Asiatic-Pacific Campaign Medal with nine Stars, Philippine Liberation Medal with two stars and the Presidential Unit Citation. Served aboard the aircraft carriers USS *Princeton* CV-37 and the USS *Langley* CVL-27. After Honorable discharge from the US Navy, 1946 went to work at Naval Air Station (NAS) Alameda, CA. 1946. Transferred to Redstone Arsenal in 1953 and worked at NASA where he worked under Dr. Werner Von Braun.

"Muffett" married Mary Elizabeth (Polatty) 1947. Two children, Michael Wayne and Gregory Vaughn. Married for 65 years, Fred is a devoted husband and father.

Fred was raised to the Degree of Master Mason by his father, PM Harold E. Moffitt, in Lodge # 494, F & AM, and Altoona, PA January 4, 1946. Conferred to the Scottish Rite, Valley of Williamsport Consistory of Williamsport, PA, May 3, 1946. Fred was conferred KCCH on October 21, 1985 and received his 33 degree, October 3, 2001. Walked the hot sands of Jaffa Shrine Temple in May 1, 1946 and transferred his membership to Cahaba Shrine Temple in 1978. "Muffett" is past Director of the Cahaba Buffoon Clown Unit, 1984 and again in 1993. Past President Dixie Shrine Clown Association in 1986. "Muffett" has won many awards as a Tramp clown with his signature tear running down his cheek, his pet fly on his nose and quivering lower lip and sad droopy eyes.

MONTGOMERY II, ALEXANDER CLARK (Bouncer) was born April 30, 1960 in Southwest Missouri. He is 6th generation Master Mason raised in 1991 and is a member of Stockton Lodge 283. He is a Life Member of Scottish Rite Valley of Joplin and a member of the Abou Ben Adhem Shrine and ABA Shrine Clowns, serving as Clown Captain in 2008 and 2009.

Bouncer attended MSU in Springfield MO studying Agriculture and Archaeology. He and his family presently own 4 crop farms in Cedar County and he serves on the Board of Trustees and on the Board of Directors with the Missouri Archaeological Society.

Bouncer was married to Galene Hendrich in 1990 and they have three children: Amelia 20, Olivia 19 and Alex 8.

He served his hometown of Stockton Missouri as a Paramedic, being one of the 1st paramedics in the county and after 4 years in the field he joined the Springfield Fire Department in 1985 for a career of 25.46 years attaining the rank of Captain from 1993 to retirement in 2011!

Bouncer was brought to life in the early 1990's after putting together real skydiving gear for his character! Yes, Bouncer does fall from perfectly good airplanes!

MORGAN, THOMAS A. (Tom Tom) was born in 1923 at Center, MO. In 1949 Thomas and Gladys (deceased in 2004) were married and had two children, Janice and Judith; seven grandchildren and nine great-great-grandchildren. He served in the US Navy from 1942-1946; attended college from 1946-1951; was an electrical apprentice from 1946-1951; a journey wireman from 1951-1990 and owner of Mercury Elec. from 1955-1985, when he retired.

"Tom Tom" was raised at Western Star Lodge #24, Monroe, LA in 1953. He walked the hot sands in 1954 at El Kaurbah, and joined the Nomad Jokers Clown Unit in 1985.

He was Worthy Grand Patron OES of Louisiana in 1974. He was Director from 1989-1990. His history includes: Service to Circus and Unsung Hero Award, 2000; Dedicated Service to Nomad Shrine Club as President in 2003, 2004, 2010 and 2011.

"Tom Tom" received a Certificate of Appreciation signed by Imp. Sir Michael G. Severe in 2012. Nomad Shrine, Pharr, TX is located 150 miles south of Corpus Christie. They have seven 15-passenger vans to transport Mexican children in Hidalgo to Houston and Galveston hospitals; one day up and one day back, 350 miles each way. In 1998, Thomas made one trip every two weeks for a total of 24 trips.

MORSE, RICHARD D. (Little 1) was born in Oneida, NY, Dec. 18, 1950. He moved to Hollywood, FL with his parents in 1960. Richard graduated from McAuthur High School in 1969. He worked for the Dade County School System in the maintenance department

He started his Masonic Journey Nov. 14, 1972, was raised May 29, 1973 from Opa Locka Lodge #287 F&.AM. Richard joined Scottish Rite Masons, Oct. 23, 1973. He went through Mahi Shrine on Nov. 23, 1973 and joined the Director Staff.

In 1988 "Little 1" moved to Elljay, GA where he went to work in the carpet industry." Richard transferred to Yarrab Shrine on Dec. 7, 1988 and Oak Bowery #81, Feb. 27, 1989. Richard developed an interest in becoming a shrine clown. With the help and guidance of the Kennesaw Mountain Jokers, he went to make-up classes and classes in balloon art. "Little 1" started going in make-up and attending parades. He is presently a member of the Red Devil Clown Unit, Yaarab Shrine, Atlanta, GA.

MOYER, RAY (DC) was born February 15, 1946 in Galion, OH. He was raised in Lincoln Lodge #693, Middleton, OH, in 1978 and became a life member in 2004. Additional Masonic history includes: York Rite—Donald W. Smith chapter/council (1983), PTIM (1991), PHP (1992), life member of both chapter and council, and Commandery #82 Southside, Fort Worth, TX (1983); Scottish Rite—Valley of Fort Worth, TX (1986), Commander of the Council of Kadosh (2009), and 32KCCH (2009); Shrine—Hella Temple (1986), Moslah Temple (1987) [Clown Unit, 1993, President of the Clown Unit, 1999, Life Member, 2003], Divan (2000) [Potentate, 2004], Life Member (2005), Recorder (2008, 2012); Imperial TRAC-Team Member (2004-2008).

Ray joined the Moslah Clowns in 1993. He placed in the top ten white face every year at both Texas Shrine Clown Association and Imperial Shrine Clown Association, Louis Stamm Make Up Award in 1996, President in 1999, Clown of the Year in 2000, Red Nose award received four years, won first place for make-up and costume at Imperial Competition in 1996 and 1999, and also placed in one-man skits and two-man skits. His motto is "Keep Smiling".

Ray married Janet Court Moyer in 1970, and they have two children, daughter Debra and son Chris, and five grandchildren. He worked for The Boy Scouts of America for 36 years and retired from the National Headquarters in 2008.

MURRAY, ARNOLD R. (Doc) began clowning in 1976 in Grande Prairie, Alberta, Canada when he joined the Shrine of

North America. That unit grew to 10 from one before he moved to Calgary in 1985. He clowned with the Al Azhar Calgary Clown Unit. He served as President of the Unit, gave many educational lectures and created interest in pipe cleaner figures for use where latex balloons were banned. Under ISCA president Ed "Stripes" Whitenet, he was appointed ISCA Chaplin. In 2005 he participated on the organizing committee for the ISCA Mid Winter conference in Calgary, Alberta. His honours were receiving the "Clown of the Year Award" of ISCA in 2005; many place finishes in competitions and the Masonic Medal of Merit. As Worshipful Master of Carstairs Lodge #20 on the GR of Alberta, he helped its rejuvenation. He was Al Azhar hospital chairman for three years and became an OKET in the Order of Quetzalcoatl. Assistance was given in establishing a "Caring Clowns Association" in Calgary.

Arnold was born in Calgary, Alberta, Canada on March 1, 1929 and schooled there. At the University of Alberta, Edmonton, he obtained his B.Sc. and MD and practiced in Grande Prairie, Alberta and in Calgary. He was very privileged to practice in the former semi-remote area where he engaged in surgery, midwifery, anaesthesia, internal medicine and intensive care. Besides many appointments on the medical staff he assisted in the design, building and commissioning of a 250 active bed hospital with added one hundred nursing and one hundred auxiliary beds. He became a sustaining member of the Rotarian Paul Harris Fellowship. As a Rotarian he initiated the rehabilitation of a refinery site into a wildland park. He was a representative to the General Council of the United Church of Canadian 1964 and an elder.

June Langlands became his wife in September 1955 and they raised six children, one of which was adopted. She was a tremendous loving support throughout their marriage in excess of 50 years.

NEWCOMB, DAVID P. (Do-No, Woe-No, Dr. Do-No, Deputy Do-No) was born August 3, 1953 in Newton, MA. He has created clown personalities in every category of costume and makeup. Do-No performs sometimes as a whiteface, sometimes an Auguste. Deputy Do-No performs as a Lite Auguste. Dr. Do-No is his character personality and Woe-No is Hobo/Tramp.

Do-No and his personal clown family began clowning in 1989 at the Aleppo Shrine in Wilmington, Massachusetts. He has entertained audiences at hospitals, parades and various functions, all in support of the Aleppo Shrine, ISCA and the Sneaker Fund for Burns Research. His family of characters has earned First Place honors in every category of clown competitions including each category in Costume & Make-Up, each category in Skits, Paradeability and Balloons Sculpting.

Served as Clown Visits Coordinator at the Boston Shrine Hospital 1993 thru 1999. Served as Aleppo Boss Clown 2001 thru 2003; Membership Chairman at Aleppo 2004 thru 2005; Dean of the Northeast Clown Institute 2004-2009; President of Northeast Shrine Clown Association 2007; Earned a Red Nose award every year since joining, twenty-two so far.

He has three Gold Nose awards so far awarded Aleppo's Clown of the Year seven times. At ISCA, Do-No served the Education arena for several years, and was appointed the U.S. Director of Education in 2012. A Past Master of Norfolk Lodge and Nehoiden Lodge in Needham MA, Degree Worker for Massachusetts Consistory and Assistant Chairman of the Grand Lodge Service Committee for Massachusetts. He has served as District Deputy Grand Master for the Massachusetts Second Masonic District 2009-2010.

O'NEIL, MIKE (Crackers) was born in Minneapolis, MN on Aug. 22, 1949. After attending school, he went into automotives and worked in that field until the need to get away took him into over-the-road truck driving. He now lives in Las Vegas, NV. Mike tried the "I do-I do" but it didn't work out. He has a daughter, Leslie, and son, Ryan, and four grandchildren.

Mike began his Mason affiliation when he was raised in the spring of 1982 at Winslow Lewis Lodge #125 at Osseo, MN. He joined OES and then joined Scottish Rite in Moss, MN.

In 1993 he joined Zuhrah Shrine in Minneapolis and joined the Funston Clown Unit, where he learned to be a clown.

"Crackers" was lucky to have some great mentors and began competing. He became President of the clown unit in 2004 and 2005. Mike began attending ISCA Mid-Winters in 2006 and is still going.

PEARLSTEIN, ERNEST "Ernie" A. (Rollo) was born in Cambridge, MA on April 27, 1944. From 1961-1965 he served as a US Marine. While stationed in California, he was the opening comic act for the Righteous Brothers. He has been married to Marjorie for 22 years and they have blended their two families—together they have six children, two sons-in-law and six grandchildren.

He was raised to Master Mason June 8, 1979 and received his 32 degree Dec. 8, 1979. Joining Aleppo Temple Clown Unit in 1980, Ernie became a member of the Northeast Shrine Clown Association and the International Shrine Clown Association that same year.

1985, Ernie was installed the Worshipful Master of Revere Lodge in Boston; in 1986, Master of Euclid Lodge making him one of the few to hold Master of two Lodges at the same time. He served as Master of the First Lodge of instruction, Master, Mount Scopus Lodge 1998-2000 and Master of Euclid Lodge 24 years later in 2010-2011.

1989-1990, Brother Pearlstein was appointed District Deputy Grand Master by the Grand Master.

1993- "Rollo" was the first recipient of the Master Clown Award presented by the North East Shrine Clown Association.

1995- Ernie, was installed President of the International Shrine Clown Association in Tacoma, WA; he has held an office every year thereafter including Treasurer for three years 2004-2005-2006.

In 2005 Ernie, was elected Junior Grand Warden of the Grand Lodge of Massachusetts and received both the Joseph Warren Distinguished Service Award in 1990 and the Henry Price Medal which is the highest Honor and only given by the Grand Master in January 2005. In 2007 was appointed the Director of Grand Lodge Service's, which he holds to this day.

"Rollo" was the recipient of Humanitarian Award presented by The Supreme

Council Ancient Accepted Scottish Rite of Freemasonry in recognition of his outstanding efforts and contributions in the support of charitable endeavors on behalf of the children of the world.

Ernie was elected Chairman of the Board of Governors for the Scottish Rite Learning Center for Children in Lexington, MA and served in that capacity for four years.

In 2003, Rollo" was awarded The I.S.C.A. lifetime Achievement Award and it was presented at the Mid-Winter Session in Victoria B.C. Canada.

"Rollo" reached a great milestone when he was awarded his 4th Gold nose patch in 2010, which reflects 24 red nose patches for 24 years of active and dedicated service to our International Shrine Clown Association.

On 2011, Ernie received the Award of Merit from Shriners Hospitals for Children.

Throughout his colorful Masonic career Ernest "Rollo" Pearlstein's favorite accomplishment is his contact with the many friends and fellow Joey's he has come to know and love. "Rollo" favorite place to be is inside hospitals entertaining the patients, bringing a little joy into their lives especially those who are very young and far away from home. "Rollo" says it's truly a pleasure for him to have shared a large part of his life with you all.

PETERSON, WILLIAM (Chuckles) was born Nov. 23, 1950 in Minneapolis, MN. He and Arlette have three children: Dustin; Brandon and Heidi and two grandchildren, Emma and Madelyn Peterson. William is retired after 42 years in the auto industry as owner-manager.

"Chuckles" was raised in October 2008 in Boylston Lodge. In January 2009 he walked the hot sands at Aleppo Temple. In June 2009 he joined the Aleppo Clown Unit.

"Chuckles" received the Unit Funny Bone Award in 2010. He attained a Red Nose in 2010, 2011 and 2012. In 2011 he was Unit Clown of the Year.

PEVETO, ALFRED E. (Al) was born April 26, 1928 in Orange TX. He was married in 1955 to Winona Purgahn Peveto. Alfred worked for DuPont Company in Orange, TX from 1948 to 1985. He was self-employed from 1985 to retirement in 1999.

He was raised at Madison Lodge #126 on Dec. 7, 1956. On Sept. 13, 1960 he walked the hot sands at El Mina Temple, Galveston, TX. On 1961 he joined the Nem Loof Clowns.

He states: What a privilege to be a Shrine Clown! It has ben a joy to serve with the Nem Loof Clown Unit 50 plus years."

His most memorable times were driving the 1923 American LeFrance Fire Truck in Shrine Parades in Galveston, Houston, Port Arthur, Beaumont, Woodville and Silsbee, TX. He drove the Fire Truck to Gov. Bill Daniel's Ranch in Romayor, TX to entertain handicapped children. Nem Loof Clowns Red Bellair and "Tiny" Fowler and "Al" did this several years. Red and "Tiny" have received the visit of the Black Camel.

"Al" had the pleasure of entertaining children from Hughen School with the late Bob Hope at Yellow Jacket Stadium, Port Arthur.

"Al," along with other Nem Loof Clowns, was in San Antonio to participate in the opening of the 1968 Harris Fair.

He states he is blessed to be a clown. He was honored to serve as El Mina Shrine President in 1968 and TSA President 1968-69.

PIPES, GEORGE A. (Patches) was born on March 11, 1948 in Providence, Rhode Island and is the son of Albert and Betty Pipes. He served in the Army during the Vietnam Conflict and then attended Northeast State and Falkner University where he graduated in 1991. He married Regina Grider in 1967, has two children (Dr. Georgina Nelson of Madison and Timothy Pipes of Huntsville Alabama), son-in law Patrick Nelson, and four grandchildren (Nate, Andrew, Arabella, and Kaitlyn Nelson).

Patches is an endowed member of Blue Lodge 456, Scottish Rite, Ben Hur Shrine and life member of Srekoj clown unit of Austin Texas. He is also a member of Cahaba Shrine and Buffoon clown unit of Huntsville Alabama. He holds memberships in Dixie and Southeastern Shrine Clown associations and the Order of Quetzacoatl.

Patches served two terms as president of Srekoj clowns and multiple years as both secretary and treasurer of Srekoj and Buffoon units. In February 2010 he was elected ISCA third VP and now serves as first VP. He is honored to have served 4 years on the board of Houston, TX SHC and currently in his 6th term on the board at Greenville S.C. SHC.

PODROVITZ, THOMAS W. (Chugg'O) was born in St. Louis, MO, Feb. 27, 1975. After attending school he was hired on with the Burlington Northern Railroad as a fireman/student engineer apprentice, where he later became examined as a locomotive engineer driving trains from the coal mines across the Midwest. He married Heidi Miller in October of 2000. They resident in Abingdon, IL.

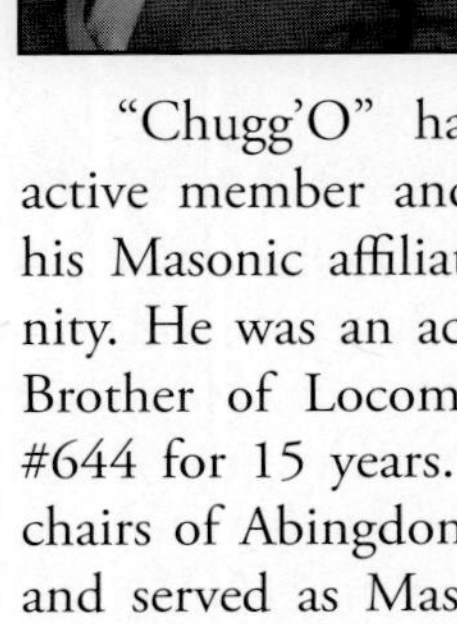

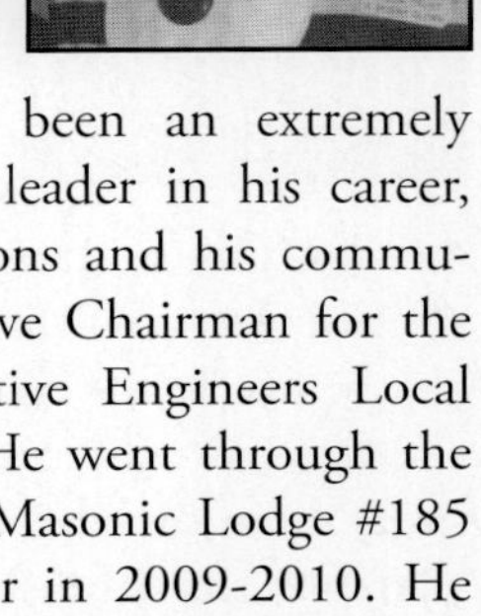

"Chugg'O" has been an extremely active member and leader in his career, his Masonic affiliations and his community. He was an active Chairman for the Brother of Locomotive Engineers Local #644 for 15 years. He went through the chairs of Abingdon Masonic Lodge #185 and served as Master in 2009-2010. He served as "Most Wise Master" Chapter of Rose Croix in the Valley of Moline Scottish Rite in 2011. He served as "El Bon" Shrine Club President in 2011 and 2012.

He became secretary/treasurer of the Fun Makers Clown Unit. He is also an active member in Illinois Council #1 Cryptic Masons, Warren Chapter #30 of Royal Arch Masons and was dubbed a Sir Knight of Galesburg Commandary Post on Feb. 28, 2009.

Chugg'O followed in his grandfather and father's footsteps. His father, Steve Podrovitz, of Leakey, TX was a past master of Leakey Lodge AF &AM in Leakey, TX and was a member of the horse patrol of Moolah Shrine in St. Louis, MO as well as the Valley of St. Louis AASR. Masonry has been an extremely important part of their lives and family history over the years.

Chugg'O's life has forever been changed from the joys of clowning and magic for small children. As an active member he spends between 150-200 hours a year clowning for the handicapped on special train rides sponsored by various charities. He's active in all local small town parades with his tiny vehicles to keep the happiness alive for the children to see, as he once saw as a kid when the Shrines paraded through town in various parades. Keeping the Shriners alive and in the hearts of the community across the small towns of the West Central Illinois is Chugg'O's goal. Chugg'O is proud to be an active member of the Mohammed Shrine in Peoria, IL.

POIRIER, JAY P. (Lugnut) was born in Lewiston Maine April 17, 1979. He is a graduate of Lewiston High School class of 1998 and furthered his education at New England College, where he received a Bachelors degree in Business Administration. He is currently employed as Assistant Manager for NAPA.

Jay joined Tranquil Lodge AF&AM #29 in Auburn Maine in 2010 and currently sits as the SR. Deacon. He joined the Scottish Rite and received my 32 degree, then joined the York Rite where he currently sits as Master of the First Veil. He became a Kora Temple Shriner in 2011, becoming an active member of the Kora Klowns and proudly receiving the "Rookie of the Year" award in 2011. He attended Clown College at North East Clown Institute in Plymouth Massachusetts.

When not clowning, he enjoys spending time with friends and family, especially his two-year-old Godson Luc. He also enjoys old cars, camping, and snowmobiling with his Bro.

RAFTER, DAVID W. (Laffter) was born in New Westminster, B.C., Canada, August 19, 1947.

In October 1981, he started his travels to becoming a master mason in Meridian Lodge #108, Grand Lodge of British Columbia and the Yukon with his father's support. He continued on through the York Rite; Royal Arch Triple Tau Chapter #21 (which amalgamated with Composite Chapter #24 in 2011) and Columbia Perceptory #34, then Joined Gizeh Shriners #85 in May 1984 in Kelowna B.C. He joined Golden Ears Shrine Club #32 and became President in 1993. With some persuasion from Noble's Peter "PeeTee" Thornburn and Leonard J. "Oh-Oh" Wyllie, he joined the Vancouver Clown Unit in 1991. Over dinner with his niece, the clown name "Laffter" was born. His wife Kathy (Past Queen Daughters of the Nile Zarah Temple #72, 1997) is his strongest supporter in clowning and of the shrine, as are their families.

REED, TED (Razzle) was born July 28, 1943 in Lancaster, OH. He attended Eastmore High School in Columbus, OH and graduated from Lancaster, OH High School in 1961. Ted served in the USMC from 1961-1965. He has been married 39 years to Maureen "Mo." Their son is Fredrick Duke Reed.

Ted worked for the Federal Government (DOD and IRS) from 1965 to 1993, when he retired. He and his wonderful wife, "Mo," currently live in Florence, KY.

In 1965 he was raised in Barstow Lodge #682. He walked the hot sands at Syrian Temple and joined the Syrian Shrine Clowns in 1999.

"Razzle" is a past director of the Syrian Shrine Clowns. He said he has won "bunch of awards but not as many as "Bingo."

RICE, ELWOOD "AL" (Woody) joined the Shrine on the 22nd of May, 1976 in Charlotte N.C. Demitted to Ben Hur in 1996, and joined the Srekoj Clown Unit in March 1996.

He received the Red Nose Award in 1997, 1998, 1999, 2000, 2001, 2002, 2003, 2004, 2005, 2006, 2007, 2008 and 2009. So far he has received two Gold Nose Awards. He has been in every Circus since 1997, and has attended 85 parades.

Al has visited to the Austin Children's Hospital more than 150 times to give out toys and love, has visited the Shrine hospitals in Houston and Galveston each year and sometimes twice, and also has visited the Childrens Hospital in Boston.

He has placed in the top 10 in Competition every year since 1997 and took 3rd place in San Antonio in 2002, 3rd place in Tyler in 2003, 1st place Fort Worth in 2004, 2nd place in Mesquite in 2005 and 1st place in Tyler 2007. All of these were in the T.S.C.A. Senior Compitition. He was in the hospital in 2006 and could not compete.

Al has been a registered member in the T.S.C.A. and Imperial since 1997 and has attended T.S.A. seven times and attended the Imperial session in Dallas, Las Vegas, and Boston. He has preformed at 10 birthday parties for children, collecting $50 to $150 for each party and all of the money collected was given to the Srekoj Clowns for the Sneaker Fund. He has also worked at all of the bucket shakes for the Clowns and Temple except 2001 and 2006 when he was in the hospital. He was president of the Srekoj Clown Unit in 2001 and again in 2004 and Vice President in 2000, 2003. 2005, 2008 and 2009. He also served as Chaplain of T.S.C.A. for the year of 2010.

RODRIGUEZ, RUBEN OCTAVIO ROSAS (Toselin) was born in Mexico City on Nov. 2, 1956, lives in Mexico City, is in charge of the IT area of the Management of Lines 1, 3 and 4 of the Metro. He married Ma Ana Rosa Torres Guzman on June 2, 1979 and they have five daughters of whom four are living: Jessica Adriana; Cynthia Mariana; Celeste Roxana and Ilse Alejandra, and also granddaughter Andrea Mariana.

On Aug. 5, 1980 RLS started February 5 No. 34 Mante City, Tamaulipas, exalted Dec. 11, 1984 RLS Chilam Balam No. 21, Royal Arch Chapter Nov. 26, 1987 City of Mexico No. 1, 2003 High Priest and High Priesthood May 28, 2006; Thrice Illustrious Master's Council No. 2 Mexico City in 2006, Generalissimo in the Ivanhoe Commandery of Knights Templar No. 2, from participating in Eye Foundation Life Sponsor to Grand Master Club, go to Nov. 23, 2004 Shriners a founding member and president 2010 of Unity Clowns, Tacos to the Attack, International Membership Lodge of the Holy Land #50 in Israel Nov. 2, 2003, Grand Secretary of the General Grand Chapter Royal Arch Masons United Mexican States 2008-2010, Grand Scribe, Great King of General Grand Chapter of Royal Arch Masons and Grand Captain General of the Grand Commandery of Knights Templar of Mexico 2012-13.

SALOUKAS, BILL I. (Box Car Billy) was born in 1939 in New York. In 1989 he and Kathy were married. Bill is founder and CEO of Broad Waverly Staffing Services in Red Bank, New Jersey since 1972.

Mr. Saloukas is recognized for his outstanding knowledge, contributions and ethics in his profession evidenced by receiving numerous awards and designations. In addition to his professional responsibilities, he serves on various Boards, conducts speaking engagements, lectures at local retraining facilities and provides time and financial resources for community and civic organizations. He is a member and past president of Red Bank Rotary. He served as Director and is a charter board member for Mid-Atlantic Association of Personnel Consultants. He has served as: Director, Greater Eastern Monmouth Area County Chamber of Commerce and Red Bank YMCA. He is a Board Member of Ronald McDonald House.

He is listed in *Who's Who in Finance and Industry in America* and *Directory of Distinguished Americans.* He has received: International Vocational Service Award, Rotary International; Community Service Award, National Association of Personnel Consultants; Paul Harris Fellowship Award and Paul Harris Sapphire Fellowship Award, Rotary of Red Bank; 1998-99, Rotary District 7500 Award; 2000 Volunteer of the Year Award, Eastern Monmouth Chamber of Commerce and 2003 Community Service Award, Mid-Atlantic Association of Personnel Consultants.

"Box Car Billy" is a member of the Crescent Masonic Temple and Crescent Clown Unit. He has received the Red Nose Award for service to the community and was named Clown of the Year.

SCHULTHEIS, NORMAN C. (Pickles) was born in St. Louis, MO, April 3, 1938. He graduated in 1956 from Hancock High. After graduating, he worked five years for Stix, Bauer and Fuller Department Stores. He went to work for A-Able Key Company and in 1962 became an apprentice locksmith. In 1974 he opened his own shop called The Dutchmans. In 1984 he closed down his shop and worked for other companies. He retired in 2010 at the age of 72 years. He and Carolyn were married in 1963. They have two children, Kelly and Mark and four grandchildren: Kayla, Justin, Michael and Molly. Rylee is their great-grandchild.

"Pickles" was always a clown as a hobby. For 35 years he clowned for the church functions, birthday parties, etc.

Norman was raised on June 11, 1996 at George Washington Lodge #9. He walked the hot sands on Oct. 12, 1997 at Moolah Temple. In 2006 he joined the Moolah Clowns Unit.

"Pickles" is a Past Master of George Washington #9 in St. Louis, MO (2005-2006); a member of the Scottish Rite, Valley of St. Louis – 32° K.C.C.H. He is a volunteer worker (Membership Services), working 25-1/2 hours a week starting in 2009. Presently he is 1st Vice President of the Unit and is scheduled to become President.

SEARS, GARY V. was born in Pueblo, Colorado and has lived in the area his entire life. He is married to Donna; they have four children and six grandchildren. During his career Gary worked in retail management and tax preparation services.

Gary was raised a Master Mason in Silver State Lodge #95 in Pueblo in 1992 and served as Worshipful Master of Silver State in 1999. He also served as Worthy Patron of OES #34 in 1998-1999. He is a member of the Southern Colorado Consistory and he was honored with the IGH 33° in 2009.

He joined Al Kaly Shriners in 1992 and has always been an active clown. He Served as President of the KalyKlown Unit in 1995 & 1996 and Secretary from 2004-2011.

He was elected to the Divan of Al Kaly Shriners in 2008 and served as Potentate of Al Kaly Shriners in 2012.

SEMANIUK, GARY (Bubbles) joined the Al-Shamal Shrine Clowns in 2000. He asked his young daughter for a name

recommendation and she came up with "Bubbles". His Shrine Clown dad "Dizzy" took him under his wing and his life as "Bubbles" started. "Bubbles" was president of the clown unit in 2008. Although not as active as he would like to be due to an elected Supreme Line position with Job's Daughters International, "Bubbles" does as many parties, move outs and Edmonton special events as he can. "Bubbles" is happy and proud to be a member of the Al-Shamal Shrine Clown Unit and to have the opportunity of clowning with the greatest clowns.

SHAPIRO, STEPHEN PAUL (Makabau, the Clown) was born Oct. 3, 1942 in Middletown, CT. He attended schools in Middletown (MHS-Class 1960), graduated from Long Island University (C.W. Post 1964), and graduate school in New York. He married Carol Zeidenberg and they were blessed with three wonderful children: Beth; Michael and Robert and two grandchildren, Nathan and Maya. They live in Middletown, CT and winter in Pembroke Pines, FL.

Stephen was raised to the sublime degree of Master Mason in February 1964 at St Johns Lodge #2, and served as Worshipful Master in 1974 and 2000. He took degrees of Scottish and York Rites in New York City, and was made a Noble of the Mystic Shrine at Mecca Temple in New York City in 1966, where he was introduced to Clowning.

Stephen took great pride in traveling to hospitals, entertaining kids of all ages and bringing that important Smile to their faces as "Makabau, the Clown". For the next quarter of a century, Makabau was always found at some hospital, clowning around with his magic and balloon animals, always there to help.

Stephen joined his family's business and Middletown landmark, Shapiro's Department Store in 1966, and helped grow it into the largest store in the area. Stephen's parents and grandparents (all Masons) instilled in him that when you were in business you must "Give Back" to the community. Stephen became active in nearly every charitable organization and worked tirelessly.

Stephen remained active in Masonry, being appointed District Deputy in 1982 and 1983; Grand Representative to Israel since 1981, and still serves in that capacity; Brotherhood In Action Committee, President of the Ritual Cast for the Shrine degree work, Potentate's Aide, Treasurer of the Shriners Temple Building, Board of Directors of MasoniCare (CT Masons Home and Hospital); Recipient of the Pierpont Edwards Medal for a life of Distinguished Service (CT Masonry's highest award).

Stephen served his community as leader and member of the Middletown Town Council for 16 years. He served 14 years as a member of the City's Planning and Zoning Commission. For his Outstanding Service to the City, Stephen was named a "Hometown Hero" of Middletown, CT and a day and park was named in Stephen's Honor.

Stephen also received the Downtown Clergy Associations Award for Altruism; the Commission of the Arts Award for Service to the Arts and was named the Man of the Year Award by the State's Jaycees.

SHERIFF, RICH (MaGee) lives in Long Island, NY. He joined Kismet Shrine in 2005 and jumped right into the clown unit. The senior Joey's of the unit taught him to put on make-up and general clowning for street and Competition. "MaGee" received awards in skits and general clowning from M.A.S.C.A, N.Y.O.S.A. and the Northeast Clown College, where he received the degree of Craftsman clown.

"MaGee" was awarded the Kismet Shriner of the year in 2006. He was elected as Boss Clown in 2006 and 2007. He states: "But of all the trophies and awards I received, none can compare to the greatest reward of all – the smiles on the faces of the young, old, sick and healthy when they see MaGee."

SOLIS, RUPERT C. (Cy-Lo) was born Sept. 22, 1960 in San Antonio, TX. He and Trish were married in 1983. Rupert has worked in Food Industry since 1986 and is currently account manager for Hydrite Chemical Co.

On Feb. 3, 1996 "Cy-Lo" was raised at West Lodge. He walked the hot sands at Medinah Temple and in 2002 joined the Medinah Clown Unit. In 2003 he joined as "Cy-Lo," an Auguste Clown, and served as Treasurer in 2007-2008.

"Cy-Lo" was awarded Unit Clown of the Year in 2008; GLSCUA Clown of the Year in 2009 and served as ISCA Secretary from 2011-2012.

STOKES, KEITH (Toby) was born on Jan. 18, 1923 in Edgar County, IL. He and wife Reba have two children, Dale Stokes and Darla Oltmanns. Keith is retired and lives in Florida.

"Toby" began clowning in 1974 as a member of the walking Shrine Clowns of Ansar. He served Central Illinois. Upon retiring to Florida, "Toby" used his clowning to serve hospitals, church day care centers, nursing homes, etc. He started teaching and has taught 1,010 clowns under Toby the Clown Foundation, a non-profit 501(3)(c) of which he is the founder. The corporation has the American Clown Museum located in Lake Placid, FL. Its' library holds all of the past issues of *Clown Alley* magazine.

"Toby" has served as teacher and judge for the Shrine Clowning community. He helped start Red Nose Relief as a founding director, also a non-profit corporation based in Atlanta, GA. He has won many awards in competition; however, his latest award came from Clowns of America, the Lifetime Achievement Award.

SZEREDY, JAMES (Chi Chi) was born Sept. 12, 1944 in Southbridge, MA. He is a life member of Harry S. Truman Lodge No. 649, Naples, Italy, and was raised on Nov. 16, 1974. He walked the hot sands on March 27, 1976 at Moslah Temple in Naples. In 2007 he joined the Cahaba Buffoons of Cahaba Shrine Center (life member), Huntsville, AL.

James became a clown in 1988 with the El Maida Shrine Sidewalk Circus, El Paso, TX. He served as member/secretary/director (two years). He is current unit secretary and chairman of the ISCA 2013 Mid-Winter to be held in Huntsville.

He is married to Kathie and they have two children, Christine and Noble Jim Jr., and three grandchildren, Gabrielle, Mason and Stazya. James is retired from the U.S. Army and a Defense Contractor.

TAYLOR, SAMUEL E. (Lucky) was born in Taylor, TX, August 29, 1947. He has an Associate of Science degree in Engineering Design Graphics and works for a Civil Engineering Firm and teaches at Austin Community College in the evening in Austin, Texas. He is married to Erica and they have blended a family of five children, seven grandchildren, and five great grandchildren. They reside in Austin and spend leisure time on our boat, sailing on Lake Travis.

"Lucky" belongs to Onion Creek No. 220 Lodge and Ben Hur Temple in Austin, Texas. He has served as Secretary and President for the Srekoj Clown unit, and was the President of the 2009-2010 Texas Shrine Clown Association. He joined the clown unit in 2001 and has earned eight Red Nose and one Gold Nose awards. He participates with his fellow clowns in the Austin, Dallas, Houston, and San Antonio circuses and various parades. He competes in the Texas Shrine Clown Mid-Winters, ISCA, and Imperial competitions in whiteface, auguste, character, and skit. Fortunately, Texas has two Shrine Hospitals only a few hours away for the Ben Hur clowns to visit and has also visited one in Hawaii. Belonging to this great organization gives him a lot of pleasure and satisfaction in helping the children's hospitals.

THRASHER, RICHARD G. (Butch) was born in Middletown, CT on April 10, 1939. After graduating from high school, he joined the US Air Force in January 1958. During his military career, Hutch served in the US, Canada, Vietnam, and Germany; he retired in 1981.

Butch was raised a Master Mason in April 1971 at DeWitt Clinton Lodge in Sandwich, MA. During his assignment to Germany, he became a member of the Scottish Rite, sitting in the Valley of NATO, Orient of California, later becoming a member of the Mystic Shrine in Aahmes Temple of Oakland, CA and eventually appointed as an Ambassador to Europe.

His first action was to become a member of the Rhein Pfalz Funster Clown Unit, the only Shrine Clown Unit in Europe under I.S.C.A. His untiring and unselfish efforts became quickly known to all, and within two years he was destined to become its President. Last, but by far, not the least. Noble "Butch" always found time to support local DeMolay and Rainbow activities. He was Dad Advisor for Unity Chapter Order of DeMolay and was also contributor of time and talent to Pauline Assembly, International Order of Rainbow for Girls, both of Kaiserslautern, Germany. In 1977 Butch was honored for his hard work and dedication by being selected Clown of the Month for I.S.C.A.

In 1978, after returning to the US, Butch became a member of the Valley of Fall River, MA, followed by him joining Aleppo Temple in Wilmington, MA where he became a member of the Aleppo Clowns and was appointed Assistant Boss Clown of the Cape Cod Unit.

Butch was responsible for the Aleppo Clown College, in addition to teaching makeup application at the college. He then became an instructor with the Northeast Shrine Clown Institute in Plymouth, MA, again bringing his expertise of applying makeup to novice Auguste clowns.

In 1998 Butch completed the NESCI judge's certification course for makeup, skit, and paradability. Over the years, "Butch" 'fared well' in Northeast Clown Convention competitions, taking 1st, 2nd and 3rd placements in the Auguste category. In 2000 "Butch" earned Mast Clown status at the Northeast Clown Institute.

Butch's second career as an Airfield Manager USAF civilian was from June 1982 to September 2008, giving him a total of 50 years with the US Air Force. He is presently enjoying retirement on Cape Cod, MA.

UMLAUF, JAMES C. (Jimbo) was born in Johnstown, PA June 20, 1935. He served in the United States Air Force, and is retired from Philadelphia Electric.

A Shriner since 1975, "Jimbo" served Crescent Shine as Illustrious Potentate in 2002. A Clown since 1977, he is Director Emeritus and Treasurer Emeritus of the Crescent Clown Unit. "Jimbo" is a member of Newtown Lodge #427, Woodside, PA, and Lehigh Consistory, Allentown, PA 32°. He has been an Associate Member of the Board of the Philadelphia Shriner's Hospital for three years.

"Jimbo" is past Secretary-Treasurer of MASA, and has served three Presidents as Director General. He earned his Master Clown Certificate at the Northeast Clown Institute, and has won many awards as a Tramp Clown.

Jimbo has two sons; Jamie who is single and lives with him, and Edward who is married and has three children: Michael, Madisen and Ashley.

UTHOFF, STEPHEN A. (Spanky) was born in 1945 in St. Louis, MO. He has two children, Lisa and Laura and grandchild Alexia. Stephen retired in 2006 after 25 years as a carpenter and home building superintendent. He and significant other, Bonita, reside in Dittmer, MO.

"Spanky" was raised in Shawnee Lodge #54 on April 26, 1997. On June 14, 1997 he walked the hot sands at Moolah Temple and then joined the Moolah Clown Unit. He has participated in several competitions, parades and face painting.

"Spanky" was president of Moolah Clown Unit in 2002. He has received the Smile Maker Award and a Gold Nose.

WHIGHAM, KENNETH (Diamonds) has been clowning since 1978. He is a member of Yaarab Shrine in Atlanta, Georgia, and Anezeh Shrine in Mexico City, Mexico.

He is a member of Yaarab Red Devil Clown Unit, Yaarab Shrine Clown Association, Anezeh Taco Clown Unit, International Shrine Clown Association (ISCA), Southeastern Shrine Clown Association (SESCA), Clowns of America, a Life Member of World Clown Association, and a member of International Clown Hall of Fame.

He was raised a Master Mason in August 1976 in Georgia at Morrow Lodge #734, where he is a lifetime member. He became a Scottish Rite Mason in May of 1977, a Shriner in June 1977, Royal Arch Mason in November 1979, and he is a Scottish Rite KCCH. Offices he has held: Chaplain for SESCA, 1998-1999; Chaplain for ISCA, 2002; President of Tara Shrine Club Clown Unit, 1980; President of Yaarab Shrine Red Devil Clowns, 1998; President of Southside Scottish Rite Association, 1985; Worthy Patron OES, Morrow #531, 1984-1985; President of Yaarab Shrine Clown Association, 2003 & 2004; President of SESCA, 2007-2008; and current Secretary of Yaarab Shrine Clown Association. He was voted into the Red Devil Clown Hall of Fame, 2003. He was awarded ISCA Clown of the Year for 2004. In Jan. 2011, he received Yaarab Shrine Merit Award No. 377.

He has won numerous first place awards in competitions for makeup and costume, balloons, and skits. He is a certified ISCA judge. His goals are for the benefit of clowning and to help relay the art of clowning to others.

Noble Kenneth Whigham and his Lady, Susan, are both retired and living their golden years in Cedar Bluff, AL.

WHITESIDE, WESLEY (Sniffles) was born May 25, 1976 and raised October 26,2002 as a Master Mason, and joined the Hadi Shrine Funsters. Sniffles is married to his wonderful lady Tara and currently has one daughter Aubrey. Sniffles is a clown of many faces, he currently does Auguste, Whiteface, Character, Happy Hobo, and Tramp faces. In 2007 Sniffles was honored to be part of the 4th generation bucking car team with the Hadi Funsters. He currently drives the well know vehicle in many parades across the U.S. and Canada. In 2011 he served as President of the Hadi Shrine Funsters. Sniffles was also honored by the Great Lakes Shrine Clown Association in 2008 as Clown of the Year and is a recipient of the ISCA Red Nose Award.

WILBANKS, JOHN E. (Hambone) was born Feb. 25, 1938 in Dayton, TN. John has four children: Robin A.; John Jr.; Tim A. and Rodney D. His grandchildren are Ashley and Katie. John and his second wife, Joan S., live in Orlando, FL. John served in the USMC, worked at Lockheed Martin and was self-employed as a builder-contractor. He retired in 2001.

John was raised in June 1989 at Charity Daylight Lodge 7541. In June 1989 he wanted the hot sands at Yarrab Temple and the same month joined the Red Devils Clown Unit.

In 1991, "Hambone" was president of Red Devils Clown Unit and in 2009 served as president of ISCA.

John is a 32-degree and belongs to York Rite.

WOODARD, HARVEY (Woody) was born in Waco, TX, Jan. 14, 1931. He lived in several small towns near Waco until 1939 when his family bought a home in the small town of Lorena, 13 miles from Waco. Woody lived there and graduated high school in 1948, worked several different jobs in the area and went to work for his father in Dallas as an electrician apprentice. Forced to leave because of business slowdown he returned to Waco. While in Dallas he commuted back to Lorena and became a Master Mason in July 1955. Returning to Lorena he met and married his first wife, Helen, and had two daughters. They were divorced after 15 years. Both of his wives were good seamstresses and made all his costumes. In 1957 he went to work for the Waco Fire Department He retired there after 34 years as Captain of Engine Company 11.

He was active in his Lodge. He served in every office except Marshall; Secretary five years, treasurer five years, tiler three times, chaplain two years. He received the Golden Trowel Award from his lodge Jan. 22, 1997. Harvey joined the Scottish Rite Valley of Waco as a charter member in 1965 and Karem Shrine in October 1969 and Karem Shrine Clowns in April 1970. He became master of the lodge and President of the clown unit in 1973. He served 16 years as secretary-treasurer of his clown unit. His unit elected him "Unsung Hero" in 1999 and he received a certificate from TSCA.

His Masonic history is: charter and endowed member Scottish Rite Valley of Waco; plural member Tranquility Lodge 2000; endowed member M. Denton Stanford Lodge #594, Lorena, TX; endowed member Waco Commandery #10 Knights Templar; endowed member Waco Royal Arch Chapter 45; endowed member Grand Council of R. & S. M. #33, Waco; member Scottish Rite Research Society; member Texas Lodge of Research Waco; member Texas York Rite College #14, Waco; charter Member of Scottish Rite Wisdom, Strength and Beauty; member Karem Shrine Waco; member Karem Shrine Hillbilly Clan 111.

When he joined Karem clowns he also joined Texas Shrine Clown Ass'n, and National Shrine Clown Ass'n., later to become ISCA. When Karem started up the Crown Of Honor program he was one of the first nine recipients. He joined the Shrine Hospital Transportation committee and the Scottish Rite Transportation committee, taking patients to Dallas Scottish Rite Hospital 100 miles away and Shrine Orthaepedic Hospital in Houston 180 miles and Shrine burns hospital in Galveston 220 miles. He made 34 trips before he stopped. He received a Certificate of Merit from the Shrine Hospital Transportation committee.

He served on many committees in Karem and he and his wife, Jean, served several years on the shrine ballroom decorating committee.

In October 2005 he received his 50-year pin from his lodge and in February 2006 went to Tecumseh, OK and saw four of his cousins, all past masters receive, their 50-year pines.

Woody did not fare so well in costume and make-up competition but did quite well in skit competition. His 3-man skit won 1st in ISCA in Jackson, MS. And a year later won 1st place in Imperial in Toronto with the same skit. He and his unit have won several skits and finished in the top 3 several times. He attended his first TSCA midwinter in 1971 and has missed only one since. He served as TSCA secretary in 1995-96.

He also has attended several ISCA midwinters.

During his years he became an 18 and 1/2 gallon blood donor. Though not as active at 81, he still pays dues and attends as much as possible in lodge, clowns and square dancing. In his younger years he made cotton candy with other members of his unit with their machine for local schools and churches and other organizations He paraded all over the State of Texas, made thousands of balloon animals, visited hundreds of hours in hospitals and schools. He earned four Red Nose awards before old age crept up on him.

On the personal side, he is remarried to Jean with two adult stepsons. Woody and Jean have eight grandchildren and 13 and 1\2 great grandchildren. With this crew Woody says he is growing his own audience. They are avid square dancers since 1977 and have held office in several clubs and have twice been presidents of the Heart Of Texas Square and Round Dance Association and held other offices since 1995. Once Woody's supplier did not deliver on name tags so he bought a machine and now works at home part time making name tags for square dancers, shriners, red hat ladies, etc.

Woody is proud of the many friends he has from the clowns of Texas and ISCA and square dancers and wishes he could start over and do it all again.

WRIGHT, JAMES K. (Jake) was born in Huntsville, AL and, within a year, the family moved to Decatur, AL. He attended school there and graduated in 1951. Soon after he joined the US Marine Corps and immediately got a tax payer paid trip to Korea.

Upon his discharge and return home he married his Lady, Barbara. They have been married for 56 years. They have a son and daughter and five granddaughters, who have all been supportive of his love of clowning.

He attended Auburn University and upon graduation went to work for Southern Railway and worked his way to Atlanta. In 1969 he became a Master Mason in Glenwood Hills Lodge No. 703.

In 1985, after the merger of the Southern and Norfolk and Western railroads, he was transferred to Roanoke, VA. In 1988 he joined Kazim Shrine and the Kazim Klown Unit. Following his retirement and return to Atlanta in 1990, he ultimately joined the Yaarab Shrine Red Devil Clown Unit.

He served the Unit as President for two years and as Chaplin for several years. He also was President of the Southeastern Shrine Clown Association in 2002-2003 and served as Chaplin in 2007-2008.

There were two things he felt deeply about: (1) all clowns have egos—speak carefully around them and never criticize their performances, and (2) being a Shrine clown requires a commitment—be prepared to be the best clown you can possibly be when representing our great fraternity.

And finally to all of his many Alabama friends, WAR EAGLE!!!

ZAGOREN, LAUREN ARTHUR (Sir Ziggy) was born June 10, 1948 in New Brunswick, NJ. Ziggy, AKA Lauren Arthur Zagoren, started his clowning career when he met Clara Bell the Clown from the "Howdy Doody Show." Ziggy was 4 and Clara Bell was huge in his black and white costume. Ziggy ran and hid – quiet Clara Bell did NOT RUN AFTER HIM. Ziggy was hooked. Years later, he became Class Clown and a Thespian. Zig was mesmerized by circuses as a child and after college worked briefly as a "roustabout" while hitching across America. He learned Circus Etiquette.

Ziggy was raised June 1, 1984 in Mount Olivet Lodge, Cambridge, MA. He went through all the chairs and served as Master in 1992. During his tenure, he was instrumental in the lodge receiving the first Grand Master's Award. He holds two life memberships in Mount Olivet Lodge in Massachusetts and Fort Myers Beach Lodge #362 in Florida. He is a life member of the Scottish Rite and joined the Aleppo Clown's in 1985. He served as the Aleppo Clowns Hospital Coordinator and perfected techniques for "Hospital Clowning" while there. Ziggy was presented in 2007, Aleppo Temples Clown Life Membership: "For your charitable efforts in clowning and bringing smiles to children all over the world."

Ziggy was made the 3rd "Master Clown" after Rollo and Pinky by the North East Shrine Institute where he taught Advanced White Face for Competition. He trained in the early 90s to work as an official ISCA Judge. He had taken first for Single and Multiple Balloons, Skits and White Face, Auguste and Character and always appreciated-Clowns strutting their stuff!

Ziggy was chosen in 1990 by ISCA, World Clowns and COAI to clown as an Ambassador in Hungary, Poland and Russia. There he was groped by a drunken Russian while performing in Drag as "Miss Sally." He served four ISCA Presidents as their Northeast Deputy; Membership Chairman and Sneaker Fund Chairman. He also served ISCA as an International Ambassador for clowning. In 2008, Zig served as Boss Clown for the Fun and Frolic Unit, Araba Temple, Fort Myers, FL.

Ziggy is a certified Laughter Yoga Instructor. He created a program in Southwest Florida for people with Parkinson's disease. His therapeutic method of incorporating laughter and humor had a proven effect. Thus, adding to the quality of their lives. Zig often performs at one of the largest hospitals in Southern India. He created a program where he visits children on the pediatric ward. He learned his craft from "old clowns" and has met and practiced with clown notables: Frosty Little" and Kenny Ahern from Ringling Brothers" and "Grand Ma" from the Big Apple Circus. Patch Adams invited Ziggy to tour with him.

Ziggy's Karma is to CLOWN. His clowning during the past 25 years has expanded around the globe. He has clowned in circuses, parades, carnivals, hospitals, medical buses, orphanages and schools. His clowning has brought him to India, Europe, the Caribbean and villages around the globe. Children of all ages have shown him that we are all members of a huge family. He has truly learned that laughter is a universal language that all beings need to experience GOD'S LOVE.

"Stay cool-you fellow fools. Be Happy and Smile."

INTERNATIONAL

The Charlotte
A SIZZLING RECORD

OASIS

Black Camel

The Clown's Last Walk-Around

As we went about our daily lives, the Black Camel sadly came and claimed more of our own. Sadly, many ISCA clowns have passed on over the last 25 years. The following biographies were provided specifically for this book – both the ISCA and publisher regret any errors or omissions.

BERG, LLOYD (Bogey) was born in the state of Ohio, February 14, 1918. He married his sweetheart, Harriet, in Ohio. They were married over 59 years. They had three boys and many grandchildren. They moved to California and other places due to his occupation as an electrician.

"Bogey" joined the Masonic Lodge in Ohio in 1948. He moved to Tri-Cities, WA in 1961 joined the Scottish Rite, and El Katif Shrine of Spokane, WA. "Bogey" joined the Columbia Basin Shrine Club, Dirty Dozen motorcycle unit, helped start the clown unit at CBSC in 1974 and became an Honorary President of CBSC. He served as President and Sec/Treas of CBS Clowns and enjoyed taking the kids to the hospital in Spokane, WA.

He was devoted to the Sneaker Fund and served as an Ambassador for the ISCA many times.

He was visited by the Black Camel in 2008.

BROWN, JIMMY (Jimbo) passed away at age 81 on Dec. 20, 2012 after a brief illness. Jimbo was a quiet and unassuming clown, however when his make-up was on, he became alive and had a special way with children that he entertained. He was very active in the Yaarab Red Devil Clowns and was inducted into the Red Devil Clowns Hall of Fame. At the funeral, his son, Ricky, when informed of the other three Red Devil Clowns who had recently passed away, said that they were all called home for the kindergarten children who were victims in the school shootings in Connecticut. He will be missed by all.

CALLAHAN, JAMES (Foots) was born Sept. 1, 1940 and his last walk-around was Oct. 22, 2010 at the age of 70 in Clayton, GA. Jim was a long time member of the Yaarab Red Devil Clowns, serving as president in 1985 and was an ISCA member for many years. He was inducted into the Red Devil Clowns Hall of Fame in 2004. He was also president of the Georgia Shrine Clown Association. Jim left behind a loving family.

CHEEK, CHRIS (Cheeko the Clown) passed away in 2011 at the age of 59. He was a long time member of the Red Devil clown and served as secretary as well as clowning for over 21 years. He was particularly fond of participating in the Brain Tumor and Grant A Wish Foundations every year. A member of the U.S. Army, achieving the rank of Major, he saw active duty in Iraq, Desert Storm and Desert Shield during his career. He also was involved as a leader in scouting and mentored 18 scouts through the rank of Eagle Scout.

CLIFF, LLOYD H. (Tater) was born July 23, 1923 at West Suffield, CT. He walked the hot sands in June 1984 at Sphinx Temple, Hartford, CT, and joined the Funsters on Nov. 29, 1984. He became a life member in May 1995. Married to Althea, the Black Camel called on May 17, 2007.

CREW, MICHAEL (Woody) passed away on January 31, 2013 at the age of 70. Michael was an active member of the mason, steel drum unit and with the El Riad Clowns in Sioux Falls SD. Michael grew up in South Dakota where he went to school and then attended USD in Vermillion, finely finishing up his degree from the Harvard Law School. Michael worked on capital hill but took time to put on his happy face and entertain the kids. The music will play on and the spot light will shine but Woody has gone, he will be missed.

CURTISS, RICKY P. (Pinky the Clown) passed away on June 26, 2012. He was well known around Abdallah Shrine because of his love of the color pink and because of his whimsical sense of humor. He was a pillar of strength within the Abdallah Shrine Clowns, serving over the years in numerous positions from secretary to president. Pinky also served as the Secretary/Treasurer of the Central States Shrine Clown Assoc. in 2004-05.

He was born on Dec. 12, 1953 and was self-employed as a construction project manager. He was a member of the Overland Park Masonic Lodge and a passionate member of the Abdallah Shrine Clown unit.

He was married to Diana and had one son, Paul, two stepdaughters, Patti and Christa, and ten grandchildren.

DUNMIRE, JOE A. (JoJo) was born Dec. 5, 1924 in Sioux City, IA. He joined Lovell Lodge #36 and was raised April 16, 1947. A member of Korein Temple, he walked the hot sands on May 30, 1981. He joined the Calliope Clowns in 1987. Joe transferred to Independence Rock Lodge #56, Past Master. He was a Scottish Rite Mason, member of Casper Consistory Club, and

was a second generation Mason—he and his father, George J. Dunmire, were both raised on April 16, 1947 at Lovell Lodge #36.

Joe was visited by the Black Camel on October 12, 2010. He was married to Arlyne, and they had three children, Jolene, Coelene and Dawn, grandchildren Kristen, Dray, Amber, Joe, Zach and Adrian, and grandchildren Eddie, Cristopf, Katelyn and Carter.

FIELDS, JERRY (Mister Smokey) clowned with the Yaarab Red Devil Clowns and Peachtree Cloen Alley for 55 years and was regarded as the patriarch of clowning. He was inducted into the Red Devil Clowns Hall of Fame in 2004. He was a past president of the Red Devil Clowns, Southeast Shrine Clown Association, Southeast Clown Association, and Peachtree Clown Alley of which he was a charter member.

He was the ISCA Sneaker Fund Chairman for the Red Devil Clowns for many years and was awarded special recognition for all of his service to the Sneaker Fund Philanthropy.

His last walk-around was Oct. 22, 2010 at the age of 81.

GILL, WILLIAM F. (Willie the Clown) was born Feb. 16, 1922 in Biloxi, MS. While living in Port Neches, he petitioned Masonic Lodge #1163 A.F.&A.M. He continued through the Degrees, becoming a member of the Scottish Rite. On Nov. 15, 1958 he became a member of El Mina Shrine Temple A.A.O.N.O.M.S. of Galveston, TX.

Soon after, Bill joined the "Foot Patrol" of El Mina, and during one parade noticed a small bunch of clowns that did not march in a straight line — no, they were having fun, talking to the spectators and making the children laugh. In 1973 he joined the Nem Loof Clown Unit and that was the day Willie the Clown was born. Willie was elected president of the Nem Loof clown unit in 1978. He was generous to a fault when it came to supporting the Shriners Burns Hospital in Galveston.

GRAY, GORDON A. (Gordie) of Camas, WA, passed away on Jan. 27, 2005 at the age of 82. A lifetime Camas resident, Gordon was a WWII Prisoner of War while serving his country in the U.S. Army. During his tenure in the Army, he received three Bronze Stars and numerous other military honors. After the war, Gordon went to work for Crown Zellerbach, where he worked until his retirement.

Gordon loved his family, riding motorcycles, and was a member of the North Bank Masonic Lodge #182 F.&A.M. As a member of the Masons, Gordon served as both a Pastmaster of North Bank Lodge #182 F.&A.M., and as Past District Deputy of District #19. He was a member of the Lackamas Chapter #152 Order of East Star, a member of the York Rite Bodies, a member of the Afifi Temple of the Shrine, and a Shriners Clown.

Gordon is survived by his wife, Demetria "Dee" Gray; two nephews, James Gray and Steven Gray; two nieces, Teri and Dena; and one great-nephew and five great-nieces.

GREENE, WILLIAM VAUGHN JR. (Tugboat) of Vancover, WA, passed away at the age of 68. He served in the U.S. Navy during the Vietnam conflict.

Bill is survived by his mother, Annabelle Greene; brother, Jerry (Yvonne) Greene; special friend and companion of ten years, Maxine Sullivan; and his extended families.

GRILLS, HERB (Herbie) passed away on Dec. 18, 2011 at his winter residence in Arizona. Herbie was created as a Noble of the Mystic Shrine in Rameses Temple June 28, 1975. He was a member of the Sudbury and Hamilton Shrine Club and a life member of the Guelph and District Shrine Club, and served as president of Guelph District Shrine Club in 1989. He also served as Chaplain to the ISCA in 1994. His first Mid-Winter competition was in Galveston, TX and he never stopped after that.

After moving out west, he affiliated with Al Shamal Temple, Sept. 6, 1994 and immediately became a member of the clown unit. He was the first Canadian Chairman of the ISCA Sneaker Fund, 1996-2000. He was also an integral part of the original planning, development and implementation of the Al Shamal clowns "Ancient Order of the Red Noze" degree.

GRUBER, DR. LEE (Doc) passed away Dec. 19, 2012 at the age of 75 after a long illness. He was a member of the Yaarab Kennesaw Shrine Club, and active Shrine Clown for many years and was involved with the Boy Scouts of America. After graduating from Life University in Kennesaw, GA, he became a chiropractor and an instructor at the university. He made the gymnasium facilities available to the Red Devil Clowns for competition.

HAWKINS, JOHNNY SR. (Hawkeye) age 70, of Powder Springs, GA, passed away on Feb. 14, 2011. He was an active member of Kennesaw Shrine Club and more especially the Kennesaw Jokers, a club clown unit of Yaarab Shrine Center. He was a competitive Shrine

Clown from the time he became a Kennesaw Jokers member, where he served as president. He enjoyed drag racing as well as clowning. He was a devoted supporter of our Shrine Hospitals. He left behind a wife, two sons and their families.

JACKSON, BOB (Woody the Clown) passed away in 2011. He worked tirelessly for the Shrine, was the President of the Central States Shrine Clown Association and the Patient Transportation Chairman for Abdallah Shriners.

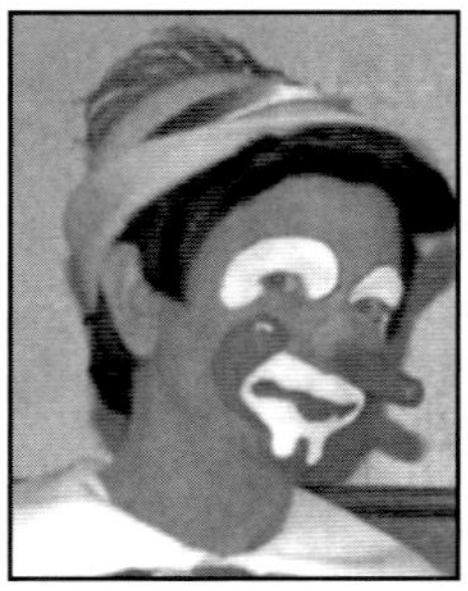

Besides being a championship clown, he worked as an antique furniture restorer and was an avid gardener. In addition to being an active member of Abdallah Shriners, he was a Past Master of Peace Lodge No. 243 in Louisburg, KS, and a KCCH in the Valley of Northeast Kansas, Scottish Rite in Overland Park, KS.

JENNINGS, DOUGLAS CHARLES (Raggs) passed away March 23, 2012 at the age of 72. Doug was born Jan. 8, 1940 in Kanas City, MO, the son of Douglas and Leone Jennings. He attended Washburn University and the University of Kansas. On April 20, 1968 he married his wife of nearly 44 years, Mary Ann, at St. Paul's Episcopal Church in Kansas City, KS.

In 1967 he was initiated into the Masonic Lodge and Abdallah Shrine in Kansas City. He transferred to the Arab Shrine in Topeka in 1972 and was instrumental in the formation of the Arab Shrine Keystone Kops, serving as the first director.

Later he joined the Arab Clown Unit as "Raggs", the tramp. He served as the clown unit treasurer for more than 30 years and was named Treasurer Emeritus. He was a good recruiter of Shriners and was awarded the Gold Medallion. He won a number of awards throughout the years in Central States Shrine Clown Assoc. skits, clown makeup and costume competitions. He was serving as chairman of the Arab Shrine Endowment Board and was an associate member in the Arab Golf Unit.

Doug was chosen as Arab Shriner of the Year in 2005.

JOHNSON, CHRIS K. (SPARKLES) a native of Rockford IL and member of Tabala Temple was visited by the Black Camel on Oct. 15, 2012 in Nashville TN. After rising to the degree of Master Mason in Loves' Park Lodge No. 1145 on April 19, 1972 Chris joined Tebala Temple on December 5, 1973, he was only 23 years old. Chris was elected to the ISCA line in San Antonio TX and worked his way through the ranks to President in 1987. He was inducted as President in Evansville Indiana on Feb. 28, 1987.

Chris spent most of his life in Rockford IL where he owned and managed a six store dry cleaning business appropriately named Sparkles Cleaners. After retirement Chris and his Lady Judy (Judimac) moved from Rockford to Austin Texas area for a short retirement before moving on to Nashville Tennessee for medical treatment.

During his time in the ISCA Chris was dedicated to serving others through clowning. He performed as both Sparkles a fun loving Auguste Clown and as Sparky a down and out Tramp Clown. He came to prefer Sparky and in his non-clowning life worked a lot with homeless men, helping them to better their lives.

As managing editor of *Clown Alley* from 1988-1996, Chris tried to encourage all Shrine Clowns to enjoy the wonderful camaraderie of the organization. He was an advocate of education to help clowns develop their clowning skills and included articles on all aspects of clowning including routines and clown history in the magazine.

Dedicated to the Shrine cause, Chris Johnson lived his Masonic Oath and helped many individual clowns and units achieve their professional skills and build their Sneaker Fund raising goals. Sparkles and Sparky received many awards including ISCA's Life Time Achievement Award and Emeritus Clown Alley Editor Award. Sparkles touched many lives both in and out of the Shrine.

JONES, FRANK (Digger) was born May 3, 1945 in Old Saybrook, CT. He walked the hot sands in 1981 at Sphinx Temple in Hartford, CT, and joined the Funsters in Nov. 1984. He became a life member in May 1995. Married to Rosemarie, the Black Camel called in March 2006.

KALOUSEK, LEROY STANLEY (Elroy the Clown) passed away June 17, 2012. He started his clowning life as a whiteface clown, but as years progressed he changed to a tramp clown. Known throughout the Central States Shrine Clown Association, he served as president of the CSSCA in 1988-89. He was also a member of Abdallah Shrine.

Elroy was born Feb. 3, 1918 in Kansas City, KS. He was a graduate of Wyandotte HS, class of 1936. He attended Kansas City Junior College then the University of Kansas before entering the U.S. Navy. He was a veteran of WWII (Pacific Theatre) and the Korean Conflict, retiring in 1963. He was a board member Emeritus of the USS Yorktown, CV-10, Mount Pleasant, SC. He was a Cherokee Indian Chief of the Y-Indian Guides. He was a Scoutmaster of Boy Scout Troop 380, a member of the Wyandotte No. 3 Masonic Lodge, Scottish Rite. He is survived by his wife of 56 years, Mary V. Kalousek, three children and two grandchildren.

KENDALL, WALTER E. "BUD" (Troubles) was born in St. Louis, MO. He and Rosa Maria Kendall were married Feb. 14, 1978. During WW II he earned two Bronze Stars. In 1950 he acquired Blust's Jewelry, which he operated until retirement on Jan. 1, 2000. His stepdaughter, Ramona Thornton, now owns Blust's Jewelry, which was established in 1915. "Bud" was a Horologist.

In 1950, "Troubles" was raised in Craftsman Lodge. He joined Moolah Temple, and walked the hot sands in 1978. In 1980 he joined the Moolah Clown Unit. "Troubles" was the Clown Director and Emeritus from 1990 to 2008; President of Central States Shrine Clown Association, Potentate Aide and Emeritus from 1990 to 2008; in 1996 was an Ambassador; in 1997 served as President ISCA and was Director of Royal Order of Jesters, 1994, Court 81. He also helped teaching costume and make-up and judging seminars with ISCA.

"Troubles" earned several clown

competitions awards from Central States Shrine Clown Association and ISCA competitions. He also received numerous Red Nose and Gold Nose Awards and over 40 1st, 2nd, and 3rd place for costume/make-up and skits.

Walter E. "Troubles" Kendall received the call of the Black Camel on April 13, 2008.

KINCHEN, WILLIAM (Wee Willie) of Cartersville, GA passed away May 18, 2011 after a long illness. He was known as a fierce competitor and a good friend. Formerly a member of the South Clayton Shrine Club, he later joined the Yaarab Red Devil Clowns, where he served as president.

He was honored as an inductee into the Red Devil Clowns Hall of Fame. Admission to the Hall of Fame requires a clown to have 20 years of service. His wife, Alice, was also very active in many clown activities.

KNICKERBOCKER JR., HAROLD A. (Skip) was born Aug. 27, 1930 in Manchester, CT. He walked the hot sands in June 1985 at Sphinx Temple, Hartford, CT and joined the Funsters on March 26, 1986. He became a life member on Oct. 24, 1996. Married to Janice, the Black Camel called on Oct. 16, 2009.

KROEGER, J. DOUGLAS (Happy the Clown) was born in 1923 in Louisville, KY. He and Lady Dorothy have four children.

Doug entered the Shrine at Nile Temple, Seattle, WA in 1962. Shortly thereafter his employer, Boeing, transferred him to New Orleans. He became "Happy the Clown" in 1963 in Jerusalem Temple. He retired from Boeing and clowning in 1988; 25 years of great clown adventures.

Happy was in many Shrine Circuses featuring the Wallindas and other great entertainers. Happy appeared on a TV show and was praised by Dom Deluis who, along with Happy, entertained the TV audiences and those in the studio.

Mardi Gras was one of the top activities for clowns in New Orleans and the surrounding communities. Happy enjoyed entertaining children, especially the kids in the Shrine Hospital in New Orleans. Happy was president of the Jerusalem Clowns and moved on to Philadelphia to continue his clowning for 14 years until retirement. After retirement Happy had many gigs, the best of which was roaming a women's prison entertaining 400 women. Happy was in the prison for over two hours among women in for minor crimes and one for murder. All the women were ladies and gave Happy many hugs.

Although he does not list a Shrine Clown group, his FEZ indicates he is a member of Sahib in Sarasota, FL. He does still do "a gig" when the opportunity arises.

Douglas Kroeger passed away June 1, 2011.

LINDQUIST, BUD (Bud, The World's Tallest Midget) passed away Dec. 13, 2012 at the age of 76 in Lake Arrowhead, Waleska, GA. Bud came to the Yaarab Red Devil Clowns Unit from the Za-Ga-Zig Shrine Clowns of Des Moines, IA.

He was a very active and competitive clown and served as President of the Red Devil Clowns and was inducted to the Red Devil Clowns Hall of Fame in 2004. He attended as well as judged at SESCA and ISCA conventions. He most recently judged the competition at the SESCA Convention in March 20212 held in Atlanta. In the early development of the ISCA *Clown Alley* magazine, he served as the Executive Editor for a short time. He will be greatly missed.

LITTLE SR., DAVID B. (Egore) was born Dec. 24, 1934 in Old Saybrook, CT. He walked the hot sands on Dec. 9, 1995 at Sphinx Temple, Newington, CT, and joined the Funsters on March 28, 1996. He became a life member on Nov. 16. 2006. Married to Pat, the Black Camel called on Feb. 7, 2009.

MARKS, C. CHARLES JR. (Eyes) passed away Aug. 18, 2011 after a long illness with diabetes. He was a long time Shriner and a member of the Historical Motor Unit until the unit folded, and he became a member of the Yaarab Red Devil Clowns. He was a past president of the Red Devil Clowns. He achieved what is considered the highest honor when he was inducted into the Red Devil Clowns Hall of Fame in 2006 for twenty years of service. He is survived by his wife Rachel, sons Wesley and Keith and his family.

MARSHALL, FRANCIS G. (Feffy) was born April 24, 1943 in Meriden, CT. He walked the hot sands in Dec. 1991 at Sphinx Temple in Newington, CT and joined the Funsters on May 28, 1992. He was a Past Master (1995 & 1996) at Unity Lodge #148, New Britain, CT, Connecticut Grand Lodge Association Marshall of District 5B in 2001 & 2002, and the Funster Chief in 2001 & 2002. Married to Kathy, the Black Camel called on July 21, 2010.

MEROLA JR., ANTHONY T. (Patches) was born May 18, 1937 in Manchester, CT. He walked the hot sands in Dec. 1980 at Sphinx Temple, Hartford, CT and joined the Funsters on Feb. 22, 1981. Married to Fran, the Black Camel called in Oct. 2002.

MORAN, WILLIAM T. (Wille-T) passed away Aug. 28, 2012 at Kindred Hospital in Louisville, KY at the age of 85. He was a member of Edmonds, WA Masonic Lodge, Scottish Rite of Seattle, and Nile Shrine. He became a clown in 1981. Wille-T was active in all clown activities. He served as president of Nile Clown Unit many times. He was Secretary of PNSCA for James Thoren and became president of PNSCA in 1989. Through his activities with clowns Bill became Circus Director of Nile Shrine for 12 years.

MUELLER, DON (Sunflower) passed away in Nov. 2012 at the age of 84 and was a member of the Yaarab Alpine Club in Helen, GA before joining the Yaarab Red Devil Clowns, where he was an active member. Don was Hospital Chairman for the Yaarab Temple and made over 260 trips to the hospitals in Greenville and Cincinnati.

Don was known as a quiet, easy going individual, and his character, Sunflower, probably came about from his bright costume and personality.

PEACOCK, JOHN "JACK" (Jjoops) passed away at the age of 67 on Feb. 1, 2012 following a courageous battle with cancer. He was a dedicated and devoted member of his church, lodge, the Shrine, Royal Arch Masons, Scottish Rite, and the Order of the Eastern Star.

He was initiated in Lynn Lake Lodge No. 170, Manitoba, Canada, Feb. 26, 1969. He affiliated with Gateway Lodge No. 164 in 1977 after moving to Edmonton, becoming their Worshipful Master in 1980. While at Fort McMurray, he affiliated with Fort McMurray Lodge No. 195 in 1983 and on his return to the Edmonton area, he affiliated with Baseline Lodge No. 198 in 2005. He was appointed Grand Steward for the Grand Lodge of Alberta in 2009 and made a Honorary Life Member of Fort McMurray Lodge No. 195 in 2010.

Jack became a Noble of Al Azhar Shrine in 1977 and later a charter member of Al Shamal in 1985. He was first a member of the Oriental Band and became a clown after his move to Fort McMurray. He served their unit as president, move out coordinator and several years as the secretary.

He was married to Fran, and had a daughter, Christine, and two sons, Toby and Robin.

RAMSEY, DR. GORDON BENDER (Doc) was born July 9, 1909. Dr. Ramsey served as an Army dentist in the Pacific

Theatre in WW II, and retired as a Lt. Colonel after serving 20 years in the Air Force Reserves. He was married to Martha Elizabeth Robinson Ramsey, and they had one daughter, Mrs. Claire Elizabeth Tischer.

During his career, he was a dentist, he wrote and taught a school program for Dental Assistants at State Technical School in Memphis, and also worked part-time as a truant officer at Memphis City Schools.

"Doc" Ramsey was raised in Masonic Lodge 919 in Kentucky on May 7, 1943. In Memphis he was first a member of Stonewall Lodge, then moved his membership to Oakville Lodge. He was also a member of Eastern Star at Oakville Lodge. His wife and daughter were members of the Daughter of the Nile and Eastern Star.

He joined Al Chymia Temple at Memphis, probably in the early 1950s. He was a member of Musketeers and the Clown Unit. His costume was usually as a hobo and he went by "Slim." Daughter Claire Elizabeth represented the Temple in the Cotton Carnival as Princess in 1957.

"Doc" served as President of the Clown Unit, President of S.E.S.C.A and was elected President Emeritus of the Unit.

The Masonic Lodge and Shrine was his life. He was very dedicated and was there almost every time the door opened. He believed wholeheartedly in the work.

Dr. Gordon Bender "Doc" Ramsey received the visit of the Black Camel on Nov. 1, 1981.

RIGGS, ROBERT LEE (Bebunk) 89, passed away Nov. 9, 2012 at Hillcrest Nursing Facility. He was born July 14, 1923 in McLean County, KY to Fred and Martha Riggs. He was preceded in death by his beloved wife, Martha J. Gipe Riggs, who passed away in 2002.

Robert was a member of First Christian Church for many years. He was a 32nd-degree Mason who belonged to the Hadi Shrine Temple. As a member of the shrine, he took on the identity of "Bebunk" the clown. He was known for his love of children and his kind, warm-hearted nature. Robert was young at heart at was known as Owensboro, Kentucky's oldest boy. He brought joy to many people.

Robert had two daughters, Barbara Latimore and Nancy Cox, five grandchildren and seven great-grandchildren.

RINER, RICHARD B. (Sparky) was born May 29, 1934 in Rocky Hill, CT. He walked the hot sands in May 1994 at Sphinx Temple, Newington, CT, and joined the Funsters on Sept. 22, 1994. Married to June, the Black Camel called on Dec. 30, 2000.

ROSS, THOMAS E. (Tommy Duck) was born March 6, 1948 at Pratt, KS. He served in the US Army from 1967 to 1969 with 18 months in Vietnam. On Dec. 3, 1983 he and Pat were married.

In May of 1973 Thomas was raised in Oak Forest Lodge #832. He walked the hot sands on Nov. 17, 1973 at Medinah Temple. He joined the Medinah Clowns Unit in July 1998.

Thomas was Master of Oak Forest Lodge #832 in 1994. He was Deputy Shrine Club Director; President of Illinois Central Shrine Club for 12 years and Appearance Chairman for Clown Unit for 13 years. In 2009 "Tommy Duck" was made Ambassador to Medinah Temple. In 2010, he was Sneaker Ambassador at Large for Eastern States. He earned two Red Rose awards.

Thomas E. "Tommy Duck" Ross was called by the Black Camel on July 21, 2010.

RUSSELL, JAMES L. LT. COLONEL (Dune Buggy) was born in Nashville, TN, June 5, 1938. Attained his BS Agriculture, Middle Tennessee State University 1960. He entered active duty US Army, 1961.

James is a graduate of Infantry Officer Basic Course, Ordnance Career Course, Command and General Staff College. He is a retired Lt. Colonel, US ARMY Reserve.

"Dune Buggy" retired Veterinary Drug Sales, Elanco Products Co., Div. Eli Lilly & Co. He is a contract employee of Georgia Peanut Commission special promotions as Dune Buggy the Clown, Peanut Circus Shows. He has been a consumer spokesman for the peanut industry since 1980. Performing 500 shows annually, entertaining over 500,000 children per year as a professional clown, magician, balloon sculpturist. Dune Buggy was rated #7 in 1982 and #5 1983 nationally by *Clown Chatter* magazine.

He is an author, Dean of Clown School, Lecturer, Editor *Clowning Around* magazine, World Clown Association 2000-Present, World Clown Association, "Clown of the Year" 2004. The only clown in the world to hold elective office in all four major clown organizations. James is a Life member of COA-COAI, Regional Vice President.

He is a Charter Life Member WCA Regional Director, Ambassador of Clowns IBM Order of Merlin with Shield. SAM. James is a Life Member, AL SIHAH Shrine Temple, Macon, GA Royal of Scotland. He is also a Life Member NSCA-ISCA, Past President 1973-74, Chairman of two ISCA Mid-Winters, Macon and Columbus, GA

Sneaker Fund was started during his Presidency. The first check for $800.00 was turned over to Imperial Sir Jacob Wingerter in Bridgeport, CT in 1974. Noble Abe Flaks presented the idea of the Sneaker at the Atlanta Imperial Session 1973. NSCA voted and adopted the project.

James passed away on Jan. 25, 2011 at the age of 72.

WHITENETT, CLARENCE EDWARD (Stripes) was born June 28, 1925 in Holyoke, MA and passed away peacefully at the age of 87 at the Red Deer Regional Hospital on Nov. 16, 2012. His career was a school teacher, principal and assistant superintendent in various communities in central and northern Alberta, Canada.

Ed was a member of the Masonic fraternity, serving in many local and district offices as well as a member of Eastern Star. He was a member of Al Azhar Shriners, Calgary, Alberta and Al Shamal, Edmonton, Alberta. He was a past president of the Battle River Shrine Club, Camrose, Alberta and the Red Deer Shrine Club, Red Deer, Alberta. Ed's enjoyment in the shrine was clowning. He was president twice of the Pacific Northwest Shrine Clown Association and president of the ISCA, Shriner's International in 2005-06.

Ed was survived by his wife Doreen.

WINDBIEL, MANFRED (Choo Choo) passed away at the age of 74 on Sept. 16, 2011 after a courageous battle with cancer. A cherished husband and father, he was married to Louise for 53 years and had five children: Debby, Kerry, Coreen, Jackie, and George, 18 grandchildren, and 10 great-grandchildren.

Fred was very dedicated to the Masonic fraternity, having served as Worshipful Master for both North Star Lodge No. 167 and Dormer Lodge No. 19. He served as District Deputy Grand Master in 2004-05. He is a past Grand Guardian of Job's Daughters International. He was a member of the Gizeh Vancouver Clown Unit under the clown name of "Choo Choo", a name he acquired as a result of his past railroad career. Choo Choo was an active member of the Shrine Pacific Northwest Clown Association.

ZIMDARS, RICHARD (Goldy) passed away Dec. 9, 2012 at the age of 81 after a long illness. Richard was originally a member of Tripoli Temple in Milwaukee before becoming an active member in the Yaarab Red Devil Clowns in Atlanta. He enjoyed dual membership in other temples as well. He had clowned since 1977 and was active as a competitor and a judge for GLSCA, SESCA and ISCA. In 1982, he was selected by the Circus World judges as the 2nd "Best All-Around Clown" at the Mid-Winter in Orlando, FL. He was inducted into the Yaarab Red Devil Clowns Hall of Fame in 2009.

"Sparky" Macaulay and his granddaughter, Erin.

The Damascus Shrine Clowns in 1987.

The Zor Flambeau Clowns.

El Mecca Clowns. Back row: Steve Lawson, Max D. Eaton, Dean Wiarda, Doug Starbeck, Del Miller, Bob Thompson. Second row: Roger Tesch, Bud Foster, Bob Morris, Wil Clark, Blair Brewer, Dave Susong. Front row: Joy Hays, James Buchwald and Jerry Irwin. Members not in picture are Ken Erickson, Jack Fliehler, Jack Hoffman, Bill Morse, Bud Waychoff, Richard Holen and Harry Boardsen.

The Kena Klowns.

ISCA Membership Roster

as of January 2013

Names listed include the member's name and clown name

-A-

Carl T. Aaron (Sergeant Shriner)
Terry Aaron (Chopper)
Michael Aaron (Muggsy)
Louis Abbotoni (Palou)
Donald Achen (Bucky)
Tom Acker (Tender Tommy)
Larry Ackerman (Little Willie)
Steven Ackermann (Bubbles)
Jack Acre (Tub)
James Adams (Candyman)
Peter Adams (Toppy)
Leroy Adams (Sparky)
Jeffrey Adams (Wow-E)
Michael Aders
Shaun Adkins (Burpee)
Jim Ahlquist (Buttons)
Ron Alberty (Babe)
Elmer Alderdyce (Elmo)
Steve Aldi (Snickers)
Nathanail Alexander
John Alexander (Tiny)
Clive Allan (Topper)
Kelly Allen (Juggles)
Wendell Allen
David M. Almquist (Choochoo)
Glenn Almy (Country)
Barry Alpern (Strawbarry)
Mark Alvarado (Kuko)
William Amspaugh (Steins)
Albert Anderson (Bently)
Dale Anderson (Checkers)
Harlan Anderson (Dinger)
Mark W. Anderson (Joker)
Melvin Anderson (Prince Andrew)
Roger Anderson (Skis)
Orren Anderson (Buttons)
Donald Anderson (Hearty)
Jack Anderson
Dick Andres (Dickie)
Jay Andres (Puddles)
Brad Andrews (Shutterbug)
Mike Andrews
Gary Angell (Duffer)
Paul Apostelos (Popeye)
Edward Aranda (Gears)
Guy Arbez (Gigglzz)
Rick Arends (Trickle)
Paul Arft (Poncho)
Terry Armentrout (Q-T)
Jeffery Arnold (Band Aide)
Thomas Arnold (Tom)
Carl Arron (Sergent Shriner)
Louis Arroyo (Flat Foot)
George Robert Astin (Buddy-B)
Sam Astin
Joel Asunskis (Lunch Pail)
Lorne Attenborough
Dennis Augustin (Klown 1)
Sidney Austin (Kilowatt)
John D. Autry (Fire Plug)
Frederick M. Ayers (Windy)

-B-

Ron Baas (Hulapopper)
E.C. Babbert (Ears)
Thomas E. Babbs (Knucklehead)
Brad Babinski
Ronald Bach (Pa Pa)
Tim Bachman (Bubbles)
David Bahmer (Tic Toc)
Les Bailey (Harlie)
James Bailey (Smilin Jack)
Robert Bailey
Harry Baillie (Bobby)
Joseph Baird (Jo Jo)
Charles Baker (Chuckles)
William Baker (B B)
Bob Baker (Bumbles)
Stan Baker (Papi)
Tom Balfour (Tomie)
Darold Ball (Disco)
James Ball (Jeb)
Gordon Bane (Gizzy)
Christopher Bang (Jolly)
Robert Banka (Huggy)
Michael Barboza (BB Blue)
John Bardes (Sparky)
Bob Bardy (Wilbee)
Richard Barker (Momo The Hobo)
Newell Barker (Sureshot)
Newell Barker (Sure Shot)
Daniel Barkley
Harry Barnes (Skip)
Brian P. Barnes (Shaggy)
Dennis Barnett (Uncle Witty)
Lynn Barnett (Spanky)
David Barnett (Shorty)
David Barnhart (Barney)
Rod Barrand (Brandi)
Alan Barrett (Smokey)
Kenneth Barrett (Bumblebee)
Fred Barron (Gumpy)
Charles Barron (Fuzzie)
Richard Bartlett (Joey)
Robert Barton (Tuitt)
Al Basner (Yum Yum)
Sam Bass (Zipper)
Robert Bassett (Peaches)
Mark Bassett
Doug Bastendorf (Snickers)
Philip Bateau (Mopsy)
John Bateman (Toto)
Robert L. Bateman (Bubi)
Charles Bates (Wire Nut)
Roy L. Baver (Smokey)
Jim Baxter (Jimbo)
Bob Baxter (Tater)
Richard Beall (Uncle Richie)
Ricky Bean (Trix / Rags)
William E. Beard (Windy Willie)
Ralph Beasley Sr. (Buttons)
Robert Beck (Pa Paw)
Barry Bede (Speedy)
Cody Ray Beech (Nic Nac)
Dennis L. Belford (Mtl Muffin)
William Bell (Ding-Dong)
Alan Bell (Ding Dong)
Dick Bement (Bozo)
Kevin Bemiss
Alan Bennett (Pokey)
William B. Bennett (Bilbo)
James Bennett (Ginjo)
William Bennett (Willie)
Andrew Bennett
C.J. Bennett (Wheels)
Gary Bennett (Gee Bee)
Donnie Benson (Fluffy)
Woodruff Bentley (Woody)
Robert N Benwell (Spike)
Archer Benzel (Kopper)
Kim D. Berg (Digger)
Gary Berger (Raw Dawg)
Dave Bergeson
Eric Bergstrom (Lug Nut)
Mark Berillo (Bubbles)
John Berry (Shef)
Warren Betts (Buttons)
Carey Wayne Beverly
Robert Bickel (Bobo)
Dale Bieber (Bago)
Alden Bietz (Giggles)
Benny Bigler (Bengy)
Don Billings (Duddle)
David Bills (Re Boot)
Tony Birchall (Big Toe)
Billy Bird (Bling Bling)
James Birdwell (Nickel)
Tracy Bishop (Dr Not Yet)
Richard Bishop (Smiley)
Scott Bishop (Scooter)
Chris Biskner (Chrispy)
George Bisson (Fingers)
Bill Black (Billy)
Carl (Bud) Black
James Blackburn (Bimbo)
Vernon B Blackburn (Jingles)
Jeff Blair (Scoop)
Mike Blais (Bow)
Douglas R. Blajszczak (Atila)
Jim Blake (Jimbo)
Jim Blake (Buzz)
Michael Blankenship (Po Po)
David Allen Blanks (Jester)
Darrell Blenniss (Opa)
James Blevins (Prof. Tuddy)
Brian Block (Bo Bo)
Bruce Blodget (Moochie)
Richard Blowers (Top Hat)
Ed Blum (Zounds)
Karl Boehl (Popcorn)
Richard Boettger (Shaker)
Donald Bohannon Jr. (Bobo)
Joey Boheman (Bucko)
Michael Bohlman (Clueless)
Jacques Boily
Joseph J.R. Boivin (Jeanno)
Ray Bolding (Togo)
John Bolton (Hartz)
Dayton Bolyard (Uncle Buck)
Farley W. Bomar (Fabo)
Richard P. Bond (Huggy)
Robert Bone (Bones)
John G. Booker (Tic Toc Doc)
William Bookwalter (Boo-Boo)
Jack Bope (Bope)
Randy Bope (Curly)
Donald J. Bordelon, Sr. (Sparky)

David B. Borgeson (Let You Know?)
Robert Bornstein (Dapper)
Drew Borske (Scraps)
Peter Bosse (Dr. Lottafun)
Robert Bossen (Bozie)
Timothy Bossert (Boz)
Leroy Bossier (Patches)
Richard C. Bosworth (Curly)
Murray Botterill (Tag)
Scott Boucher (Scooter)
Ernie Boulicault (Shamrock)
William Bovard (Bovy)
Gene Bowie (Bow Wow)
Jerome H. Boxer (Spuds)
Richard Boyce (Apples)
Ronald Boyd (Shoestring)
Robert Boyd (Poncho)
Glen Dale Boyd (Blimpo)
Terry Boyer (Stinky)
Chad Boyles (Checkers)
Gene Bracewell
Henry Bradley (Spike)
Bart Bradley
Derrick Bradley (Dusty)
Martin Bradt (Shuffles)
Christopher Braeuel (Teddy Bear)
Dexter Bragas (Check Mate)
Stan Brake (Happy Too)
James Brakefield (Uncle Sam)
David Brannon (Taterbug)
Les Branson (Mr. More)
Bruce C Brege Jr. (Brucie)
Dennis Breheny (Shorty Circuit)
Larry Breland (Crumby)
Travis Breuer (Happy Jack)
Ben Brewer (Kidder)
Les Bridges (Fancy)
Ron Briggs (Digger)
Robert Brinkley (Splotchee)
Larry Brisbois (Dandy)
Antonio Brisco (Brisco The Clown)
Harold L. Brock (Dusty)
Matthew Brodeur (Dusty)
Richard Brodeur (Hoppy)
John Bronius (Boomer)
Michael W. Brooks (Tunes)
Craig Brooks (Hollywood)
Norm Brooks Bee Bop)
Randol Brookshier (Kolohe)
Bob Brotherton (Loop Hole)
Isaac Brower-Berkhoven (Brockli)
James Brown (Putz)
Greg Brown (Buttons)
Fred Brown (Noodles)
Larry Brown (Uffda)
J. C. Brown (Bumbles)
Duncan Brown (Dr Dunc)
Brian Brown (Poo Poo)
Daniel Brown (Spanky)
Jason Brown (Joe Boo)
Ronnie Brown (Useless)
John P. Brown (Copper)
Carl M Brown (Charlie Bro)
Don Brown (Snoozo)
Verlon Brown, Jr
Verlon Brown, Sr
Turl D. Browning (Turtle)
Bill Broyles (Bill Bo)
Martin W. Bruce
Johnny Brunac (Twee Dee Buttons)
George Bruner (Bruno)
Rick Brunsdon (Tex)
John Bruski (Grumpy)
James Bruton (Jim-Bo)
Joe T. Bryan (Hopscotch)
David Bryant (Bumps)
John Bryant (Seaweed)
Allen Bryant (Boomer)
Lawrence V. Bryant (Fat Rita)
Sandy Buchan (Sundae)
John Buchanan (Buzzer)
Chris Buckius (Yippy)
Jason Buckley (Mac Smilie)
Bob Bukowski
Mike Bulger (Slap Shot)
Larry Bumgarner (Bum Fuzz)
Kenneth Burcham (Peanut)
Dwayne Burckhard (Snippy)
Mark Burgad (Buzzy)
Jim Burger (Kazoo)
Gary Burke (Smirky)
Lon Burke (Cactus)
Dennis Burkholder (Skooter)
Lawrence Burleigh (Specs)
Peter Burlock (Digby)
Ron Burnett (Doormat)
Kyle Burns (Dimple)
Bob Burr (Nickels)
Kenneth Burse (Lamb Chop)
Fred Burt (Freddy)
Bob K. Burt (Okie)
Kent Bushard (Gizmo)
Frederick Buss (Punch)
Clarence Butler (Skooter)
Rob Butler
Charles Butler (Fudd)
Jim Butler (Jimbo)
William Butrica Sr. (Willard The Wiz)
Bobbie Byers (Boo Boo)
John M. "Mike" Byrd (Salty)

-C-

David D Caddick (Digger)
Frank Caffey (Rusty)
James Cagle (Bubba)
G. Eugene Cagle (Trouble)
Melvin Cain (Chunky)
Richard Cain (R.C.)
Patrick Calabro (Oops)
Jim Calcutt (Steamer)
Scott Caldwell (Kazoo)
Jerry W. Callahan (Hollihan)
Steve Callaway (Pops)
Mike Calli (Cappy)
William Callister (Decie)
John G. Calver (Bernie)
Dale Calverley
Warren R. Campbell (Beans)
Graham D. Campbell (Beeper)
Patrick Canavan (Dr Cuddles)
Earl Canfield
Bill Canning
Gene Cantrell (Sawdust)
Harry Cantrell (Harry O)
Nazario Cantu, III (Tucan)
Luis Cardenas Luigi Pekas)
Mark Cardin (Salty)
Joseph Cardone (Willy Nilly)
Jack Carey (Chuckles)
John Carey (Snowball)
Jackie Carl (Little Toot)
Brian Carlson (Uni)
Harold Carmichael (Flash)
Duncan Carmichael (Butch)
Edward Carmona (Kwoko)
Milan Carnes
Edward H. Carney (Gusto)
Stephen Caron Jr (Ruffles)
Fred Carpenter (Reddy)
Steve Carroll (Sparky)
Robert Carter (Ducky)
Morris Carter (Candy Man)
Jeff Carter (Cee Jay)
Ricky L. Carter (Ziggy)
Richard Caruso (Fuzzy)
Bill Case (Jiggs)
Bill Case (Toot)
Lee Casey
Thomas M. Casey (Tom)
Stan Casner (Ta-Ta)
Javier V Castaneda (Choo Choo)
Michael Castelan (Poppy)
Carlos Castro (Jollee)
Juan Castro (Papo)
James A Causey (Giggles)
Damon Cavan
William Cayton (Gofer)
Laurel Celander (Hey)
Kermit Centers (Frog)
Robert Cepielik (Jingles)
Chester Chabot (Pansy)
Michael Chambers (Tags)
Frank Chambrovich (Dimples)
Ron Chaple (Flower Pot)
James Chapman (Crackers)
William Chappell (Smilo)
James Chastain (Jimbo)
Patrick Cheng (Tappy)
John Cherry (Sunnie)
Robert Chesser (Strike Out)
Shelby A. Chestnut
Paul Chhina (Goofey - Golfer)
Phillip Choat (Goober)
Harry Choate (Hoogey)
Ron Choina (Cappy)
Keith Christensen (Kaysee)
Donald W Churchill (Nibbles)
Daniel Cialariello
John A Cinotto
Michael Clark (Bucket Head)
Tom Clark (Tea Sea)
Ronald Clark (B R)
Ross Clark Sparky)
Nick Clausen (Pooky)
Charles Clauss (Chazz)
Chris Clauss (Kringle)
Charles A. Claypool
W.R. Clayton (Tobby)
Al Clegg (Poppi)
Mike Clemenhagen (Clem)
Craig Clendening (Flash)
Jed Clifford (Shamrock)
James Clinton (Pee Wee)
J. B. Cloud (Jellybean)
Oscar Cloutier (Clyde)
Toby's Clown Foundation (Toby The Clown)
Roy Clugston
Tom Clukey (Clukey)
James Cobb (Klutz)
Craig Cobb (Ding-A-Ling)
Kevin Cobb (Kevo)
Donald Cochrane (Muggs)
Mike Coffey (U Who)
Daniel Cofone (Dok)
David Cohen
Howard Cohen (Cuz)

James Cohen (J-Bob)
Cary Cohn (Ump)
Andrew Coiley (Camo)
James Coker (Bubbles)
Joe Curtis Cole (Ol Coach)
Dion Cole (Rumples)
Douglas Collier (Kuku)
Jim Collins (Slapshot)
Fredric R. Collins (Mr. Hapi)
Robert L. Collins (Happy A Clwn)
Scott Collins (Scooter)
David Colson (Wormy)
Jeff Colson (Midget)
Ricky J. Colwell (Pogo)
Bob Comer (Plow Boy)
William Condon (Willie)
Leroy J. Conley (Lumpy)
Bob Conrad (Tin Cup)
Joseph Consolo (Judgie)
Ross Contella (Mr Bibbs)
Edward Coobs
Craig Cook (Dinky)
Michael R. Cook (Rusty)
Ken Cooke (Koo Kee)
Walt Jr. Cooley (Hick)
Kelvin Cooper (Coop)
John Cooper (Jay-Jay)
Bill Copley (Gramps)
Jesse Copple (Oops)
Bobby Joe Corbell (Lum)
Nelson K. Corbin (Baby Face)
Paul Cormier (Haystack)
Norm Cormier (Giggles)
Timothy Cornell (Wheels)
Gary Cornell (Blue Note)
Ray Cornett (Bail Out)
John L Cornett (Smurf)
Jerry Correll (Yoyo)
Thomas Cory, Phd (Hugger)
Robert Cosh (Roco)
Tommy Coskey (Zero)
David S Coughlin (Solly)
Mitchell Coulthard (Frost Byte)
Don Coutoumas (Angus)
Jonathan Cowen (Y-U-Ask)
Bruce Cowie (Smiley)
Jim Cox (Frenchee)
Charles Crabtree (Flatfoot)
Jerry Craft (Cheesy)
David Crane (Junior)
Paul E Crane, Jr. (Chef Kris Ko)
JC Crawford (Squatty Body)
Ken Crawford (Bugsby)
Ron Crawford (Rosee)
Floyd Creekmore (Creeky)
Robert A. Crego (Re Go)
Robert Crisp (Box Car Bobby)
Doug Crocker (What)
Leon Crockett (Growly Bear)
Dana Crockett (Clipper)
Adrian E. Croissant (Fatso)
Milo Cropley (Gampy)
Dean Crowley (Shamrock)
Ron Crowley (Handy Hobo)
Travis Crum
Richard Cruz (Popo)
Bruce Cuco (Patches)
Kenneth Cullum (Popcorn)
Stephen Cummins (Smoothie)
Charles Cumpstone, Jr.
Ryan Cunningham (Bengal)
William Cunningham (Inky)
H. David Cunningham (Binny)
Jeff Curry
Carl Curty (Twinky)

-D-

Paul Dafoe (Paul-O)
J. Dalby (Colonel)
Harry Dapre, Jr (Chuckles)
Arron Kai Daquio (Dags)
Ray Dark (Radar)
Jesse E Daugherty (1st In 10)
Bill Davidson (Billy Bob)
Jon A. Davies (Boxcar Jonnie)
Fred Davila (Confetti)
Roger Davis (Jojo)
Jim Davis (Snooky)
Tom Davis
Ralph Davis (Sir Ralph)
Rick Davis (Pap)
Kevin Davis (Bobo)
Mike Davis (Scotty)
C. Ron Davis (Duffer)
Butch Davis (Huh)
Kenneth E. Davis (Kadee)
Alex Davis (Oh! Boy!)
Joe Davis (Uh! Oh!)
Ralph L. Davis
Kevin Davis (Scooter Scoot)
Scott Dawson (Shaggy)
Ross Dayton (Funny Bone)
Robert De Graff (Bugs)
Mark Dean (Wally)
Terry Dean (Ima Cop)
Michael Deavilla (Yowza)
Darrell Debo (Dee Bo)
Don Deboard (Speed Bump)
Lanny Decker (Lilweasel)
James V. Defonso (Fonzi)
Lloyd Degonia (Skippy)
Nicholas Delcimmuto (Popcorn)
Wayne Dell (Relic)
Scott Dell (Happy)
Kenneth Dellhime (Gold Dust)
Kris Delong (Poe Goe)
William H Dement (Whistlestop)
Lee Demerchant (Mokanic)
Harrie Demers (Bobo)
Robert Demery
Bryan Deming (Squiggles)
James Demoss (Jammer)
Edward Dempsy (Smelt)
Remeo Denghel (Shaggy)
Dave Denis (Busta)
Irv Denune (Fuzzy)
Neil Depue (Peppe)
Henry Desenberg (Teddy Bear)
Ken Devore (Green Bean)
Val Devuyst (Bubby)
Arlen Dewall (Squeaker)
Ken Dewey (Crasher)
Goldie Dewitt (Goldi)
David Dickson (Twinkle Toes)
James Diem (Hopper)
Lawrence E. Dietz (Klipper)
Bob Dill (Dill Pickle)
James Dillinger (Pork Chop)
James Dingman (Dinger)
Paul Disbennett (Not Yet)
Bob Disher (Chuckles)
Bob Disler (Dizzy)
Joe Disper (Sunflower)
Lloyd Ditmars (Ditto)
Jeff Dixe (Pa Pa)
Peter Doebener (Buttons)
John Doman (Whiskers)
Joe Donato (Sparkey)
Greg Dortch (Boomer)
Darryl R. Dortch
Randall Douglas (Woo Woo)
Fred Dow (Snicklfritz)
Ray Dowd (Choo Choo)
Edward Dowling (Pea Pa)
Jack Dowling
Michael D. Downey (Kit Karson)
Charles Drennan (Lucky Chucky)
Jeff Dresch (Noodles)
Fred Drew (Derf)
Tom Drudi (T-Kat)
Shawn Dube (Disco)
Ian Duchart (Imotay)
Johnny B. Dudley (Do Rite)
Robert Duffy (Chappy)
Mike Dugal (Doogie)
Erv Duke (Little Toot)
Leon Dumstrey-Soos (Go Go)
Rod Duncan (Puddin)
Robert R Duncan Sr. (Pappy)
Brandon Dunn (Snickers)
Gary W. Dunwoody
Jim Dura
Edward H Durham (Lemon Drop)
Walter J Dury (Phoo Phoo)
Gerard Dwan (Qwerty)
Denis Dyer (Fuz)
Richard Dyess (Okie Dokie)
Charles Dyke (Creepy Mouse)

-E-

Jim Eaches (Smiley)
Dan Eacret (Darned)
David E Earlam (Davee)
Freddy Easley (Crickett)
Guy Eastberg (Sparky)
Phil Easterman (Chipper)
George Eaton (Jolly)
William Eaton (Billbo)
Gus Eckert
Wm. S. Edge
Dwight Edmonson
Ralph Edwards (Li'l Ralphie)
Jeff Edwards (Skippy)
Chris Edwards (Bitz)
Michael Edwards (Big Topper)
Rich Eilsworth (Pookie)
Phil Elery (Whut?)
Robert Elkin (Waki)
Phillip Elkins (Philly)
Chris Ellard (Kwivers)
Ron Ellenson (Roneee)
Todd Elliot (Sky Hook)
Richard Ellis (Sporty)
Dan Elmore (Cravin)
Gregory Elmore (Elmo)
Howard Eloe (Howdy)
Mike Elsbernd
Roger Elsbury (Rainbowillie)
Paul Emerson
Jeff Emge (Fuzzy)
Anton Endler (Rosebud)
Orville (Jim) England (Rainbow)
Ryan Engle (Pappy)
Maurice English (Mo)
Bill Enloe (U-Hoo)
John Enloe (Tater)

Richard Entrican (Zero)
Brad Epling (Smiley)
Richard Epstein (Checkers)
Ian Erdos (Bakin)
Dave Erickson (Bogie)
David Erickson (Bogie)
Kenneth A. Ericson (Knickers)
Fernando Escabi (Echo)
Victor Estrada (Bubblies)
C. Mich Ethier (Fuzzy)
Reggie Eugley (Jasper)
Robert Evans (Pip)
Paul Evans (Billy Bob)
Lester Evans (Mr Clown)
James E Everett, Jr. (Doctor D)
Scott R Ewell (Turbo)

-F-

Tom Fairchild (Scooter)
Mike Falkenstein (E-Moe)
James Fankhanel (Happy Frank)
Robert Fanning (Checkers)
Tim Farrar (Yo Yo)
James Farrell (Kuffs)
Brian Farries (Prince Apple)
Robert Farrington (Robo)
John Farris (Farriswheel)
Robert A. Farrow (Mayday)
Harold Farrow (Boss Hog)
Ray Fautheree (Gadget)
Carl Fauver (Prof. Perkins)
Willard E. Fawcett, Jr.
Steve Fay (Fayzo)
Tony Feagley (Peenuts)
Larry Feinstein (Chappie)
Dennis Feister (Rocky)
Howard Feldman (Toots)
Richard Fellows (Ladders)
Patrick Fenner (Bucho)
Richard Ferber (Duffy)
Jim Ferguson (Bumps)
Richard Ferguson (Twinkles)
Michael G. Ferguson (Scooby-Doo)
Richard Ferranto (Seal Beam)
Ralph Ferree (Jingles)
Gil Ferrer (Zippy)
Christopher J. Fetko (Loki)
Harry Fiebig (Trubble)
Dan Fierimonte (Monte)
Graham Finch (Soda)
Ronald L. Fine (Mugsy)
Donald Fink (Stinky)
Douglas Fink (Finky)
Raymond Fink (Ramondo)
Daryl Finley (Hi Pockets)
Dennis W. Fischer (Nitro)
Charles Fischer (Fishy)
Dick Fisher (Mr. Buttons)
Timothy Fisher (Shutter Bug)
Bobby Fisher (Bofish)
Peter Fisher (Merlin)
Robert Fitch (Bingo)
Mike Fitzgerald Kopper)
John D. Flaherty (Shamus)
John Wilson Fleming (Bigfoot)
Wayne Fleming (Sparky)
Enrique Flores (Kikin)
Chris Fluharty (Billie Bob)
Matthew J. Flynn (Wood-E)
Terry Font (T-Bone)
Michael Ford (Splatter)
James Ford Jr. (Pockets)
John Forden (Nuttin)
Nick Forgit (Pocket Change)
Ron Forney (Funny)
Doug Foss (Dr. Funn E Bone)
Stephen W Foster Sparky)
Donald Foster (Taffy)
Donatien Fournier (Dee Cee)
John R. Fowler (Checkers)
Lyle Fox (Foxy)
Earl Frady (Squirrel)
Doug Fralick (Popkorn)
Clint Frank (Cuddles)
Michael Frankel (Mickey)
Charles D. Franklin (Felix)
John Fraser (Teez)
Chris Fratello
Dwight L Frater (Happy)
Norm Frazier (Stormin)
Glenn Frealy (Ip)
John Frederick (Barley)
Travis Freeman
Felix Freeman (Flat Top)
Raoul L. Frevel
James Kevin Frey (Chip)
Scott Frink (Smitty)
Jim Fritz (Fritz)
Kent Fronk (Bagger Vance)
Douglas Fry (B B)
Dietrick Frye (Gramps)
Jim Frye (Squeek E)
Jack Fuller
Donald Fuller (Dr Chuckles)
Paul Fulton Gimpy)
William Furlong (Fuzzy)
Robert Furmidge (Fuzzy)
Michael R Fussell (Butterbean)
Charles A Fustish

-G-

Douglas Gabel (Bullseye)
Don Gaddie (Pazazz)
Andrew Gagliano (Sun Shine)
William J. Gainey (Jolly)
Robert Gale (Robby)
Jerry M. Gallman (Buster Brown)
Mark Galloway (Dizzie)
Mike Galvin
Sherman A Gamble (Spangle)
Jerry G. Gantt
Dane Garcia (Dizzy)
Eric Garcia (Gizmo)
Ricky W. Gardner (Rozco)
Keith Gardner (Kgar)
Gary Garfola (Choo Choo)
Robert Garner (Chipper)
Allen Garnett (Boomer)
H.C. "Bud" Garrison (Bayou Bubba)
Nicholas Garrity (Niko)
Brad Gasmund (Tiny)
Richard Gauer (Pepper)
Robert Gean (Bones)
Edward Gee (Dusty)
Steve Gehring
Dan Genners
Earl Genter (Buzzy)
Michael Gentry (Howie Diddit)
Claude D. Gentry (Slapstick)
Bill Gentry
James Gentry Sr. (Cabbage)
Thomas George (Spangles)
Lou George (Kaboom)
Daniel George (Porkey)
Jonathan F. George, Sr. (Dimples)
Robert Gerhard (Deputy Dawg)
James German (Beep Beep)
Dennis Gesel (Mr. Fix-It)
Bill Gher (Duster)
Jim Gibson (Skeeter)
Larry Gibson (Qwakkers)
Dave Gienger (Gramp's)
Kenneth Gilbert (Babycakes)
Edward Gilchrist (Mr. Ed)
H. Rusty Giles (Dusty-Rusty)
Jeffery "Jeff" Giles (Patches)
Jonathan Gill (Zig Zag)
Kenneth L Gillespie (Dizzy)
Neil Gilligan (Honker)
Michael Gingrich (Chatter Box)
Dominic Gionfriddo (Dizzy)
Philip Giorgetti
Marius W. Girard (Su_Iram)
Sam Giroux (Root-N-Tootin)
Fred Gischler (Hobo Freddy)
Michael Givler (Nails)
Warren Glass (Firecracker)
Gregory Gleason (Hoss)
Dick Glessing (Happy)
Joseph Glorioso, Jr. (Sir Raggs)
Larry Glover
Stephen M. Glushakow (Buttercup)
Jim Godsey (Scooter)
Kenny Godwin (Lightnin)
Terry L. Godwin (Tater)
James P. Godwin, Jr.
Al Goehring (Funzo)
Bruce Goin (Beegee)
Terry Goins (Choo Choo)
Howard E Gold (Goldy)
Larry G. Golden (Surfer Dude)
Nick Goltra (Repete)
Ron Gongaware (RL)
Edmund C. Goodfield
Jerry Goodman (Goody)
Rex Goodman
Calvin Goodman (Tiny)
Delbert Goodwin
Keith Goolsby (Sneaky)
Robert Goosen (Goose)
Robert Gordon (Buzz B)
N. Angus Gordon (Cookee)
Donnie Gosselin (Silly Goose)
Steve Gotham (Stevo)
Richard Gottschlich (Gotcha)
Ken Graham
Jose Grajales (Pipiolo)
Lindy Graves
Roger L. Gray (Poor O Roger)
Alfred Gray (Freckles)
Ken Grayson (Happy)
Joseph Grbac (Meatball)
Scott Greaney (Turkey Lips)
Willie Green (Kraker Jak)
Richard Greene (Putter)
Bill Greenen (Hey Hay)
Laurence Greenlee (Larz)
Robert Greer (Tiny)
Curt Gregory (Banty)
Emil Greiner (Gizmo)
Mike Grenadier
Paul Griffin (Griffy)
Robert P Grimaldi (Bucky)
Terry Griswold
Harold L. Grogan (Buckshot)
Louis Gross (Gee Wiz)

Jarrod Grudzinski (Tiny)
Kevin Guest (Mungo)
Jim Guest (Gabbyhobo)
John N. Guidry (Band-Aid)
Brian Gulbranson (Bubba)
Harlan Gurney (Spud)
Larry Gustafson (Gustie)
Nick Guthro (Happy)

-H-

Micah Haas (Scooter)
Van Haas (Jasper)
Howard Haber (Pappy)
Ken Hadsall (Akey)
Carlton Haenel (Buster)
Ronaldo (Jack) Hager (Red Nose)
Chris Hahn (Chilly)
Leland Haidsiak (Buster D Clw)
Fred Haines (Snappy)
David Halderman (Pappy)
Ken Halford (Cheezie)
Jason Hall (Jay-Dee)
Allan Hall (Dutch)
Sam Hall (Stretch)
Charles Hall (Chuckles)
Don Hall (Gingles)
Keith Hall (Pearly)
Reg. J. Hall (Reggie)
James A Hall (Jimbo)
George Steven (Hall)
Scott Hall (Po-Po)
Eric R Hallam (Golf Bawl)
Gordon Hallberg (Uncle Giddy)
Scott Hallock (Scotty)
Matt Hallowell (Mertie)
Clay Hamblen (Cliffy)
Dwight Hamborsky (Joker)
George E. Hamburg
George Hamburg III (Zippy)
Terry Hamilton (Hambone)
Mark Hamilton (Snorkel)
Donald Hamilton (Milty)
Nell Hamilton
John J. Hammond
Jerry Hampton (Sketter)
Luther J. Hampton (Redbaron)
Robert A. Hancock (Sci)
Ralph I Haney, Jr. (Popcorn)
Howard Hankin (Blinkee)
Michael Hankin (Hankee)
David Hankins (Hot Rod)
James Hann (Tynee)
Scott Hannan (Jingles)
Roger A. Hanney (Ringo)
Roger Hanson (Robd)
Larry Hanson (Billy The Clown)
Dennis Hardin (Gabby)
John Hardin (Jellybean)
Kevin Harding (Goose)
Dan Hardwick (Kupkake The Kop)
Dennis Hardy (Denbo)
Mark Harford (Ol Cheery)
Vernon Harger (Fuzzee)
Harold Hargiss (Carrot Top)
Mike Hargrave
Ronald Harke (Crackers)
Scott Harm (Cruzer)
Don Harmon (Choo-Choo)
Peter Harmon (Jet O)
Robert Harper
William Truett (Harrelson Stripes)
Paul Harrington (Happi Harri)
Melvin Harrington (Boo)
Jon W. Harris (Spinner)
Gene Harris (Geno)
Gary Harris (Puppers)
Jeff Harris (Uncle Buck)
Bill Harris (B No)
John Harris, III (Cracker Jack)
Jim Harrison
Don Harrison (Bucky)
Bill Harrison (Billy Buttons)
Blair Hart (Nifty)
Coy L. Hart (Blicko)
Dave Hartley
Bruce Hartman (W C)
Dan Hartman (Sidekick)
Ken Hartman (Red)
Ken Hartman (Red)
Cliff Hartmier (Mister Stripes)
Les Hartshorn (Skeeter)
Nick Hartwell (Skootz)
Dave Hartwig (Buckles)
Floyd Hartwig (Twig)
Rick Hartz (Hooter)
French Harvey (Patches)
Donald Haskins (Toby)
Tommy Hass (Tombo)
Rex Hasty
N. Dale Hatch (Slapshot)
Warren Ray Haviland (Short Cut)
Warren L. Hawkins
Doug Hawley (Duper)
Jeff Hawley (Bingo)
John Hayes (Hack)
Tommy F. Hayes, Jr. (Mingo)
Chris Headley (Gizmo)
Stephen Hearn (Pumpkin)
Maurice Heater (Abu Benny)
Don Heidenburg (Kasper)
Jake Heidrich (Sappy)
Wayne Heimsoth (Shorty)
Charles Heine (Punkin)
Hal Heizer (Tuit)
Bob Hekel (Bubber)
Leonard Helfrich (Holler)
Eddie Henderson (E-Walk)
Mike Henderson (Hendie)
Glenn Henderson (Henny)
Al Hendren (Mishka)
William Henley
James A. Henricks, Jr.
Douglas Hensley (High Pockets)
Ervin L. Hensley (Bug Dust)
Bart Hensley (Plunger)
Donald Henson (Lil Bit)
Ed Herbest (E C)
TC Cameron Hercus (Jasper)
Henry B. Hering, Sr. (B Kuz)
Jim Herman (Jimbo)
Pablo Hernandez (Don Palin)
Dorian Heroman (Brsh/Mtygrw)
Arturo Herrera, Jr. (Snaps)
John Heslop Sr. (Shiner)
Daneal Hess (Sparky)
Rod Hessler (Rocket)
George Heyen (Chuckles)
James Higdon (Dink)
Emmett Higginbotham (Popa Boo)
Stanley Higgins (Sque Key)
Charles R. Higgs (Blinki)
Russell Hildebrand (Rosco)
Don Hill (Trouble)
Kevin Hill (Eclipse)
Chester Hill Jr. (Joekey)
Dan Hillenbrand (Cookie)
Dave Hillerud
Gerald Hillman (Uncle Geezer)
John Hilyard (Dixie Dale)
James R. Hinde (Dandy)
Fred Hinde, Jr. (Band Aid)
Michael Hines (Grapes)
Jason Hinkle (J Bird)
Danny Hinton (Spirit)
Jim Hirl (Hwey)
Eric Hitchcock (Wrench)
Albert Hittle (Rollo)
Leonard W. K. Ho (Lenny Da Hobo)
Donald Hobbs
Ronald Hobensack (Hobe)
Carleton Hodge (Hugs)
Richard Hodge (Ricko)
Doug Hodges (Cowboy)
Gerry Hodges (Smiley)
William Hodgson (Koko-Nut)
Randy Hodnett (Rowdy)
Ari Hoeksema Dr. (Sigmund Fraud)
Darwin Hoff (Quackers)
Paul Hoff (Tiny)
Craig Hoffman
Larry Hoffman (Lucky)
Rod Hogan
William Hohmeyer (Shortcakes)
Steve Holbrook (Inky-D)
Robert B. Holck (Hokie)
James Holderfield (Mr Ups)
Kenneth Holderfield (Doodle Bug)
Rodney Holdren (U Hoo)
Cliff Holland (Cliffie)
James Irby Holland (Choo Choo)
Haldean P. Holland (Hoppy Poppy)
Randall Hollinger (Cuffs)
Rodney Hollinger (Pockets)
John Hollowood (Harpo)
Joe Roy Holloway (Jodie)
Robert Rodney Holmberg
Dale Holmen (Darrell)
Fred Holmes (Peanut)
Dean Holmes
Robert Holscher (Bob - O)
Ralph Holstrom (Abiff)
Jeff Holt (Turtle)
Alan Holt (Snickers)
Lynn Holt (Sunny Sunflower)
Thomas Hooks (Smilee)
Jason B. Hopkin
W. Kirk Hopkins (Boho)
Michael L. Horning (Kaboos)
Morris Horowitz (Moe Moe)
Bob Horowitz (Topper)
Danny Horton (Popcycle)
Azan Hosein (Zar Zar)
Tom Houchins (Buckshot)
L Lew Hounsell (Rainbow)
Charles F. Houska, IV (Speckles)
John Houston (Pinky)
Kelton Houts (Whoops)
Mike Howard (Howie)
Arthur Howard (Pa Pa)
Ken Howard (Howard)
Eugene Howard (BB)
Tracy Howard (Tiny)
Arthur Howell (Oscar)
Willie Howell (Chilly Willy)
Walter R. Howerton (T-Bird)
Gene Howes (Fat Slats)

Kurt Howes (Chopper)
Terrell Howes (Red-Top)
James Hrejsa (Jaymus)
Mathew Hubbard (Hubbabub)
John Hubbard
William Huber (Willy)
Chuck Hudson (Cheetoe)
Billy Hudson (Bilbo)
Jerry Huffman (Patches)
William M. Hughes (Dub)
Donald Huguley Jr. (Hugs)
Curt Huhn
John Hull (Homie)
Tim Hull (Vaso)
Lloyd Hultman
Richard Humes
Charles Humes (Poppy)
Chad Humphreys (Chap Stick)
Joe Humphreys (Bubba)
Troy Huneycutt (Paint-Bucket)
Jerry Hunsberger
Mike Hunter
Michael Hunter
Ralph Huntington (Wheels)
Steven Hurlburt (Whirly)
Linden Hurlbut (Beards)
Raymond Huson (Hughee)
Bryan Hutchcraft (Hubcap)
Roy Hutchins (Poppy)
Jerel H. Hutchinson (Rusty)
Doug Hutchinson (Bobo The Hobo)
Mike Hutton
William A. Hylton (Poppy)

-I-

Herry Ilcken (Rainbow)
Gerald Innis (Dusty)
Charles Insley (Chazz)
Brian Irwin (B.J.)
Michael Ito (Ted E Bear)
Lawrence (Jay) Iverson (O-No)
Jim Iverson (Jinks)
Lewis Ivy (Shorty)

-J-

David Jack (Dee Jay)
Ray Jackson (Frisco)
Bob Jackson (Woody)
Perry Jackson (Jax)
C.H. Jake Jacobs (Skooter)
Jon A Jacobs (Ashis)
Mort Jacobs (Kernel)
Jack Jacobs (10 Fingers)
Ted H. Jacobsen (Profy)
Roy A. Jacobson (Meat Ball)
Edward Jakubowsky
James James (Jiggles)
Bill Jamieson (Tiddlie Winks)
Louis F. Janke (Cotton Candy)
Bruce Jardine (Noodles)
Fant Jarrett (Dandy)
Delmar L Jefferson (Jeffie)
Gerald Jeitner (Donuts)
Tom Jelberg (Jelly)
Joe Jenckes (Lucky Lewey)
Greg Jenkins (Fixit)
Doug Jennings (Rags)
Dave Jensen (Digger)
Waldon Jensen (Augie)
Peter Jensen (Repete)
Irving Jimenez (Bolita)
Paul Johnson (Lefty)
Gary Johnson (Pockets)
Tyler Johnson
Barry Johnson (Coco)
Matt Johnson
Tom Johnson (Uno)
David Johnson (Bo)
Richard Johnson (Rhineheart)
Aaron Johnson (Mr Bojangles)
Brian Johnson (Heybuddy)
G Darrell Johnson (Jo Jo)
J Kevin Johnson (Johnny)
Barney Johnson (Kooter)
Chris Johnson (Sparkles)
Megan Johnson
S. Gene Johnson (Peaches)
Todd Johnson (Toddles)
Will Johnson
James J. Johnson Jr. (Jolly)
Jason Johnston (JJ)
Christopher R. Johnston (Bam Bam)
Al Johnston (Jumbo)
Glen Johnston
Charles L. Johnston, Jr. (Sea Shell)
Fred Joiner (Bossa)
Joe R. Joity
Higgins Jonathan (Swee' Pea)
Jack Jones (Bubbles)
Jeff Jones (Sir Limpsalot)
Robert Jones (Alley Oops)
George Jones (Poppa Bear)
George Jones (Georgie)
Timothy Jones (Timmers)
Doug Jones (Tiny)
Randy Jones (Spazz)
Edward Jones (Tee Jay)
Robert A. Jones (Bunky)
Wayne A. Jones (Fireball)
Stephen Jones (Bud)
Steven Jones (Herbie)
Darrell Jones (Pappy)
Ronald Jones (Joker)
David Jones (Choo Choo)
Roger Jones (Butch)
Alan Jones (Honey)
Robin Jones (Bobbin)
Jack Jones
Laurance Jones III (Buzz - Bee)
William D. Jones Jr. (Bo)
John Jones III (Sleepy)
Steve Jordan (Dandy)
Samuel Jordan (Happy Sam)
John Joseph (Jay Jay)
Richard Joy
William Joyce (Willie)
N. Gray Joyner (Looney)
Gary Julian (Hill Billy)
Mike Junkin (Moose)

-K-

Ted Kaiser (Whiskers)
Richard Kaiser (Dimples)
Raymond Kalita (Klutz/Pierre)
Wayne Kamper (2 Speed)
Mark Kaplan (Dizzy)
Edward Kaplan (Emundo)
Norm Karaszewski
Ken Karnes
Joseph M. Kasnia, Jr.
Johnny L. Katz (Uptown)
Louis J. Katzenberger
Barry Kaye (Homer)
Robert W. Kaylor (Redeye)
Craig A. Kazin (Doc)
Tom Kean
Emerson Keay (Bucky)
Jay Keeler
Greg Keeling (Weezer)
Ross Keenan (Slippery)
Mark Keiser (Nosey T. Clown)
Pat Kelley (Pooch)
Alfred Kellner (Alfalfa)
John J. Kelly (Silly)
Tim Kelly (Recycles)
Clark Kemmerer (Clark Ee Poo)
Michael J. Kemp Sr. (Wild Child)
Bob Kempf (Kookie)
Chris Kempf (Donut)
Rosa Maria (Kendall)
Bill Kendrick (Uncle Sam)
Brian R Kennedy (Flat Foot)
Randy Kennedy (Slick)
Cory Kennedy
Ray Kennedy (Hobo Joe)
Chris Kennedy (Krazy)
Donald Kent
Clark Kent (Colors)
William Kerakos (Bingo Bill)
Harry Kerkheide (Toko)
Steve Kern (Knucklehead)
Jim Kern (I Dont Know)
J. Ken Kerpan (Klutz)
Sean Kesterson (Ship Wreck)
Harry R. Ketchabaw (Harry Bear)
Jim Ketcherside (Jimmi)
Clarence E. Keto (Lemonaide)
Frank Kiblinger (Can-Do)
John R. Kidder (Flip-Flop)
Garnic Kidwell (Pockets)
Roger Kilby (Top Hat)
Don Killmer (Angus)
Samuel Kim (Mik-Mas)
Kurt Kimberling (Guido)
Ron Kina (No No)
Mike Kinard (Doc)
Rudolph E Kincke (Gadget)
William Kinden (Buck)
Stephen King (Matey)
Robert L. King (Bo-Shag)
William P King (Willy P)
James S. King (Noodles)
Gene King (Stutter)
Vern King (Pogo)
David King (Joe Buford)
Wayne M. King (Sparkles)
Michael King (Hubba Bubba)
Gariel "Bud" King (Flambeau)
Geoff A. King (Sticks)
Bryan Kinkade (Shades)
Donald R. Kinney (Puddles)
Eric Kippenbrock (Tinker)
John K. Kirby, Jr.
Vern Kirchhoff (Stretch)
Kevin Kirkbride (Sweet- P)
Fred Kirke (Jingles)
Bob Kirklin (Wiley-Bob)
George Kirkpatrick (Smiley)
Timothy Kirshman (Bo-Bo)
Harold L Kisner (Jelly Belly)
James E Kleck
Ken Klein
Paul S. Kleinberger (Fuddi-Duddy)
Edmund Kleiner (Candy)
John Kline (Doodles)
Abe Knapp

John Knecht (Astro)
Scott Knechtel
Albert Knelle, Jr. (Fastball)
Matt Knight (Nutt)
Wayne Knight (Bogey)
John Knoepfler (Skates)
James Knott (Frisky)
Robert Knowles (Rocky)
Chad Knowles
Bill Knowles (Patches)
Jerral Knox (Jelly Bean)
Gary Knubley (Stueee)
Terry Knutson (Stinky)
Dan Kobasa (Ko-Bee)
John Koedel (Bunkey)
Joseph Kohen (Joko Koko)
William Kohl
E Robert Kohler, Jr. (Patches)
Derek Koleas
Albin J. Konchar (Beany)
Joseph Konklewski (Cool Beans)
Larry Konopasky (Rgdy Andy Jr)
Joseph Koonrad (U-No)
Stephen Koonrad (Darnook)
Jerry Kopenhaver (Sloopy)
Jason Kosolofsky (Koko)
Jim Koudelik (Scruffee)
Clarence Kraft Caboose)
Robert Krahn (Pippin)
Bill Krantz (Hush Puppy)
Robert W. Kraus (Sinker)
John G. Krebs (Opa John)
John Krodel (Spinner)
J. Douglas Kroeger (Happy The Clown)
James Krokosh (Klik)
Fritz C. Krouskop (Fritzer)
Chad Kundert (Stinky)
Greg Kuntz (Whistle)
Ron Kwiatkowski (Ok)

-L-

Gary La Gasse (Binky)
Marvin Laack II (Toothy)
Anthony J. Lacava (TJ)
Wayne Lachut (Fudgie)
Lawrence Lackey (Pasquli)
Harold Lafave (Capt Rivet)
Dennis Lahue (Motor Mowth)
Hugh H. Laird (Racer)
Scott Lakin (Snarfie)
Richard Lamb (Buttons)
Gary Lambert
John Lambros (Oil Can)
Gary Lamon (Bingo)
James E. Lampley (Mater-Juice)
Richard Lang (Saxo)
David Lang (Max)
Charles Lanoue (Whistler)
Bill Lansdale (Roscoe)
Peter Lantka (Chick Pea)
Roger Larkins (Muskrat)
Dave Larrett (Kubbie)
Pete Larson (Knickers)
Lowell Larson
Arron Larson (Ozzy)
John Larue (Long John)
Lori Larue
Dana Latch
Donald Laughlin (Smirky)
Gordon Lauzon (Bondo)
Ron Lawford (Bubbles)
David Lawrence
Jesse Lawrenz
Bruce Lawry (Rolly Polly)
Keith D. Lawson (O'gee)
H Steve Lawson (Doodles)
Louis Le Blanc Babo)
Jerry Leach (Burt)
Ron Leaverton (Wide Track)
Paul Leavy (Pinchy)
Donald Leblanc (Backhoe)
Ron Lebold (Jazz)
Joel Lebow (Stitches)
Jack Ledger (JJ)
Hoover Lee (Puhi)
Dennis Lee (Banjo)
Ronnie Lee Um Pah Pah)
Tony Lee (Spaz)
Richard Lee
James A. Lee (Snips)
Dr. Briant H. Lee (Phudsie)
James Lees (Big Daddy)
Joel Lees (Buckwheat)
James Legier (Legs)
John Lehman (Gambinee)
E G Leipheimer, IV
Bernard J Lemieux, MD
David B. Lempky (Fotoman)
David W. Lempky (Buscuit)
Mike Lennon (Koo-Koo)
Jason Lensing
W. M. "Bud" (Leonard)
Michel Levesque (Kami)
Gary Lewis (Shoofly)
Bruce Lewis (Nickels)
David F Lewis (Yeeehaw)
Greg Lewis (Nikko)
Ed Lewis (Tater)
John Liberty (Spanky)
Hutson Light (Skippy)
Clark Likness (Doc)
Jon Lindberg
Charles Lindberg (Rosebud)
Matt Lindelof (Homey)
Michael Lindsay (Spunky)
Malcolm Lindsay
Dennis Lindsay (Butterfinger)
Bill Lineaweaver (Will Ee)
Paul Linnell (Uff Da)
Scott Lipps (Lippsy)
Errol C Lipschitz (Lippy)
Jim Litchford (Jimbo)
Rick Lively (3-Putt)
Robert Locke (Combo)
Paul Lockhart
Gerald Loftin (Doodle Bug)
Kenny Loftis (Sparky)
Mark Lollis (Pappy)
William London (10 Can)
Andy Long (Kopper)
Bruce Long (Boo Boo)
Richard Loomis (Grampee)
Steve Looyson (Spex)
Charles Lord (Chuckles)
Thomas Lorentz Sr. (Uncle Dippy)
John C Lorne Jr. (Pockets)
Emanuel Loulis Sr. (Sidetrack)
David L. Lourwood (Whiffer)
Larry W. Love (Wiskers)
Doug Love (Patches)
Nick Love (Liberty)
Danny Love (Chief Pappy)
Dana Lovell (Swish)
Phillip B. Lovell (Ducky)
David Lovett
Merrill A. Lovvik
Justin Lowder
Eric Lubberts (Looby)
Wayne Luebe (Wainbow)
Leo E. Luettjohann (Pop Eye)
Allan Luke (Peeps)
Phil Lunn (Bummer)
Nicholas Lutz (Nick)
Philip Lycett III (Pete)
Jerry Lynch (Alphie)
Johnny R.E. Lynch (Jrel)

-M-

Gregory Mac Kay (Scotty)
G.L. Mac Rae (Rails)
William Macculloch (Fuzzy)
Bill Macdonald (Buttons)
Alfred Macdonald (Sport)
Alan Machmiller (Monkey Wrench)
Harold Maciver (Hobo Hal)
Everett V. Mack (Sparky)
Rod Mackay (Poor Rod)
Lloyd Mackay
Will Mackay (Patty-O-Furniture)
Malcolm Mackenzie (Gonzo)
Donald Mackintosh (Ducky)
Thomas J. Macready (Clipper)
Ken Maddison (Jelly Bean)
Alan W Madsen
Howard W Magan, Jr. (Cuzn Clem)
Jerry Maggard (Shabby)
Troy Magnuson (Popcorn)
Don Mah (Bloomer)
James Mahaney (Hobo)
Bob Maien (Pot Shot)
Roger Mallberg
John Malmstrom (Bubbles)
John Maloney (No Dough)
Philip Malonson (Reco-Ve-Ree)
Jim Malott (Twigler)
Pat Manary (Shamrock)
Donald J. Maness
Anthony Mangez (Booger Bug)
Barry Mangrum (Patches)
Gary Mann (Snicker)
Charles Manning (Knuckles)
Robert Mantle (Checkers)
Kenny Manzi (Pee-Wee)
Roland Maracle (Rollo)
Larry Marean (Zippy)
Jack Marine (Bunky)
Gordon Markley (Sunny)
Joseph P. Markovitch (Jo Jo)
Jeffery Marlowe (Smiley)
Loren Marlowe (Curley)
Ivan Marquez (Bombacha)
Steve Marsh (Swampy)
Brian Marshall (Blue)
James Marshall (Jim Bob)
James D. Marshall (Jingles)
Jay Marshall (J-Bird)
John Marshall (Wilber)
Duane Marshall (Skidz)
James Martin (Twister)
Ed Martin (Chuckles)
George Martin (Radar)
Robert Martin (Poindexter)
Dale U. Martin (Marty)
Leonard Martin (Slip Joint)
Larry Martin (Soup)
Ronald Martin (Zipper)

Mel Martin
Agustin Martinez (Windies)
Joseph Martinez (Kookie)
Reuben Martinez (Boo Boo)
Harold Martinson (Marty)
James Darrell Mashburn (Bisquit)
Norm Maske (Stormy)
Earl Keith Mason (Smilely)
Jeff Masson (Jeffro)
Jack Masters
George Mather (Z-Clown)
Gary Matican (Huggy)
Andrew Matlins (Iggy)
Paul Maxwell (Rodeo)
Eldred Maxwell
J.D. Maxwell (Splats)
Douglas E. Maxwell
David May (Gismo)
Glenn May-Anderson (Archie)
Kelly Maygard (Sparkles)
Tim Mayner (Sundance)
Don McCauley (Pistol Pete)
Lyle McDowell (Mumbles)
Ken Mc Kenney (Si)
Don McNeil
Alan McAdams
David C. McAndrews (Bongo)
Donald L. McAndrews (Gentle Ben)
Harvey McAninch (Strawberry)
Ronald McAtee (Fizz-Ed)
Paul McCallum Puffy)
Louis McCann (Mac-A-Doo)
Cameron McCannell
Dean McCard (Cup Cake)
Jim McCarroll (Nervis)
Jim McCash (Gooch)
Manning McCauley (Nifty)
Wayne McClelland (Hay Seed)
Michael E. McComas (Short Stack)
Ken McComb (Chumly)
John McCorkindale
William McCormick (Bumfuzzle)
Dr. Michael McCosh (Dr. Magick)
David McCreery (Yoyo)
Stanley McDaniel
Jerry McDaniel (Skipper)
Randy McDevitt (Noze)
Rod McDonald
Roger McDonald (Spud)
James M. McDonald (Moo Cow)
Robert McDonald (Aggie)
John McDonough (Irish)
John McDougal (Dougal)
Jack McDowell (Anchor)
Brian McEachern (Noodles)
Stephen McFadden (Chip The Clown)
John J. McGarry (Wrinkles)
Alan McGhie
Nyle McGill (Cinders)
Edgar McGonigal
Lloyd McGowan (Yogi)
Jack McGregor (Spud)
Tony McHale
Ralph McHam (Ralph-O)
Steve McIntyre (Mose)
Dan McKee (Harp)
Wayne McKey (Howdy)
Ralph McKinnon (Boss)
Steven B McKitrick (Li'l Mac)
Daryl McLaughlin (Whut?)
Jim McLaughlin (Happy)
Jerry McLaughlin (Mac)
Tim McMahon (Roscoe T Clown)
John McManus (Her-Bee)
Richard McNabb (Checkers)
Don R. McNeil
Craig McPPhee (Krazy Krazy)
J Dennis McQuade (Todo)
Barry McQuillin (Happy Jack)
Greg H McRae (Puff Puff)
Terry McShane (Speedy)
Robert McWilliams (Pancake)
Douglas McWilliams (Rover)
Michael McWilliams (Grease Monkey)
Doug Mead (Boo-Boo)
John Medaglia (Chooch)
Francisco Medellin (Boris)
Sam Medsker (Orange Beard)
Tim Meeker (Squeaky)
Howard F. Mehringer (Giddy)
Michael Meinke (Jo Jo)
Vrej Mekhalian (Pasha)
Andrew Mellman (Chili Pepper)
Horace Melton (Papa Ho)
Douglas Menard (Jojo)
Lawrence Mendel (The Dude)
Henry Mendez (Snickers)
Bill Mendola (Wild Bill)
Sheldon Menin (Spanky)
George Mergen (Wabbit)
Jason Merideth (Pudding)
David C. Merrell (Curly)
Olen Merry (Catfish)
Clifford E Metz (Rover)
Clifford Metz (Rover)
David Meuller (Petals)
Robert Meyer (Korky)
Donald Meyers Jr. (Doodle)
Steve Mhoon (Raid - R)
John Micallef (Mr. Scooter)
James Michel, MD
Dennis Mickelson
Larry Middendorf (Pockets)
Ray Milan (Sunshine)
Joseph Milazzo (Jo Jo)
George Milder (Sweet-Hearts)
Mark D. Miles (Retro)
Robert Miller (Blaze)
Steve Miller
Willett Miller
John H. Miller (Dirtee)
Richard Miller
William Miller (Sneekz)
Walter Miller (Scorpo)
Joel Miller (Jewls)
Kelly Miller (Flounder)
Gregory Miller
Edward Miller
Michael E. Miller (Whiskers)
Robert Miller (Ice Bucket)
Blaine W. Miller Jr. (Divot)
Robert Millman (Cup Cake)
Terry Mills (Bubbles)
Robert Milot (New Bee)
Albert Minahan, Jr. (Freddy Free Meal)
Tony Minnicks (Freedom)
Jerry Minor (Hitch)
Edward Scott Mishoe
Randall E. Mishoe
Terry Mislark (Bingo II)
Herbert R Mitchell (Candy)
Mike Mitchell (Alley- Oop)
James Mitchell (Apple)
Jim Mitchell (Jimbo)
Merlin Mitchell (Magic)
Phil Mitchell (Mitch)
George A. Mitchell (Buns)
John W. Mitchell, Jr. (Daffy Doc)
Bob Mittler (Bobbie)
Kenneth Mitz (Mitzo)
Ray Modisette (Tootsie)
Ray Modlins (Bubba Pee)
Lewis K. Molnar
Richard Montee (Ribbitz)
Robert Montgomery (Topsy)
Clark Montgomery (Bouncer)
John Montoya (Buttons)
Billy Ray Moore (Skillet)
Steve Moore (Speckles)
Wm. Gordon Moore
Randy Moore (Topper)
Dennis Moore (Roony)
Harry Moore Jr. (Dimples)
William Moran
P.C. Moran (Diesel)
David Morey (Happy)
Ken Morey (Krackers)
Raymond Morgan (Sparks)
Robert Morgan (Jiggs)
Oliver Morgan (Mr Messy)
Jimmy Morgan
Gary Morin (Clumsy)
Michael Morin (Par-Tee)
Darryl Morphy (Oh Boy)
Sanford Morris (Ootz)
John Morris (Checkers)
Dick Morris (Hi Bye)
David Morris (Clipper)
R. Wayne Morris (Dr Wikiwiki)
Sonny Morrow (Sonny)
Donald Morse (Bus Driver)
Richard Morse (Little One)
Robert Morton (Jungo)
Sherman Morton (Sammy)
Donald L. Morton (Cookie)
Phillip Moss (Jingles)
Shawn Mott (Patches)
W.G. Mounce (Wee Willie)
Ray Moyer (D.C.)
Rob Much (Bubbles)
Lee Mueller (Greenjeans)
Ed Mummey (Gudder)
Dennis Mundt (Pokey)
Jack Muralt (Doc)
James Murphy (Murf)
Daniel Murphy Shamrock)
Tylor Murray
Arnold Murray (Doc)
Duncan Murray (Cuddles)
Brian Mushrow (Ko- Ko)
Melchior Myers (Mell)
Michael Myers (Snellie)
Robert J. Myers (Tinker)
Clifford Myers (Sparky)
Clyde Myhill (Sparky)
Albert Myshrall (Bunyon)
Walter Myslewicz (Wally)

-N-

Richard M. Nadeau (Kracker)
Rajen Naidu
Korosh Namini (Kay-Cee)
William Naquin Jr. (Shoe)
James Nasby Madd (Max)
Eugene W. Nead (Gene-O)
Matthew Neal (Dr. Chubby)

Norm Neely (Pee Wee)
Melvin F. Neil (Choo Choo)
Billy Neimeyer (Precious)
J.C. Neimeyer (Twinkie)
Billy Neimeyer Jr. (Shadow)
Michael Nelson (Tic-Kits)
Larry Nelson (Poppi)
Larry Nelson (Bear)
John E. Nelson (Demo)
Roy Nelson (Pete)
Brian Nelson Ronbo)
Ronald L. Nenaber
Thomas J. Nervegna (Loopy)
Teri Neubert (Mr 'B' Good)
Jake Neuman (Gunner)
Bruce New (Newt)
Joe New (Jo Jo)
David Newcomb (Do-No)
Billy Newcomb (Blue Nose)
Russell Newell (Happy Hobo)
Wesley Newman (Baloo Baphoon)
Larry Newman (3 Putt)
Harold Newton (Happy)
Jim Nichols (Sparky)
David Nicholson (Dandy)
Kenneth Nichter (Radical)
V.J. Nickolas
Steve Nielsen (Crackerjack)
Paul Niemczyk
Chad Michael Nix
John C. Nobles
Lorne Noiles (Gizmo)
Rex Nolen (Junior)
Lloyd Norman (Oops)
Charles H. Norris (Dreamer)
Henry A. Norris Sr. (Wavy)
Larry Norvell (Rusty Neck)
Charles Nowak (Six Bits)
Paul Nunn (Gnl Hafas)
Bob Nustad

-O-

Michael O'Brien (Lucky Charm)
Dan O'Connor (Doc)
Matthew Oakes (Ty-Dy)
David Oaks
Robert Oberman (Anchoovie)
B.J. Odom (Beezer)
Charlie Odorizzi (Hypnos)
Carlos Odriozola (Botarga)
Raymond Offutt (Beep)
Douglas Ohms (Snickers)
M. Burton Oien
William F. Okesson Jr. (Happy)
David A Olivares (Howie U)
Ron Oliver
Jimmie Olson (Buttons)
Mike Oneil (Crackers)
Larry Oram (Bubba)
Robert Orednick
Donald D. Orton ('Oli 'Oli)
Rusty Orwig (Rusty)
Gregory Osborne (Pozi)
David Oshefsky
Leslie G. Osterman (Bouncey)
Conrad Ostwalt (Rainbow)
David Ottinger (Bones)
Mark D. Overbaugh (Banko)
Ralph Owen
Clay Owen (Biscuit)
Grant C. Owens (Screwball)
Doug Owens (Happy Jack)
Frank Owens (Frank O)
Kenneth Owens
John Oxrider (Smiley)

-P-

Patrick Padian (Pockets)
Thomas Palko (Pepper)
William Palmer (Hot Dog)
Charles J Palmer (Chappy)
Tye Pameticky
Gordon Panchuk (Lucky)
James Pandolfo (Bubbles)
Chester Paris (Tux)
Tom Park (Conal)
Norman Parker (Whatever)
Charles M Parker (Buck E)
Ed Parker (Bussy)
Dewayne Parker
Larry Parker
Bob Parker (Bannack Bob)
Dwain Parker (Dusty)
William Parks (Tic-Toc)
Joseph Parkton (Chuckles)
William Kim Parkyn (Unkle Willie)
Ralph W. Parsons (Papo)
Randy Patchett (Crash)
Kirit Patel (Sleepy)
Drew Patten
Jerry Patterson (Patches)
Dave Patterson (Dave)
Tim Paul (Timbo)
Eddie Paul
Harvey Paulson (Hooter)
George Pavey (Bunny)
Edward Payne (Pita)
Mark Payne (Winkles)
Wally Payne (Klumze)
Ken Peach
John Peacock (Jjoops)
Ernest Pearlstein (Rollo)
Kirk Pearson Jr. (Moose)
Kirk Pearson Sr. (Krusty)
Brian Peck (Boo)
L. Keith Peck (Bogie)
Steven Peck (Hobo Bill)
John Pecotte (Rags)
Wayne Pedigo
Patrick Penley (Patches)
Wayne Penley (Skittles)
Dale Pennington (Sluf-Fun)
Frank E. Pennington (Chase)
Hugh Pentney (U E)
Mike Pepler (Mikey)
Martin Perfit (F O U)
Perry Perkins (Doc Rock)
Luther Perkins (Perky Doc)
Lynn Perkins (Perky)
Curtis Pernak (Sloppy)
Frank Pernak (Hammy)
Jack Perrine (Gizbo)
Douglas Peters (Homer)
David J. Peters (Leftovers)
Edward Peters (Squeezer)
Herb Petersen (Pete)
William Petersen (Willie)
William Peterson
Franklin D. Peterson, Atty At Law (Franklee)
Gary Petty (Donuts)
Al E Peveto (Al)
Byron D. Pewitt Jr. (Oopsy)
Larry R Pfeiffer (Hatman)
Jerry Pherson (Peep)
Mike Phillips (Cookie)
Tom Phillips (Flips)
Russell Phillips (Rusty)
John Phillips (Deckster)
Tommy Phillips (Bird Dog)
Jimmy Phillips
Fred Phillips (Buckey)
David Pianezzi (Sunshine)
Robert Pickett (Wrench)
Hugh Lee Pickle (Gerkey)
Roy Pidcock (Ragz)
Patrick Pieper (Plunger)
Ken Pierce
Jay Pifer (Poppy)
Roland E. Pigeon (Rollo)
Drew Pincus (Kwotes)
Jerry L. Pingle (PJ)
Howard R Pinkham (Fizz-Bo)
Albert Pipes (Spike)
George Pipes (Patches)
Rick Pirog (Shorty)
Peter Pizzorno (Petee Boy)
Leo Plato (Jo Jo)
Rob Plummer (Dr Floppy)
Terry Plummer (Pinky)
Thomas Podrovitz (Chugg'o)
Jay Poirier (Lugnut)
Frank Poissant (Squeaky)
Virgil Polak (Coach)
Dave Polen (Smiley)
Douglas Pope (Dopie)
Leon Portman (Joy)
Greg Post (Jiggs)
Norm Post (Cinders)
Tom Pott (Tapper)
Donald Powell (Eagle)
Ed Prange
Warren Pready (Wheels)
Eugene Prentice (Geno)
Charles Prescott (Biffo)
Larry Pressman (Cookie)
Terry Price (Rusty)
Jim Price (Bing-Go)
Marvin Privette (Put Put)
Charlie Prock (Charlie Brown)
Barry Proctor (Dusty)
Jerry Proctor (Dr Malpractice)
Peter Proudlock (Wizz Bang)
George Pruden (Puddin)
Charles Pruitt (Dapper)
Jack Arnold Pulis (Honkee Kat)

-Q-

Norman Quaas (Joker)
Rick Qual
Matt Queau (Mr Q)
James N. Quinn (Doddles)
John Quintana (Hilti)
Tony Quintana (Rascal)

-R-

Todd Rackley (Donut)
Ted Radcliffe (Capt Salty)
Mike Radford (Murph)
Scott Radford (Ritz)
Leonard Radle (Spanky)
John A. Radziunas (Razzi)
Walter Rae (Skookum)
David Rafter (Laffter)
Doug Rafters (Raffy)
Everett Rainer (Tex)
John Raines Jr. (Shadow)

Richard Raitt (Red Dog)
Bill Ralph (Ralphy)
Duane Ramberg (Rumpy)
Ruben Ramirez (Rocky)
Dan Randall (Derby Dan)
Jack Randall (Shorty)
James E. Raney (Snapshot)
Richard R. Rausch (Doo Dad)
Michael Rawls (Yogi)
Charles Raymond (Pee Wee)
John Ream (Peanut)
Ned Reed (Squeaks)
Jerry L. Reed (Stitches)
Michael Reed (Alfalfa)
Lawrence J. Reed, Sr. (Shorty)
Luke Reicks
Floyd Reid (Pockits)
Thomas J. Reidy (Tipsy)
Dan Reim (Trouble)
Gary Reiners (Grits)
Ed Reinhardt (Maverick)
Chance L. Rennic (Horse Shoe)
Richard Rennison (Turbo)
Kevin Reuther (Sparky)
Rick Reyes (Tater)
Bob Reynolds (Hobokin)
Chris Reynolds (Smokey)
James Reynolds Jr. (T. J.)
Dusty Rhodes (Sparkey)
Elwood A. Rice (Woody)
Tom Richards
Andrew Richardson (Big Un)
W R Richardson (Bloomers)
Dan Richardson
Verne Ricker
Charles Rieder (Tuna)
Donald Rigby (Chuckles)
Dean Riggin (P K)
Robert Riggs (Bebunk)
Floyd Rinker
Scott Risley (Smiley)
Robin Ritter
Nick Roach (Whitey)
Kenneth Roan (Zero)
Larry Roberts (Rascal)
Richard M. Roberts (Big Hat)
David Roberts (Biskets)
Robert E. Roberts (Rock)
Larry Roberts (Doodles)
Gary Roberts (Dimples)
Robert Roberts (Bobo)
Geoff Roberts (Flip Flop)
Richard J. Roberts (Box Car)
Clayton Robertson (Pabo)
Scott Robertson (Strypes)
John Robertson (Tango)
Jim Robertson
George Robinson (Georgie)
Mike J. Robinson (Jolly)
Robert J. Robinson (Sunshine)
Jim Robinson (Pockets)
James Robinson (Checkers)
Mike Robitaille (Dew Gee)
Michael Robshaw (Gumpy)
Joe Rocco (Rocco)
Leon Raul Rock
Larry Rode (Ziggy)
David R. Rodriquez (Wassup)
Darrin Roe (Will-Bee)
Arthur Roeber
Paul Rogers (Gismo)
Al Romani (Bundy)
William J. Romer (Wee Willie)
Darryl Romero (Chaunchy)
Roy Rommelman (Noodles)
Frank W. Root (Frankie)
Travis Rorher (Duffer)
Ruben Rosas (Toselin)
James E. Roschal (Rowdy)
Robert E. Rose (Kranky)
Bob Rosebro (Robo T' Hobo)
Harry J. Rosenbaum (Fphooozziye)
Stanley Rosenberg (Stringbean)
Jeff Rosier (Pinto)
Adrian Roskom
James Ross
Pat Ross
George Rotas (Jingles)
Marvin Roth (Dumy)
Kevin Rothermel (Dipper)
Ken Rotter (Bubbles)
David Rouleau (Woo Hoo)
Bill Rouse (M-Ber)
Tom Rousseau (Flash)
Kevin Roustazad
Grant Routzohn (G)
Duane Roy (Ya You)
Shad Roys
Adam Rude (Rudy)
Victor P. Ruff (Ruffee)
Benjamin Ruhs (Digger)
Florencio Ruiz (Sleepy)
Gary Rushworth, Sr. (Dobber)
Joseph Rusnak (Hobo Joe)
Jim Russell (Laddie)
Zachary Russell (Pookee)
Steven Russell
Bill Russo (Rascal)
Eric Rust (Popcorn)
Matt Rutledge (Cookie)

-S-

Khalid Sabri (O' Doc)
Shane Salisbury (Stumpy)
William Saloukas (Box Car Billy)
Howard Samiya (Chop Stix)
Mike Samiya (Jappo)
Charles E. Sammons (Cracker)
Richard Sams (Sammy)
Eduardo A. Sanchez (Sneaky)
Dennis Sand (Fluffy)
Dr. Stan Sandomirsky (Dic Doc)
Carlos Sandoval (Sunshine)
John Sands (Cupcake)
Macmillan Sandy
Ted Sanford (Rno/Sdk)
Dean Sauerwein (Sweetie)
Mel Saunders (Momo)
Dave Saunders (Cotton)
Cy Saunders (Papa Cy)
Garry Saunders (Pyro)
Ronald L. Saunders (Ronzo)
Richard Saunders (Pockets)
Ray W. Saur (See Saw)
Fernando Sauri
Joseph Savaglio
John A. Saville
Donald Sawatzky (Twinkle Toes)
Jackie Scarbrough (Sir Clarence)
Chad Schabe (Zippy)
David Scheidler (Jibber Gabber)
Frank Schepers, Jr (Scheps)
Nick Scherbenshe (Slick)
Fred L. Schilb (Choo Choo)
Ron Schlank (Ronnie)
Dick Schlechter (Buttons)
Steve Schlittler (Doddles)
Gary Schlussler (Peaches)
Robert Schmidt (Homer)
Brian Schmidt (Putter)
Kent Schmitz
Vernon Schmitz
Erik Schuett (Shoes)
Rolf C. Schuetz (Sloppo)
Norman C. Schultheis (Pickles)
Tom Schultz (Schultzie)
Richard Schulz (Jelly Bean)
Silvain (Dan) Schulze (Dookie)
Frank W. Schurwon (Bootz)
Ron Schwans
Lester Schwartz (Mo)
Dennis Schweinsburg (Radish)
Herb Schwidkay (Herby)
Jerry Sciullo (Dots)
Mack Scott
John Scott (Snookums)
Claude Scott (Scotty)
Gary Sears (Panhandle Slim)
Lou Ann Seavey
Robert Sebold (Sparky)
Herman Seibert (Lucky)
Lucas J. Seibert (Tweety)
Robert Seidel (Tiny)
Frank Selby (Anonymous)
Lanny Selby (Snee-Kee)
Gerald L. Seldon Sr. (Poppy)
William Self (Spanky)
Jeffery Selke (Hayseed)
Max Sell (Inky)
William G. Selsam
Gary Semaniuk (Bubbles)
Ralph Semb
Keith Seplak (Lucky)
Michael G. Severe
Randy D. Severson (Rizzo)
Charles Sewell (Radar)
Anthony Sexton (Troubador)
William Shaffer (Wee Willie)
Desmond Shairp (Shar Pee)
Stephen Shapiro (Makabau)
Mark Sharp (Sharpie)
Kenneth Sharp (Harley)
Bob Sheets (Bo Bo)
James G. Shekell (Sunny Jim)
John Shelley (Whirly Berd)
Dave Shelton (Myagi Clown)
Danny C. Shelton
Robert Shelton (Homey)
Dave Shenkoff (Whiskers)
Jerry Sherman (Booppa)
Doug Sherman
Richard Sherriff (Magee)
Matthew Sherrill (Ringo)
Jack Shinn (Pa-Po)
William G. Shoe (Shoeclown)
Craig Short (Popcorn)
Michael Short (Shorty)
David Shoultz (Fred Dee)
Jeff Shreaves (Mookie)
Wayne Shriver (Wayno)
Donald Shuler (Buzz-Zee)
Brian Shuler (Fingers)
Chuck Shull (Zero)
Merle Shull (Fuzzy)
Jason Shuman
Richard Shumilak (Boots)

James Sickles (Buttons)
Jerry Siemens (Snoopy)
Byron Simmons (Boing)
Ted Simon (Thumper)
Thomas Simoneau
Bob Simpson (Butterbean)
Dane Simpson (Homer)
Arthur Sims (O'Grins)
Bobby C. Sircy (Debbie Boy)
Edward Sisson (Smokey)
Cris Sizemore (Weelz)
Charlie Skeel (Sweet Pea)
James Skinner (Hay See)
Jim Sklenar (Hambone)
Ian Skogstad (Skogie)
Donald T. Skowronski (Pop Pop)
Bruce Slade
Allen Slagle (Pumper)
Randy Slapak (Slappy)
Greg Sleet (Starz)
Norman B. Sloan, Jr. (Corky)
Burt Slowbe (Rinkles)
Michael A. Sluiter (Mikee)
David Small, Jr. (Squiggles)
Richard Smallwood II (Outback)
Jeff Smarkel (Buster)
Freeman Smith (Smitty)
Leo Smith (Thumper)
Glenn Smith (Cubby)
Lauren Smith (Jolly)
Clyde Smith (Rowdy)
Lester Smith (Lucky)
James Smith (Tubby)
Robert Smith (Snuffy)
Ernie Smith (Squeeky)
Dwight B. Smith (Peppy)
George A. Smith (Georgie)
R. Dillon Smith (Ditchbug)
Kevin Smith (Kaboos)
Mike Smith (Jinglez)
Marcus Smith (Grumpy)
Mark Smith
Randall Smith (Smitty)
Danny L. Smith (Campy)
Matthew Smith (Uncle Sham)
John Smith (Yo-Yo)
Kevin Smith (Bubbles)
Marshall Smith (Big Kahuna)
Kenneth Smith
John T. Smith
Leo Smith (Thumper)
Sandy Smith (Yo-Yo)
Robert F. Smith, III (Choo Choo)
Sid Smithline (Abie)
Bart Smookler (Presstoe)
Dean Smyth (Dazzle)
Darryl Sneary (Stretch-O)
Harry Snyder (Chugg)
Daniel Snyder (Pickle)
Robert P Snyderman (Schlep)
Rupert Solis (Cy-Lo)
Fred Soltzer (Freddie)
Richard P. Sommers Jr.
John Sopotyk (Shmoe)
Toby Sorenson (Pea Soup)
Paul Sosnick (Smiley)
Allan D. Southhall (Pokey)
Bill Spaetzel (Spats)
Jim Spalding (Jimbo)
Craig Sparks (Patches)
John D Speedone (Speedy)
Larry Speer (Nosebleed)
Robert Wm. (Spillett Spilly)
Thomas Spindler (Funny Bone)
Steve Spofford (Super Star)
Kerry Spofford (Spiffy)
Rod Sponamore (Baxter)
John Sprague (Nickels)
Clive L. Squibb (Hayseed)
Al St Pierre (Garcon)
Archie St. Peter (Pete)
James Staedt (Boots)
Thomas L. Stafford (Ole Blue)
Jimmy Stafford (Cotton Candy)
Bret Stahler (Snap Trap)
Gerald Staiger (Stretch)
Ken Stallings (Patches)
Sam Stam
James A. Stamps (Jelopy-Jim)
Thad A. Starr (Thadbo)
Stephen C. Starr (Boinky)
Dale W. Stauss
Marvin Stavig (Dusty)
Troy Stavig (Dimples)
Edward Steel (Mr Ed)
Bill Steele (Bobaloey)
Cliff Steele (Hollywood)
Walter Steffes (Milkshake)
Zalig Stein (Popsee)
Col. Jerry Stein (Ma - Jer)
Jerry Steinman
Richard Steinmetz
Vernon Stencil (Doozie)
Bob Stephens (Captain Bob)
Joel Stephens (Katchup)
Tony Stepleton (Pecos Pinky)
Dan Sterkal
Mike Stevens (Mybo)
Allen R. Stevens (Bogey)
Donald Stewart (Happy)
Tony Stewart (T. K.)
Joe Stewart
Trent Stier (Skids)
Fred Stinard (Wingnut)
Russell Stoddard (Rusty)
Bruce Stoddart (Skipper)
Tim Stokes (Zammy)
Keith D. Stokes (Toby)
Rodney Stoltenberg (Rascal)
Joe Stom (Bubba)
Eric Stone (Guzzo)
Myron Storch (Sueflay)
Wayne Stovall (Pappy)
Ron Strang (Archer)
John C. Straub (Beans)
Larry Stringer (Foooey)
Jeffery Stroud (Tatoo)
Charles Struble
Keith Struble (Crash)
Steve Sturm (Lefty)
Roger Sturner (Bubbles)
Jeff Stygar
David Sullivan (High Tower)
Sidney Sullivan (El - Sid)
Scott Sumner (Yuk Yuk)
Curtis Sumrall (Trashcan)
Robert Sundberg (Buba)
Lewis Surber (Jellybean)
David Sutton (King Of Hearts)
Howard Svigals
Robert Swafford (Willie)
Jerry Swanbery (Swanie)
Don Swanger (Pokey)
Kevin Swartz (Bogey)
Jim Sweaney (Moose)
Gerald Sweezey (Shine)
Wayne Swenson (Buttons)
Larry Swenson (Lars)
Steven Swift (Swifty)
Don Swindle (Skippy)
Jon Swisher (Switch)
Jeff Switzer (Juggery)
Mike Szabo (Z-Bo)
James K Szeredy (Chi Chi)

-T-

Aaron Tabing (Skippy)
Greg Talley (Fuzzy)
Rick Tate (Tater)
C. Fred Tate (Rosey)
Larry Taylor (Tator)
Ronnie Taylor (Putt Putt)
Samuel Taylor (Lucky)
Kenneth Taylor (Grimee)
Willie C. Taylor (Droopy)
Gordon Taylor (Nibs)
Lonnie Taylor (Sho-Biz)
Wilfred Taylor (TC-Trashcan)
Edwin Taylor Jr. (Mr. Happy)
Ray Taylor, Sr. (Crash Keystone Cop)
Lionel Tennant (Jimbo)
Charles Tenney (Big Top)
Jon Tessier (Sylly)
Mel Tessmer
Matt Tevault (Lazy Larry)
Bob Thachluk (Tacky)
Alan Thal (Ties)
Ronald Theyers (Rondo)
Frank Thistle (Tinker)
Gaylord Thomas (Zeeby)
David Thomas (Slo-Poke)
John Thomas (Chatterbox)
Dennis Thomas (Buggzie)
Nicholas Thomas
Iseral Thomas, Jr (Okie Dokie)
Brian Thompson (Dippidi Doo)
Roger Thompson (Hubbub)
James Thompson (Jake)
Timothy Thompson (Tubby)
Steven Thompson (Ragg's)
Fred Thompson (Buttons)
James 'Mat' Thompson (Winkers)
William A. Thompson (Wild Bill)
Peter Thornburn (Peetee)
Michael Second Thorne (Hashbrown)
Richard Thrasher (Butch)
Charles H Thurber (Nimbo)
Jim Tidwell (Jimbo)
Fred Timm (Ho Ho)
George Tipton (Dude)
Eric Tjarks (Checkers)
Paul B. Toberg Jr.
Avery S. Toledo (Nium)
Parker Toler Fire (Plug)
Johnny Toliver (Flip)
Don Tootle (Toots)
Dennis Topleski (Idonno)
Brian Toth (Ah Oh)
Robert Towlson (Bumbles)
Robert Trahey (Brave Heart)
Victor Traini (Choo Choo)
Bill Trammell (Lucky)
Scott Trandem
Roger Trant (Artee)
Jay Traxel (Splatter)
Jim Treherne (Jimbo)

John Tremblay (Shabba-Dabba)
Jeffery M. Trent (KC)
James L. Tripp
John Trivette (Banjo)
Robert Trotter (Saw Horse)
Lawrence Truman (Captain Benny)
Travis Tryon
Charles Terry Tucker (Sloppy Joe)
Ken Tuckwood (Jincks)
Don Tulloch (Duffy)
Ed Tuma (Bugsy)
Richard Tumanon (I Duno)
David Turner
Jonathan Turner (Stinky)
Arthur W Turner
Robert N. Turnipseed
Jim Turpen (Ankor)
Wayne Tutty (Zoom Zoom)
Chris Twiford (Sprinkles)
Robert W Tyrrell (Robo)
Thomas Tyrrell (Mr Chip)
James N. Tyson (Crackers)

-U-

Walter Ulrich (Dandylion)
Jim Umlauf (Jimbo)
Nate Underwood (Bonzo)
Gary Unger (Smirkin)
Kevin Upshaw (Sneakers)
Joe Urban (Checkers)
Matthew Urbanic (Milt)
Constante Uson (Chibu)
Stephen Uthoff (Spanky)
Steven Uttecht (Sunshine & Chaz)
Bob Uzzell (Rerun)

-V-

Joel Vachal (Wojo)
Darryl Vachon (Robo)
Arnold Vachss (Bo Jangles)
Donald Van Alstyne (Buckaroo)
John Van Schaik (Professor)
Robert A. Vanatter, Jr. (Hobo Bob)
Tom Vanchieri (Piggy)
Attn: Bert Vanderschaaff
Victor Varela (Gori)
Jose Vargas (Choo Choo)
Spencer Reid Vass (Chef Stew)
Tim Vaughan (Coco Da Poe Poe)
Jared M. Vawter (Jiggy)
Nick Venero (Lug-Nut)
George Ventura (Bubbles)
Jay Ver Hulst (U-No)
John Vermaas
Torben Vik (Skidmark)
Randle Jay Vinden ('S Me)
John Viner (Silks)
Thomas Violett (Lookout)
Tony Visconti (Y-Not)
Gerry Viverito (Sneakers)
Richard Vivian (Honky)
Al Vogele (Whistles)
Clarence S Vogler, Jr.
William Voigt (Tutu)
Arthur Vosatka (Binky)

-W-

Thomas Wade (Brushes)
Perry Wade (Periwinkle)
Baxter Wade (Windy)
Frank M. Wadkins (Who Cares)
John Wadsworth (Sleepy)
Jack Wagner (Mr. Jack)
Patrick Waite (Trailer)
Todd Walhof (Punky)
Richard E. Walker (Pinkie)
Bob Walker (Dobby)
Don Wall (Sonny)
Mike Wallace (Sleepy)
Stanley Wallerstedt (Scrubby)
Donald Wallick (No No)
Robert Walliker (Sgt. Bobo)
Dean Walls (Dean-O)
Jim Walsh Jr. (Bubba)
Gary Walter
Harry Walters (Sleepy)
Rodney Waltman (Carmac)
Ray Wann (Curly)
T. Jack Ward (T J)
Clarence D. Ward (Bo Jingles)
Lewis Wargo (Lew Bear)
Richard Wark (Sprinkler)
Craig Warner
Stanley Warner (Buttons)
James Warnick (Jimbo)
Kent Warren (Cupcake)
Rick Warren
Ronald Wassel
Jack Waterfield
Donald Waters (Cozmo)
Chalres J. Wathen, Jr. (Buddy)
Jim Watkins (Clippetty Clop)
Arthur Watson (Coota)
Steve Watson (Petals)
E. Boyd Watson
Carl Watts (Day Late)
Curtis Watts (C'dubya)
Geoff Waygood (Goodee 2 Shuz)
John A. Waynick (Sweet Pea)
Phillip Waynick (Skipper)
Ray Weaver (Smiley)
Cody Webb (Whiskers)
Jerry W. Weber
Paul Weber (Tator)
Randy Webner (Bis-Kits)
Ronald Wedge (Curly)
Robert Weekley (Weedle)
Morris Weeks (Moe)
Charles L. Wegener Jr. (Chazo)
Rudy F. Weidenbacher (Orville)
Larry A. Weiers (Zippy)
Tom Weik
Gerald Weitz (Pokey Dot)
Robert Welch
William J. Welch
Don Weldon (Chief)
Randy R. Weldon (Wuzzles)
Jim Wells (Hot Rod)
Don Wells (Smedley)
Fred Wendt (Freddieee)
Richard Werner (Inky)
Michael D. West (Flat Hat)
Dean West
Robert D. Westenhaver (Ten Pin)
James Westerfield
Scott Western (Scooter)
Dr. D.J. Daniel Wetherup (Toot)
Josh Weyh (Pumper)
Forrest Wheeler (Muggins)
Kevin Wheeler (Gusbo)
Kenneth Whigham (Diamonds)
Tom Whitaker (Topper)
Paul Whitcomb (Paulie)
Donald T. White (Opa)
Keith White (Salty)
Jay White (Willie)
Robert White (Fetch)
Verl White (Biggon)
Kenneth White (Pudgie)
Zane P. White (Zippo)
Joe Tom White (Big Tom)
Joseph Emmanuel White (Peanut Butter)
Wilburn Roy White (Paw Paw)
Robert White (Jeeprz)
Steve Whitehead (Tiny)
Chris Whitehead (Elmer)
Bob Whitehead (O Bob)
Steve Whiteside (U Who)
Wesley Whiteside
Jimmy Whitfield (Bisket)
Guy Whitley (String Bean)
Noel Alexander Whitman (Jelly)
Wallace Whitworth (Waldo)
Bill Whyte (Bebo)
Alfred Wiggins (Wigs)
Robert Wigmore (Poppy)
John Wilbanks, Sr. (Hambone)
Glenn Wilcox
Robert Wild (Jingles)
H. B. Wilder (Mr Bones)
Kenny Wilee (Rags)
Greg Wilhite
Marcus Wilke (Razcal)
Carey Wilkerson (Cabo)
Roy Wilkerson (Oreo)
Don Wilkerson (Scooter)
Ronald Williams (Schnitzel)
Harvey Williams (Harvo)
Ben Williams (Loco)
John Williams (Dumplin)
Steve Williams (Willy)
John Williams (Pop-Pop)
C. Tom Williams (Geezer)
Scott Williams (Uncle Sam)
Gerry Williams (Wheely)
Peter Williams (Petey)
Jerry Williams (Pokey)
Victor Williams (Homey)
James Williams (Jimbo)
Ron P. Williams (Curley)
Don Williams (Chatterbox)
Jerry L. Williams (Zipper)
Ken Williamson (Kenny)
Gary Willis (Dogone)
Doug Wilson (Willie)
Robert L. Wilson (Lucky)
William T. Wilson (Moose)
Bill Wilson (A J)
William Wilson (Bubba)
Edward Wilson (Fuzzz)
Frank Wilson (Frog)
Ray Wilson (Mookie)
Sam Wilt (Sam I Am)
Bill Wimmenauer (Odie)
Fred Windbiel (Choo-Choo)
Barry Winecoff (Toyo)
John Wingfield (Doctor Chopper)
Robin Winslett (Pockets)
Gerry Wintle (Buttons)
Jimmy Wisdom
Steve Wisdom (Wiz)
Lester D. Withers (Zippo)
Jeff Witte (Ringo)
William Wohlfarth (Rainbow)
Ritchie Wolf (Deadeye)
Larry Wolf (Pa Pa)

Vern Wolf (El Lobo)
Charles Wolfe (Bugle Boy)
Andy Wolfe (Raggedy Andy)
Larry Wolford (Sparkle)
Lester Wolfson (Bow)
Jeffery Wolok (Jasper)
Larry Wolsfelt (Taz)
Eddy Wood (Sparkey)
Roland Wood (Numb - Numb)
Brady P. Woodard (Bullgigs)
Eugene Woodard (C. C.)
Woody Woodard (Woody)
E. George Woodley (Pippin)
Chuck Woods (Woody)
Howard Woolley (Fuzzy)
Raymond Worden (Chip)
David Worel
Gordon Wormsbecker (Punch)
Ronald Wortmann (Mojo)
Eric Wotring (Bubbles)
Gary Wraalstad (Gary)
Gary Wraalstad
Murray Wray (Poppi)
Scott Wright (Flat Tire)
James Wright (Jake)
W. Tommy Wright (Bobo)
Barry Wright (Doodles)
Ken Wrisley (Elims)
Ron Wurmb (Curly)
John Wylie

-Y-

Thomas R. Yarnall (Fuzzy)
Ron Yates (Curly)
Frank Yetner (Pinky)
Vernon Yielding (Bubbles)
W. L. York Jr.
Bruce R. Youmans (Gyro)
Michael W Young (Idonno)
Mike Young (Ace)
Randall Young (Toot Roar)
Donnie Young (Bo Bo)
Duane Young (Div-It)
Ernest Yull (Squid)

-Z-

Lauren A. Zagoren (Sir Ziggy)
Paul Zaharia
Sean Zamora (Popcorn)
Ron Zappone (Skittles)
Edward Zeh (Putter-R-R)
Jerry Zeldes (Pogo)
Richard Zimdars (Goldy)
Howard H. Zimmerman (Howie)
Chris Zimmerman (Lucky)
Kenneth Zook (Yellow Shoes)
Dennis Zubler (Itzy)

Dean Wiarda making another child smile.

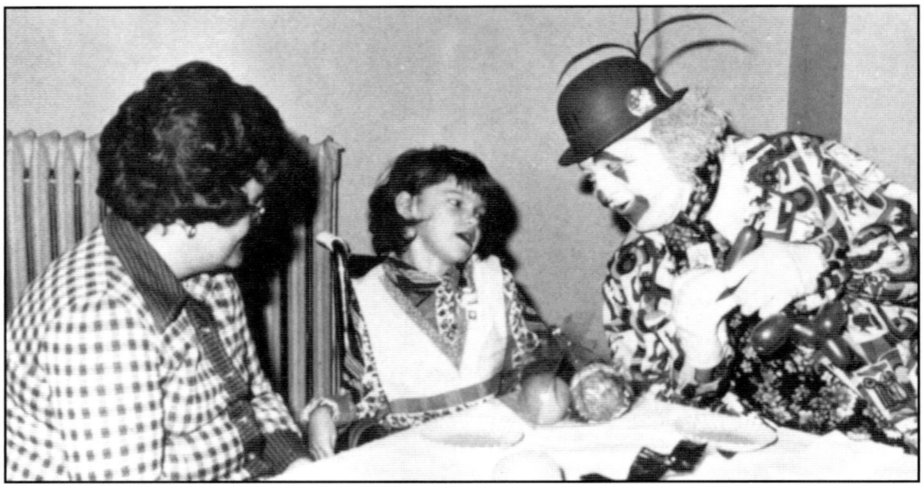

George Frost entertaining a girl in a wheelchair.

"Gone Fishing" float in the parade.

The Tigris Temple Shrine Clowns ready for the 1987 Circus.

The Nile Clowns.

Lloyd "Muggs" Webb helping at school.

Araba Clowns ready for parade.

Virginia Beach, Sept. 9, 2001, First Place – MASCA & MASA.

Virginia Beach Parade, Sept. 9, 2001.

Afifi Clowns with Red Skelton. L-r: "Henny" Hendrson, Red Skelton, "Kolohe" Brookshier and "Muggs" Magin in front.

Araba Clowns

Araba Clowns

Index

The ISCA Membership Roster, pages 110-122, was not indexed since it is in alphabetical order.